D1453226

THE UN-MELTING POT

The
Un-Melting Pot

*An English Town
and its Immigrants*

John Brown

Macmillan

First published 1970 by
MACMILLAN AND CO LTD
London and Basingstoke
Associated companies in New York Toronto
Dublin Melbourne Johannesburg & Madras

Printed in Great Britain by
ROBERT MACLEHOSE AND CO LTD
The University Press, Glasgow

For Audrey, Janie and Tootie

Contents

		Page
Acknowledgements		9
Introduction		11

PART I: THE NATIONAL GROUPS

1.	The Town	19
2.	Poland	32
3.	Latvia	44
4.	Ukraine	56
5.	Yugoslavia	68
6.	Italy	82
7.	West Indies	98
8.	India	116
9.	Pakistan	132

PART II: IMMIGRANTS IN THE COMMUNITY

10.	Employment	145
11.	Education	160
12.	Housing	175
13.	Health	188
14.	Immigrants and the Police	198
15.	Clubs, Culture and the Community	209
16.	Conclusions	219

Appendixes

| I. | Education in Bedford, January 1970 | 229 |
| II. | Immigrants – Facts and Statistics | 231 |

| *Index* | | 237 |

Plates

Page

1. The dean of Bedford's immigrants. Joe Clough in 1908. (J. Clough)   32

2 and 3. Father Marian Majewski in Dachau concentration camp, and as he is today. (Father Majewski; Bedford County Press)   33

4. Christmas celebrations by the Polish community in Bedford. (K. S. Photo Studios, Bedford)   33

5. Jaroslav Madylus studying for his A Levels. (Bedford County Press)   64

6. Mrs Emilia Slobodian in traditional Sunday dress embroidering traditional patterns. (Bedford County Press)   64

7. A Serb wedding ceremony. (Bedford County Press)   65

8. A rehearsal for Slovenian dancing in Bedford. (Bedford County Press)   65

9. A woman from South Italy. (*Daily Telegraph*)   96

10. West Indians at the Bible Way Pentecostal Church. (Bedford County Press)   97

11. A Sikh engagement ceremony. (Bedford County Press)   97

12. The interior of a Bedford lodging-house. (R. E. Fry)   128

13. Ampthill Road Junior School, where there is a high proportion of immigrant children. (Bedford County Press)   129

Tables

	Page
1. Stewartby Labour Records (Selected Dates)	147
2. Numbers of Immigrant Children in the Borough of Bedford Schools 1955–69	161
3. Immigrant Children in Bedford Schools (January 1969)	162
4. Nationalities of Occupants in Multiple Occupation since 1955	178–9
5. Number of Conditions Seen at VD Clinic, Bedford General Hospital during October, November and December 1966	191
6. Number of Conditions Seen at VD Clinic, Bedford General Hospital during October, November and December 1968	191
7. Commonwealth Immigrant Membership of Youth Clubs in Bedford (1969)	210

Map Showing the Distribution of Immigrant Children in the Borough of Bedford Schools (January 1969)   163

Acknowledgements

My grateful thanks to the hundreds of people of Bedford, of many different nationalities and conditions of life, who spared time to help me in the writing of this book; to Mrs Joan Sood for her invaluable help in preparing the manuscript; to Mr Douglas May and Mr Harry Sedgwick, Editor-in-Chief and Chief Photographer respectively of the Bedford County Press, for making many of the photographs; and to my wife for her comments, with love.

JOHN BROWN
CRANFIELD INSTITUTE OF TECHNOLOGY

A.2

First Polite Native. "Who's 'im, Bill?"
Second ditto. "A Stranger!"
First ditto. " 'Eave 'arf a brick at 'im."

25 February 1854   By permission of *Punch*

Introduction

THIS is a study of the immigrants who have come to live in a small English town since the Second World War. It has been a time of rapid change in almost every aspect of British life: in its technology, its economy, its social structure and its culture or way of life. The coming of the immigrants has to be seen against this whole process of change; and, indeed, as part of it.

The town is Bedford, about fifty miles north of London. Of some 70,000 inhabitants at the time of writing, more than one in five are immigrants; about a quarter of the children in Bedford schools are the children of immigrants; and about a third of town births are babies of immigrants. Nearly fifty nationalities are represented here, the main groups – in descending order of size – being the Italians, Indians, West Indians, Pakistanis, Poles, Yugoslavs, Germans, Latvians, Hungarians, and Chinese. There are also several hundreds of Americans, Irish and Spaniards, mainly in temporary residence. Bedford, in sum, is a microcosm of a changing society.

You are most likely to come to the town by train from London. As it slows, some miles south, a smell of brickdust assails the senses, if not the sinuses and lungs. The towering chimneys of Stewartby, largest of all brickyards, stand above its excavations like giant, denuded tree-trunks over a ravaged battlefield. Bedford, you are forcibly reminded, means bricks. Bricks have meant immigrants. And when, in haste, you quit the Midland Road Station, ugly and dirty relic of nineteenth-century achievement, you find yourself immediately in immigrant streets.

Is it town or urban agglomeration? The word 'town' implies the notion of community, of corporate purpose or being. Hard to discern much of that in Bedford. Hard to say what it is any more than where it is. It is clearly not of East Anglia, nor yet of the Midlands. It cannot claim the consequence of the Home Counties. In any true regional sense, it does not belong. As a county town, it has little of the vivid sense of character that Durham has: and it lacks the sense of community, the neighbourliness bred of adversity, of many northern towns. A few quarters have a certain charm. There are a few places of historic interest. But, over all, little sense of corporate being. A town without a centre, or, as some have said, a town without a soul. In virtues as in vices, unremarkable; a town neither for a warm welcome nor a violent rebuff. In short, a thoroughly modern town; if not faceless, at least of neutral identity. And by its very anonymity, a town eminently suited for people of all kinds, conditions and colours to live together on a basis, not of community, but of coexistence.

The purpose of this book is to explore: where the various groups of immigrants came from; how and why they came; their problems in settling; the nature of their relationships with the people of Bedford, with the people of other national groups, and with their own people; the nature of their employment and of their working relationships; the problems that their presence imposes on the social services and upon official and voluntary agencies; the new ranges of problems created by the growth of a second generation; and the ways in which their patterns of life are changing and are likely to develop in future.

There is, at present, a good deal of concern about immigrants. It is common for people, both sympathetic and otherwise, to speak and write of 'the immigrant problem', implying, at least, a certain homogeneity among immigrant groups. This has little or no basis in fact. Few immigrant groups have much in common. There is no 'immigrant problem' in a general sense. There are only the problems of separate groups susceptible to different solutions or to no solutions.

People also speak of the 'colour problem' as if the various groups we call 'coloured' were also somehow homogeneous. They are not, any more than groups we call 'white' are homogeneous. A day trip on the Channel boat to Calais should be sufficient to make that point.

The concept of the 'colour problem' even proves dangerously misleading. It implies a sense of communality between Asians and West Indians, which also has no basis in fact. Indians, for example, have no more in common with West Indians than with any other national group. The evidence of Guyana suggests, if anything, that they have very much less. Indeed, there may often be very little in common between people of the same national group, as the wide range of class/colour shades and gradations in Jamaican society makes clear.

Even awareness of colour as a determinant of human differences is nowhere near as universal as current discussion suggests. For many West Indians, such an awareness is a part of their consciousness. For many Asians, it is not. Often it comes to them only as a vicious shock after arriving in England. It is only here that they become conditioned to it.

The very use of the word 'colour', moreover, is strangely ambiguous. While national usage tends to make it a term which inaccurately lumps together Asians and West Indians, local usage in Bedford, particularly among those most in contact with immigrants, commonly restricts its meaning to West Indians only.

This is not to say that discussion in terms of colour difference is not useful or pertinent. It is simply that contemporary concern – if not obsession – with the 'colour problem' has fixed attention upon colour as if it were *the* rather than *one* source of British antipathy to immigrants.

I do not believe that British xenophobia is in reality anything like so discriminating. Does it not operate against *all* that is not congruous to its own standards, whether that incongruity, or foreignness, is expressed in terms of colour, physical appearance, clothes, language, accent, manners, class, work attitudes or even smell?[1] Whatever the nature of the difference, that which does not resemble local norms is condemnable. The greater the incongruity, the more emphatic the condemnation.

Since my purpose is to try to understand the condition of life and the problems of each of the main immigrant groups in Bedford, I therefore believe this can best be done, firstly, by considering them in a total immigrant context – the experience of each and every group, irrespective of racial grouping; secondly, by making my focus not the colour of each group but its culture. Recently, I heard a West Indian say: 'I am what I am because of my background and history.' I take that statement as my starting-point.

To attempt a general survey of the various national cultures is within neither my purpose nor my competence. I can only choose themes which may help to illuminate the immigrants' lives in Bedford. To know the West Indians of Bedford, for example, I believe one must know something of the consciousness created on the colonial plantations: for the Italians of Bedford, the effects of

[1] See pp. 193–4.

centuries of isolation, poverty and neglect in the southern Italian provinces: or for the Yugoslavs of Bedford, the bitter history of division among the South Slav peoples.

For each group, I use the forms of reference which seem best to illustrate these themes, from literature as well as from history. Certain literary works achieve levels of perception and understanding more profound than historical, political, economic or social studies. V. S. Naipaul's novel, *A House for Mr Biswas*, for example, is not only one of the great novels of our time, it is also a major act of perception about the nature of West Indian life. In this respect, its qualities resemble those of di Lampedusa's vision of Sicily in *The Leopard*, Pasternak's Russia in *Dr Zhivago*, Knuts Lesins' Latvia in *The Wine of Eternity*, or the *Montenegro* of Milovan Djilas. Certain books of personal experience achieve perception of a similar order. Carlo Levi's *Christ Stopped at Eboli*, for instance, illuminates the background of Bedford's Italian immigrants more fully than any historical survey.

The context of this study is the changing culture of our own country. Here again, I can only suggest the relevant themes: the ways in which local patterns of life yield place to national and international patterns of urban, industrial culture: the fragmentation of family and community in an age of expanding communications: the weakening of local sources of authority, priest or parent, teacher or policeman: the eroding of traditional values: the isolation of contemporary man. Such processes of change deeply affect the immigrants. Absence of community may ease the problems of settling. The eroding of values may stiffen their resolve to preserve their own ways of life. Certainly it seems that the immigrant groups of Bedford have nothing in common more than their distrust, distaste for the permissive climate of our times.

With the principles of immigrant entry into Britain I am not much concerned. The conditions of life in Bedford force attention to practicalities rather than to principles. I take it to be more relevant and more useful to discuss the relationships between economic needs and social consequences in the Bedford area. The basic situation is very simple. Local industry needs immigrant labour. In consequence, local services strain at the seam. To discuss this theme may not be popular. Academics may deplore its utility, industrialists its impertinence. It is possible that our society needs discussion of this kind.

The heart of the book is the personal experience of the immigrants. At times this is reported; at times directly quoted, usually with concealed identity. Often a device of 'representative voices' is used. Interpretations and analyses are as far as possible backed up by statistical evidence, where this is available and reliable. Though I have tried to present the 'facts', I think it will be clear that my first concern is with quality of life. This means that I cannot hope to do more than approximate to a reality that is itself constantly shifting and changing. It also means that I am subject to three other major sources of error. One is subjectivity. Another is ignorance. The third is lack of direct experience. Having at least some experience of Europe and the Caribbean, I have felt this lack most in approaching the immigrants from India and Pakistan. To them, to the other immigrant groups, to the other – British – strangers to Bedford, and to the natives themselves, I can only say: I have tried to understand.

PART I
The National Groups

I

The Town

BEDFORD is an ancient town. There are several references in the Anglo-Saxon Chronicle, and local finds of Celtic and Roman coins suggest an even earlier settlement. For long it was a frontier town between Saxons and Danes, and when Edward the Elder captured it from the Danes in 919, he fortified it and gave it the status of a royal fief. Though burnt by the Danes in the disastrous raid of 1009, Bedford grew again in size and consequence under the Normans.

The civic status of Bedford is also old, and was jealously guarded. The Rev. C. F. Farrar, in his *Old Bedford* (1926), comments that 'of all the watertight, hermetically sealed, patent Chubb-locked oligarchies and autocracies which ever flourished for centuries, commend me to the Mayor, Chamberlains, Bailiffs and Burgesses of the Vill de Bedford, as constituted by the Charter of Henry II, extended by that of Henry IV.'

The burgesses saw to it that their bastion of privilege endured. They were certainly quick to check possible competition from foreigners and strangers. In the thirteenth century, persecution of the Jews of Bedford ended with their expulsion in 1290 and the confiscation of their property. A characteristic reference in the *Blacke Booke* of 1563, a collection of local statutes, prohibits all foreigners and strangers 'from using publicly in town any art, craft, trade, mystery or manual occupation and from selling wares or merchandise within the town'. Foreigners were also prevented from buying until after the market bell had struck eleven in the morning.

The burgesses, in brief, saw Bedford as their oyster, themselves as the pearl. Even as late as 1802, a burgess refused to serve as mayor after election because he considered the council composed of persons unworthy to associate with him.

This pattern of privilege withstood pestilence, civil war and every kind of political vicissitude until the Municipal Corporations

Reform Act of 1835. And until the nineteenth century, Bedford long remained unchanged either in size or way of life. The configuration of streets in Speed's map of 1610, like the configuration of the social structure, remained unaltered during the seventeenth and eighteenth centuries. Deeply traditional in its function as a market town, its people were deeply conservative in habits and values.

Such a town could only view dissidence with disfavour, as John Bunyan found, imprisoned there between 1660 and 1672, and again during the winter and spring of 1675–6, when he began his *Pilgrim's Progress*. That this imprisonment was not imposed with rigour may also have reflected the temper of a people complacent and secure in their own standards. It is not surprising that John Wesley, who often preached at Bedford, found his congregation there, at different times, 'drowsy' . . . 'heavy' . . . 'sleepy'.

They had reason to be content. At the end of the eighteenth century, Bedford enjoyed more than a modest prosperity as a centre of trade together with the dignity of a daily coach to London. The directory of 1791[1] states that 'the trade consists generally of wheat, barley, malt and wool outwards, and coal, timber, stone and iron inwards. . . . The adjacent soil being very fruitful in corn, especially barley and the best wheat, the former is exported by its navigable river to Holland by way of Lynn, and the latter is carried by waggon 20 miles off to the markets of Hitchin and Hertford, where it is bought again, ground, and carried in meal to London.' Included among those serving this town of some 3,000 people were 6 surgeons and apothecaries, 6 attorneys, 5 peruke makers, 3 hairdressers and perfumers, 5 glove makers, 2 glove and breeches makers, 2 tailor habit makers, 2 common brewers, 39 victuallers, and 3 innkeepers: hardly an impoverished community.

In the nineteenth century, the pattern of life was distinctly modified. The population increased ninefold. In 1801, it was 3,948; in 1851, 11,693; in 1901, 35,144, about half the present population. The expansion was dominated by two forms of development: in industry and in education.

By mid-century, extensive works for the manufacture of agricultural implements, as well as breweries, had been established, industrial development being dominated by one family firm. John Howard, ironmonger and smith, had set up business in the

---

[1] I am indebted to Alderman Richard Turner for this reference.

High Street in 1813, built a shop and workshop in 1835, and his sons, James and Frederick, moved the business to its present site in 1859. The Britannia Iron Works, as it was named, devoted to the manufacture of steel ploughs and other farm implements, occupied a site of some twenty acres, and until 1881 was the only large employer in the town – at that time, of about 600 people.

The new mood of the town was reflected in the first editorials of the *Bedford Times* in 1845. 'We enter upon the career of journalist at a remarkable time. . . . Ours, if not in an allegorical sense the iron age, is at least the age of veritable iron. Railroads are the passion of the day. . . .It is an age of road-making. . . .' Indeed, Bedford grew rapidly as a centre of communications, at first for coaches, later for railways. The Bedford–Northampton railway line was opened in 1846, the Bedford–Cambridge line in 1860. Soon after the latter was incorporated into the London and North-Western network: and the Midland line opened a station at Bedford in 1868.

There was, of course, another side to the coin of industrial development. The shift of industry from home to factory meant also the shift of country people to town. For the most part, these immigrants from the country came to live in hundreds of tiny dwellings to the west of the town centre, the very area where foreign immigrants live in greatest numbers today. Overcrowding led inevitably to falling health and housing standards, and notably to a severe epidemic of typhoid fever about 1860. This, in turn, led to the Public Health Act of 1875, making provision for a public water-supply and adequate sewerage. Industrial development continued slowly during the century, although the second major industrial plant, the Queen's Works, was not founded until 1894. This was a matter of casual chance. W. H. Allen had operated a marine engineering works in London between 1880 and 1894, but after differences with his neighbours, the London and South-Western Railway, he thought of transferring his works to Derby. En route there, his train stopped at Bedford. His attention was drawn to a local football match, and then to a site nearby that looked suitable for his factory. Two hundred of his men followed him from London, and by 1914 the number of his employees had grown to 1,000 – similar numbers to those employed in the Britannia Works at the time. By this time, too, Igranic Electric and W. H. A. Robertson, a firm of small-part mechanical engineers, were also operating in Bedford.

The expansion of the Harpur Trust schools in the nineteenth

century was equal in significance to the town's industrial growth. In 1552, Edward VI had granted a licence to the mayor, bailiffs, burgesses and commonalty of Bedford to establish a free and perpetual grammar school for the nourishing and education of poor children. Sir William Harpur endowed the school in 1566, but its fortunes ebbed during the eighteenth century. When Dr Brereton took over as master in 1811, the pupils numbered no more than six. The town evidently felt little need for the benefits of a classical education; and, in fact, a writing school, later the Commercial or Modern School, was developed in the late eighteenth century to provide teaching with an emphasis on English, arithmetic and other more useful subjects.

Dr Brereton transformed the original school; and, in doing so, affected the development of Bedford quite as fundamentally as the Howard family. He was as astute as he was energetic. One of the terms of his appointment was that he was allowed to take in boarders: and since, by an act of 1798, a capitation fee was allowed for each pupil he set to work quickly to build the school's, and his own, fortunes. By 1822, the school had 32 day boys and 50 boarders. He was further encouraged by an act of 1826, which fixed the master's salary and set a capitation fee on day boys of the school, with no limit on numbers. From that time, he concentrated on increasing the number of day boys, to such effect that by 1848 they numbered 187.

School regulations demanded that pupils must be of town birth, the sons of town residents with a rental of £10 or in possession of real estate to that value. Dr Brereton's efforts thus drew into Bedford a substantial class of people from the armed services or from professional careers wishing to raise a family and to give their children a good education attractively free from expense. Dr Brereton's success was so great, in fact, as almost to break the Trust. It certainly disturbed the trustees and created a great deal of public controversy. As a result, new regulations were introduced in 1853, putting new restraints upon the master's salary. Two years later, Brereton resigned.

The Harpur Trust gave further impetus to the town's expansion after an act of 1873, by which development was extended to two boys' schools and two girls' schools, with regulations instituting a system of low fees and abolishing the need to restrict pupils to those born in Bedford. This act brought in a whole new influx of people, many from the colonial civil service and the army.

Often they were people with large families and small pensions who were willing to invest their savings in one of the largish houses built between 1873 and 1914 on condition that their children had access to educational opportunities they could not otherwise afford. The Anglo-Indians, in particular, found Bedford very much to their taste. Many were the tales of imposing halls, and of orange boxes in the further rooms.

After this rapid growth came a time of peace, even of stagnation. A population of 39,183 in 1911 rose only to 40,242 in 1921, and 40,554 in 1931. On the eve of the Second World War, Bedford's main functions were those of a market town, a minor centre for industry, and a place for genteel retirement and cheap education. Its three communities might justly be called 'traditionals', 'industrials' and 'colonials'. In varying degree they were overlapping, although they did not cohere. As yet, the brickworks, the main factor in the making of Bedford as an immigrant town after 1945, was still only a huddle of chimneys on the southern horizon.

From 1914 onwards, several groups of strangers from other parts of the country came into the life of the town. A number of Scots soldiers, billeted in Bedford during the First World War, married and settled here. The unemployment of the thirties brought in a group of Durham miners. There were also itinerant Irish labourers with a reputation for brawn and beeriness. . . .

Of foreigners and foreign immigrants, the town's experience was of the slightest. A previous mayor of Bedford, Alderman Richard Turner, born in 1881, recalls the very scruffy German band that used to play there annually; and an Italian organ-grinder, perhaps the first true immigrant, who sold ice-cream or hokey-pokey at $\frac{1}{2}d$ a piece during the summer and roast chestnuts during the winter. More significant were the handful of Jewish refugees from Germany in the late thirties, though they made few ripples on the placid surface of Bedford life.

The only immigrant of note is a man of colour. His name is Joe Clough. He has a unique place in the town's history, and it would be just to call him the doyen of Bedford's immigrants.

Born in Jamaica in 1886, he came to England in 1906 as personal servant to a rich Jamaican doctor and planter. When his master returned home, Joe became a London bus driver on the No. 11 route between Liverpool Street and Wormwood Scrubbs.[1] In 1911, he married his English wife, Margaret, two years older than

[1] See Plate 1.

himself, whose father kept a pub in the City. As an ambulance driver in France throughout the First World War, he was proud that everywhere he was liked and accepted. 'No trouble, no trouble at all nowhere. Nobody mentioned my colour. I was like a king there. They even made me captain of the cricket team.'

Demobbed in 1919, he settled soon after in Bedford, working as a bus driver until after the Second World War, and then running his own taxi business from 1949 until his retirement in November 1968. He was then 82. A flood of retirement cards and good wishes marked Bedford's affection for Joe. 'People have been so kind,' says his wife; 'I think he's the luckiest coloured man living.'

He can recall only three incidents that have marred some fifty years of life in Bedford. The first was at a corporals' dance in Kempston Barracks just after the First World War. A captain demanded drunkenly 'Who gave that damned nigger an invitation? Get him out of here.' Joe perforce withdrew. Later, he received a regimental apology. Some time after, he was temporarily laid off from his job through false reports that other drivers objected to his colour. He was quickly reinstated and everywhere won respect as an excellent and steady driver.

The most dramatic incident took place in the Second World War. Walking back from the garage one night, passing near the river, he was noticed by three American servicemen.

'Hey, see what I see? Let's get the black bastard!'

'Nobody talk to me like that. Don't think I'm a blinking mug.'

'Come on, let's pitch the bastard into the river.'

'You are not in America, you know. You're in Bedford and don't forget it.'

At this point appeared a British Army corporal, who knew Joe.

'Don't you dare touch him, he's one of us.'

'We squared up to them,' said Joe, 'and all the Americans turned away liked whipped dogs.'

Unknown to Joe, his wife 'raised Cain and Abel' with the American authorities. An American officer visited their home to apologise.

As driver, character, and private person, Joe has total acceptance in Bedford. No doubt the fact he was unique helped make it so. No doubt the pattern could never be repeated. But this is not the whole explanation. One should also reckon what he has given to Bedford. Skill and integrity in his profession: a constant and kindly involvement in community life, giving readily, demanding nothing: and with these things, a pattern of family life to disarm the harshest critic. What he and his wife have made between them is not a small thing. They live deservedly in peace and in the town's esteem.

Now things change, Joe recognises: relationships deteriorate, attitudes to colour harden, the situation everywhere becomes 'a bit niggly'. On the one hand, he regrets those immigrants whose bad behaviour taints the reputation of their fellows: on the other, the instances of local people refusing jobs to properly qualified coloured men. The time of danger, he says, will be when the new generation of immigrants are educated and come to compete with local people for the skilled jobs. 'That's when the trouble going to start.'

For many Europeans, experience of war meant experience of total breakdown of the order of their society. Their experience was thus different in nature and quality from that of most British people. Though Britain suffered a great deal between 1939 and 1945, its post-war society was – all too recognisably – a continuation of pre-war society. If the social order had been – almost insensibly – modified, it had not been subjected to radical change; and after the war Britain had no need of radical rethinking to remake herself. At the time it seemed a matter for rejoicing. Nearly twenty-five years later, we tend to see it also as one cause of Britain's post-war failure both to adapt rationally to change and to control it for the use and benefit of her people.

Final victory preserved the myth of inviolability: twenty-two miles of water had, once again, preserved us equally from invasion and understanding. The spectacle of a devastated Europe only served to reinforce native insularities. Even the belated movement towards Europe twenty years later was rooted in necessity rather than in understanding. A constant, if rarely immoderate, xenophobia enables us to dismiss in this way all ways of life, all cultures, other than our own. Is it that colour of culture is more important to us than colour of skin?

War brought little overt change to the tenor of Bedford life. For the most part, change was confined to those who had gone away: the men. The war scattered them helter-skelter, crowded them on trains or ships, brought death into sharp focus. For better or for worse, it shook them out of themselves. Afterwards, only the older ex-servicemen could be, more or less, their former selves.

The younger men, in greater or lesser degree, were unsettled in their ways and values. Many were unable or unwilling to accept the old local dispensations. Some were made rootless for ever, a few detribalised. For many, soldiering was an experience of life they would never know again. And when, after it all, the family portals clanged behind them once more, many kept the memory of war years green, refreshing it on certain nights of the year when the lads came together again. They had heard the chimes at midnight. They had seen the days.

One thing was clear: the men of Bedford were not coming home to harsh, ill-paid, unskilled or semi-skilled work such as some had been forced to accept before the war. To the skilled tasks, yes, such as they and their fathers had made their own preserves over many years, but not to unskilled work in the brickyards and in the foundries. A man does not do service for that. With light engineering beginning to fringe the town, there were other opportunities and they could think too, as never before, of moving. They were used to moving, used to downing their kit and making a place for themselves, even in the roughest places. Bedford was just a place like any other. Those without houses or children, especially, found it no great wrench to leave, provided the wife was willing.

And as there was movement out, so there was movement in, especially of people with the skills needed for the new industries or for the town's expanding services. Today, relatively few of these professional people are Bedfordians, whether teachers or police officers, executives or engineers. This influx of British newcomers, together with that of European immigrants, after the war further weakened whatever social cohesion remained in Bedford, and from then onwards it is hardly possible to speak of Bedford in terms of a 'community'.

Many of these British newcomers came to know some of the trials that foreign immigrants were to experience in later years: indifference, suspicion, lack of community. The more they, as individuals, differed from local ways, the more they suffered from local antipathy. Stories are legion: of men refused lodgings; of couples who for years have been unacknowledged by neighbours; even of a Scots youth, derided at a local school for his accent and attitude to games, driven to rebellion and expulsion.

British newcomers came mainly for skilled jobs. Yet Bedford's principal post-war need was for unskilled labour. The measure of that is the 14,000 foreign immigrants. Only wilful self-delusion can explain the persistence of the myth that 'a large number of these people are just here for welfare state benefits'.[1] It could hardly be more obvious that the prime reason for their presence in Bedford is the need of the local brick industry for people to do work that British people will not do, despite all inducements of union rates of pay.

This industry derives from the discovery of valuable beds of brick-working clay at the end of the nineteenth century. These beds form part of a great belt of clay which stretches across England from Yorkshire to the Dorset coast. 'The uniformity of the clay-beds is eminently suited to mechanical excavations and the characteristics of the clay make it particularly suitable for mechanised brick-working on a large scale.'[2] The industry grew rapidly and, after a series of amalgamations during the twenties, the London Brick Co. Ltd, the main local company and the biggest brick-making organisation in the world, was founded in 1936.

Until the war, Bedford was not greatly affected by the growth of the brick industry. The village of Stewartby had been created in 1926 to house company employees, and local recruitment problems were few. Before the war, nine out of ten young men in local villages came to work in the brickfields. During the war, most fires were damped down and out. Some works were used for camps or stores. Skeleton staffs were maintained, but most of the men went away to the forces.

After the war, of course, the demand for bricks became enormous. There was everywhere a call for rebuilding and for new building developments. From that time onwards, the brick industry has been in need of labour; today as much as ever. As far as recruiting local men was concerned, difficulties were twofold: short-term and long-term. Those who had gone away to war were reluctant to return; and, more importantly, the war had irrevocably broken local work traditions. One works manager reckons that nowadays not more than one young man in a hundred in the local villages goes to work in the brickfields.

Since the fires were rekindled, the plain fact is that the brick industry has virtually survived on foreign labour. Even today at Stewartby, largest of the London Brick Co. works, with a weekly production of 15 million bricks, foreign labour represents over 40 per cent of the work force.

[1] Letter to the *Bedfordshire Times*, 20 June 1969.
[2] London Brick Co. brochure.

Failing British labour in the immediate post-war period, recourse was first made to ex-prisoners-of-war. At Stewartby towards the end of 1947 they made up nearly one-quarter of the whole labour force. One local trade union leader still maintains they were the best workers the brick industry ever had. Repatriation in March 1948 brought their contribution to an abrupt end.

By this time a considerable number of Poles had been recruited. They were ex-soldiers who, after fighting the war against Germany, found they could not return to their own country. Following the dispensations of the Yalta Conference and the betrayal of Soviet commitments to the principle of free elections in Poland, their country passed under Soviet control. Yalta, almost certainly, is the dirtiest word in Bedford among the Poles and other groups of political refugees. 'Sell-out' and 'betrayal' are the usual epithets; and many feel that their countries at this time were sacrificed to political expediency. None feels this more bitterly than the Poles, who had fought bravely at Britain's side, notably in the bloody assault on Monte Cassino.

Though given rights of re-settlement theoretically equal to those of British ex-servicemen, the Poles soon found that the protectionist attitudes of British trade unions drastically limited their opportunities of employment. Many were forced to take the left-overs, jobs in farming or heavy industry such as the brickfields. At the beginning of 1948 there were 332 Poles – just over 15 per cent of the whole work force – working at Stewartby alone. Some 60 of them are still there today.

British post-war needs for unskilled or semi-skilled labour coincided with a growing embarrassment of numbers in the dis-placed-persons' camps of Europe. These people had come to the camps by many routes. Some had been recruited by the Germans for forced labour or for the German Army, others had fought the Germans under Draza Mihailovic, or had suffered in concentration camps, or were simply refugees who had fled from the East to avoid the 'liberation' of the Soviet armies. The displaced persons from Western European countries were rapidly repatriated, and by 1947 those who were left in the camps were mainly people from the central and eastern countries of Europe, their numbers constantly reinforced by fresh influxes of refugees from Soviet-controlled territories. Most of them, for reasons mainly political, would not or could not go home.

In this context, the 'Westward Ho!' scheme for recruiting

displaced persons for British industry was started in 1947. Germany at the time was still a scene of desolation, people living makeshift lives in broken cities. Families and whole communities had been fragmented and camps swarmed with people of every kind and faith, thrown together by chance in a common condition of rootlessness. The dominant mood was one of hopelessness and futility. In that climate refugees seized eagerly on the chance of a new beginning, particularly in Britain, for in their minds Britain was the country which had kept freedom alight. It was the country of hope. Though the mood of post-war Italy was far less oppressive, those recruited from Italian camps shared the hopes of new life.

During 1947 and 1948, some 100,000 European Voluntary Workers came to Britain. Their identity cards were stamped with the information that they were 'Permitted to Land on Condition that the Holder Registers with the Police, Enters such Employment as may be specified by the Ministry of Labour and National Service, and does not leave such Employment without the consent of the Ministry'.

The EVWs were of every condition of life. They were given work in coal-mines or farms or in heavy industries where British labour could not be found. The younger men were able to adapt with comparative ease. For the older men, particularly for those with backgrounds of intellectual work before the war and of hardship and deprivation during the war, adaptation took a great deal of courage. By sweeping all into the common lot of manual labourer, many talents were cruelly wasted, for even after the men had completed their three years of indentured labour, European academic and medical qualifications were rarely recognised in Britain.

In a paper on 'The Resettlement of Refugees after the Second World War', given in Bedford during the World Refugee Year (1959–60), Andrew Elek quoted the case of a man who had been a surgeon of international repute employed as a hospital porter: and of another who had been a lecturer at St Petersburg University prior to 1917 working as a lavatory cleaner in an industrial hostel. 'He bought a modest, older type of house and hoped to make enough money letting a room or two to see him through to the end of his life, after he became too old to work at the hostel. He was quite a remarkable man and a brilliant mathematician, but nobody cared about him because he spoke very little English. There are, of course, very many similar tragic cases.'

Some EVWs came directly to the brickfields: others joined them later from other occupations. By the beginning of 1951, over a quarter of the work force at Stewartby were EVWs, and Poles and EVWs together made up a third.

Though many were physically or mentally unfitted for heavy labour, the EVWs, like the Poles, accepted without demur the hardship of brickyard labour, the lack of privacy of brickyard hostels, the pain of exile. They demanded little and accepted all. They had learnt, many in the hardest ways, to endure. One could only soldier on waiting for 'normality' to return, for the day one could go home. 'That was naïve. We know now that there is no such condition as "normality", especially in political affairs. . . .' Foreign voices and ways, rough clothes and marks of hardship made the EVWs a people apart. Among the people of Bedford they met, at best, indifference. Seeking lodgings or relationships, they encountered suspicion and rejection. They were turned away from many doors and spurned by many girls.

There were further reasons for local antipathies. The EVWs were associated with a defeated and ravaged Europe from which the British instinctively and consciously recoiled; and they were identified as people in opposition to the Soviet Union, the gallant allies of the war years.

Less than a decade later, they were to reflect how the world can go about. By the time that Soviet tanks rolled into the streets of Budapest in 1956, the gallant allies had become powers of darkness in the popular mind. Again there was a flood of refugees from Central Europe: 25,000 Hungarians came to Britain at the end of 1956. Of these, some ten families and seventy-five single men came to Bedford.

The British are a kind people when needs are brought to their notice. Publicity easily stirs their generosity and their conscience. The spectacle of Hungarians confronting Soviet tanks in Budapest evoked a great wave of feeling for the refugees. In Bedford, they were warmly welcomed. Under the umbrella of the British Council for Aid to Refugees, voluntary services and clubs of all kinds contributed help. Two houses were purchased and each converted into three or four flats. Women's organisations decorated and furnished them. Clothing was provided, together with educational and job opportunities.

When the dust settled, the facts emerged. Yes, there had been those who had fought for freedom in the streets of Budapest, but more of them had simply used the occasions to serve personal needs: to break relationships, to avoid military service or to escape the police. A few may even have been members of the Hungarian secret police. Though some were deeply appreciative, most were demanding and resentful. The crime record of Hungarians in Bedford is unparalleled among any other immigrant group, and of the twenty-five for whom jobs were found at the brickfields, all had left within a week.

Those who had opposed Soviet armies in the past, who had by that time given nine years' unstinted service to British industry, and who throughout that time had been unhonoured and unhelped, observed the scene in silence. For them it was bitter irony.

Years later again, in 1968, a Hungarian EVW revisited his country for the first time since the war. He went expecting the worst, a country under Stalinist oppression. He was astonished that, in private at least, people were speaking freely. He was further astonished and impressed by the sense of discipline and responsibility among the youth. Returning to the country which had been his home for twenty-one years, he realised that the black and white certainties of post-war years had gone for ever. Britain herself was reduced in status and no longer a light in darkness. The whole world, indeed, seemed only shades of grey: the political control of the East balanced against the commercial conditioning of the West. The world had gone about once more, this time with new emphases. Despite it all, he was glad to go home to the country in which he had lived and worked; to which, now, his loyalties were established, to which he belonged.

Most Poles and EVWs in Bedford know now that they will die here. Most have made their solutions to life in exile by self-help and self-reliance. And because they have done this for themselves, with few hands stretched out to help them, because they have endured much in silence and accepted all, they have little sympathy for the complaints, protests, and demands of later immigrant groups. With those groups, they feel little in common; and though now they recognise that their life here is permanent, that they are truly 'immigrants', their pride leads them to insist that certain distinctions and recognitions be made. That the Poles came here as soldiers and political refugees; that the EVWs came as political refugees; that those who came after them came as wage-earners.

2

Poland

'IN Warsaw, the first of September 1939 was a beautiful day. A lovely, lovely morning. At seven o'clock I was shaving myself, preparing to go to the bank. My working hours were eight to three. That was very satisfactory. I heard then the boom! boom! of explosions. I looked out of the window. I saw lights in the sky as upon a Christmas-tree. I said to my wife, "It is war." ' The ordered pattern of the speaker's life was broken for ever, but he could hardly have guessed that he would spend his later years of life in exile and in Bedford.

That fine morning in Poland had behind it a chequered, often tragic, history. Geographical position alone had made the country a prey for Prussia and Austria on the one hand, for Russia on the other. From 1795 until after the end of the First World War, the name of Poland had been erased from the map, and its history during the nineteenth century was characterised by heroic, confused, and tragically abortive struggles for national freedom. Pride and bitterness came together to the well-known observation: 'We Poles are better at dying than at living.'

Poland was also long troubled by social divisions inherited from medieval times. While the social order of feudal society was breaking up in most western countries, the nobles in Poland increasingly usurped both wealth and privilege. At the end of the seventeenth century, an English historian wrote that 'The Polish nation is divided into two sorts of People: The Gentry or Free Born Subjects, who are hardly a tenth part of the Kingdom, and the Vassals, who are no better than Slaves to the Gentry, have received no Benefit from the Laws, can Buy no estate, nor enjoy Property any more than our Negroes in the West Indies can.' Nearly a century later, Rousseau described the Polish nation as composed of three orders: 'The nobles, who are everything; the bourgeoisie, who are nothing; and the peasants, who are less than nothing.'

The dean of Bedford's immigrants. Joe Clough in 1908 (see pp. 23–5)

2 and 3. Father Marian Majewski in Dachau concentration camp, and as he is tod[a]

4. Christmas celebrations by the Polish community in Bedford

Even after the return to national independence in the early twenties, Poland was not a country at ease. Political as well as social divisions were still acute and these were exacerbated by further divisions between the Poles and the various minority groups living in Poland. In 1939, Ukrainians, Jews, White Russians, and Germans made up about 10 million of a total population of some 35 million people.

In all of this, the unbreakable thread was Polish pride of identity and the sense of the continuity of Polish political and religious traditions. These traditions have been deeply intertwined since Duke Miesko accepted the Christian faith in 966. Poland came to distinct political existence shortly afterwards when his son, Boleshaw, was consecrated as first king of Poland in 1025. The unity of the traditions is symbolised in the legend of Our Lady of Czestochowa. This Byzantine painting of the Virgin Mary had reputedly been brought from Nazareth and was installed at Czestochowa in 1384. Heroic resistance there to Swedish invasion in the seventeenth century became the inspiration for the Polish people to expel the Swedes from their land. In thanksgiving, the king, Jan Kazimiertz, solemnly dedicated the Polish nation to the Virgin in 1656, making her queen of Poland. National legend has it that she protects Poland at times of greatest danger, as at the 'Miracle of the Vistula', when the Red Army was defeated at the gates of Warsaw after the First World War.

In September 1939, Poland found itself once more between the hammer and the anvil. Once more, it was the conqueror's intention to eliminate Poland. 'I shall make her a long forgotten name on ancient maps', was Hitler's boast. Once more, Polish resistance was heroic, and unavailing. Following the German blitzkrieg, Soviet troops entered Poland on 7 September and on the twenty-eighth of the month the country was again partitioned.

Poles took many routes to Bedford. None was more terrible than that of their priest, Father Majewski. 'I was in Polish underground movement, as chaplain. Going to visit ill persons, I have been taken by Gestapo: first to Birkenau, then to Auschwitz, Buchenwald and at last Dachau. I have concentration camp tattoo here on my arm. 154088. In one year in Buchenwald, was called 25 times to come to place for gas chambers. Each time, German officer in charge of my part of camp – 'Kapo' Fritz – kept me back. I write him still in Frankfurt. Each year since meet together Polish priests in Dachau. Each year, less. Each year, some

B

dying from experiences....' His own health has suffered grievously. A small, fat man, hands folded across his belly, smiling: a face of forgiveness.[1] Three thousand Polish Catholic priests were killed in German concentration camps, 846 in Dachau.

L., born on the Romanian border, served in the Polish Army Cadet Reserve at the outbreak of war, guarding the Hungarian border. As Germans and Russians advanced, he crossed the border and was interned. Escaping, he crossed into Yugoslavia to report to the Polish consulate in Zagreb. After a brief idyll on the beach at Split, he took a small, overcrowded cargo boat, in rough weather, to Marseilles. The Polish Government in exile in Paris became the focus for many Poles who escaped in similar ways. B., from the same village, swam the river into Romania after the Russian occupation.

'I was supposed to report to Vladivostok to a regiment there. I said to my mother, "It is time to go. I shall go instead to Paris. It is nearer".'

'And nicer?'

'Of course.'

Like most Polish exiles who escaped to France, B. and L. joined the 1st Polish Corps in Scotland after the fall of France. They returned to Europe on D-Day, where B. was badly wounded, subsequently enduring twenty-seven operations during eight years in hospital.

The majority of Bedford's 500 Poles made the journey to Bedford via Siberian labour camps, as S. did. 'I took my wife, son, and femme de chambre in a party on two lorries belonging to my neighbour. We left Warsaw fifth September 1939, six o'clock at night. That was the last time I saw Warsaw in my life. . . .' They went first to Pinsk, then on into western Poland. There they met cars, trucks, and lorries from the opposite direction. The Russians were invading from the east. 'For me, that was the end.' They returned to Pinsk under Russian occupation, then moved north to Vilna, where S. began work with refugee committees. On 10 October the Russians returned Vilna to Lithuania as its ancient capital. 'For a while, the shops were filled with the beautiful sausage, the lovely bacon of Lithuania. . . .'

The respite was brief. By spring 1940, Lithuanian hostility to Poles was growing fast and the refugee committees were accused – not without reason – of helping Poles to escape through Lithuania to Sweden and thence to Britain. In June, Russia

[1] See Plates 2 and 3.

occupied all three Baltic countries and they were 'admitted' into the Soviet Union. The next month, S. was knocked up at night by Russian secret police and taken from his family to prison. 'Cell 210. Door shut. For ten days, nothing. Just iron bed, iron table, stove, bucket for w.c., hole for ventilation.' Each week, he was taken for interrogation by an NKVD colonel, hours at a time. He was accused of belonging to the Polish underground and even of being a British spy. 'If you don't admit, you will die in this prison. You will never see your wife again.'

After being found with a piece of bone used to shape bread into chess figures, S. was given three days' solitary confinement, crouching in a small, dank hole in complete darkness. On the first day, he was given only water, on the next two days, water and a little bread. He collapsed when he was taken out. From this experience, very poor diet and lack of fresh air, his health deteriorated. At the end of the year he was offered freedom on condition that he helped the Russians against the Germans. 'Thirty-first December 1940, ten o'clock at night, I breathed fresh air again. There was sharp frost. The air was clean. . . .'

So he returned to his family, living in a rented room. All cried with joy. On the table was a large piece of bacon. He took it up and tore at it voraciously. Two days later, he kept a rendezvous on a bridge in Vilna with the NKVD. It was suggested he should go to the USA. While awaiting visas, he found a job as accountant. Then, demands were made that he should provide information about the Polish refugee committees in Vilna. He refused. Shortly after, on the 14 June 1941, there were mass deportations from Vilna to Siberia. With his wife and son, he was taken by truck to the railway station. His wife and son were put aboard a train of cattle-wagons about to leave. He was held back. As a 'political', he had been put down to go on another train to Angelsk in northern Siberia. He swore he would not be parted from his family, blustered at the station officials, and was pushed aboard the wagon with his family as the train started to move. Utter darkness in the wagon. No one knew where they were going. 'It does not matter where. We are all together. It is a miracle.'

After a week, they passed troop trains going west. The Germans had invaded Russia. In the wagons they sang Polish songs in celebration, and at the end of seventeen days came to Rubcrvka in southern Siberia. Some 1,100 Poles were taken from the train to a huge square. The camp commandant addressed them, concluding, 'Here you will work and here you will die.' The people were chosen for forced labour, and S., once more, was lucky. Since many local Russians had been conscripted, he was given a job as book-keeper. He was lucky too in that it was summer. The winter before in that region a group of Poles had lost 70 per cent of their children, 80 per cent of the old people, in the bitter weather.

The final stroke of luck was that, before winter, they heard of the agreement between Sikorsky and Maisky whereby Poles in Russia were granted amnesty, and a Polish army was to be formed. S. quickly organised a committee for his group of Poles, informed the Polish authorities in Moscow of their presence and their readiness to join a Polish army, and in October, incredibly, arranged transport for them south to Samarkand. Many Poles were collecting in this part of Russia and S. was made Polish delegate for the area of Dzambul in Kazakhstan. On Good Friday 1942, the Polish 10th Division left the Soviet Union for Poland. S. stayed on to help collect more men, though for some time he was near death with typhoid fever. Soviet attitudes were hardening quickly against the Poles at the time he crossed from Russia into Persia on 21 August 1942. His was one of the last groups to come out. Of some 2 million Poles taken into Russia, not more than 150,000 left the country. Most of those who came to Bedford had relatives who were taken into the USSR and of whom there has been no further word or trace.

At Teheran, S. parted from his wife to join the Polish Army. She found work in a Polish camp in Palestine. Many other Polish women were taken to Kenya, Uganda, and Rhodesia, some to India. They rejoined their husbands – those who were still living – after the war. The Polish 2nd Corps went into training in Iraq and thereafter joined the Eighth Army pushing up into Italy. In the bloody battles for Monte Cassino, fighting for Warsaw and their other cities destroyed by the Germans, the Poles showed their qualities once more to the world. It was an appropriate place. The monks who brought Christianity to Poland in the tenth century had included Benedictines from the monastery of Monte Cassino. Over that monastery, at 9.30 on the morning of 18 May 1944, the Poles raised their flag.

So the Poles came to Bedford as soldiers, comrades of war. For them, of course, there was no victory: only the bitter irony that the war which had begun in defence of Poland's freedom and independence had ended in a victory which confirmed the loss of that freedom and independence. In the war, they had also lost 6 million of their people. Their record in battle was proud, yet, once again, Polish heroism and sacrifice had proved fruitless, even as it had been in the Warsaw uprising of 1944, when town and people were cynically abandoned to destruction.

Their bitterness centred on the word 'Yalta'. 'There, Poland was sold out. Betrayed. We must have freedom, you understand. We must have it. . . . We came here as political exiles, not for money but for freedom. We are not immigrants. We do not want special favours, privileges, but we want recognition that we are allies. We are soldiers. We have been dying for this country. . . .'

At the war's end, Britain inevitably felt a certain sense of obligation towards the Poles who could not go home. They were accorded rights equal to those of British soldiers on demobilisation and the Polish Resettlement Corps was established to aid their transition to civil life in an alien land. In the event, as we have already seen, 'equal rights' proved paper words, for restrictive practices in British industries directed many Poles, irrespective of their backgrounds, to uncongenial jobs. The brickworks claimed many and were the main reason for some 700 Poles settling in Bedford in the post-war years.

Many lived in brick company hostels until, with groups of comrades, they sought lodgings in town. Speaking little English, cut off from their own country, most depended on their group for help and security. Some men were rejoined by their wives from Africa or from India: some married Polish women they had met in England or in Germany during the occupation. Marriages to British women were mainly among men of the 1st Polish Corps, who had been stationed in Scotland and whose English was generally more fluent than that of their comrades from the 2nd Polish Corps.

L. was one who met his wife in Germany when the war ended. Born in Poznan, she had been taken into forced labour on a German farm. They married in 1946 and in 1948 he left the Resettlement Corps to live in Essex. The couple with their baby first found a tiny room to live in, then turned squatters in an old, deserted house. In 1950, L. found employment as a cleaner in Bedford. To find lodgings was a greater difficulty. 'Each evening, I took one street. Went from house to house. I knocked. Sometimes they opened. "Any rooms to let?" Eight months I been looking. Every street was covered. . . .'

At last, he found a flat in an old, big house near the station belonging to a colonel's widow of 82. She insisted she saw the family before she accepted them. L.'s wife had to borrow a coat to create the necessary impression. The old lady told them that the rent was £3 a week. L. was then earning £4 10s a week. She wanted three months' rent in advance. (You can't be too careful with foreigners.) L. and his wife agreed, although it took their demob savings. The old lady insisted that L. carry her upstairs so that she could point out where to put the shillings for the gas. (You can't expect foreigners to grasp these things.) They did not have many shillings and often went cold. To make ends meet, L. took on an extra job. After tea, he set to each evening weaving carpets, at which he was skilled. Often, he did not finish work until midnight. As the child grew older, his wife took a part-time cleaning job to help out.

For many Polish exiles, life offered little in the early days. Uncongenial labour, hostels or rented rooms, and the constant barrier of language, often made it lonely and desolate. (Even today, some 120 Poles are still living in lodging-houses, most of them as single men.) For some time they were buoyed up by hopes of return. Many did not bother to learn English because of this. They strove, above all, to preserve their wartime spirit of community and to keep alive the idea of a free Poland. They even had their own newspaper, for the wartime *Polish Soldiers' Daily* was transformed into the post-war *Polish Daily and Soldiers' Daily*, with a circulation of 22,000.

Hope waned as divisions grew between East and West. Small wonder that many took the chance of life in the United States when it was offered them in the early fifties. Others simply retreated to heavy drinking to drown their despair. 'Loneliness was then the killer.' Those who suffered most were the older people, more settled in their ways, often with backgrounds of loss and suffering, no longer able or willing to adapt to the demands of making a new life in a new country.

The Polish Club, which opened in the early fifties, did much to alleviate their loneliness and serve as a focus or meeting-place. The Polish Workers' and Craftsmen's Union took the first steps in buying a house for a club to operate. It was essentially a place to meet and drink, and did much to create a community among lonely exiles.

As the Poles of Bedford have come to accept their stay here as at least semi-permanent, so they developed their own community with its own council, clubs, some fifteen to twenty businesses, its two doctors and its priest. Father Majewski came here in 1948. He serves some five hundred parishioners in twenty-seven places from Hitchin to Wellingborough, with three services in different places every Sunday. Until recent years he used a bicycle, then began to learn to drive. After a coronary thrombosis four years ago: 'Doctor say no bicycle, no car.' Nowadays, he has to rely on his brother's car.

His brother came to join him in Bedford in 1950. He had been a lawyer and government administrative official before the war. In Bedford, he had to take what was going and for fifteen years worked as a machine operator. Over the last few years he has found work as a clerk. In 1958 his wife and son joined him from Poland. He had never seen his son before, nor his wife since he escaped the Russians in September 1939, leaving her pregnant. After living in disguise in Lithuania, working as woodchopper, labourer and railway handyman, he was deported to northern Siberia and from there, via General Anders' army he came to Britain. From Britain he supported his family as best he could until their arrival. The son joined his father at his place of work and then, taking advantage of education and training facilities for the families of Polish soldiers, he studied medicine and has recently qualified as a doctor. The mother was not so lucky. Lack of English doomed her to the poorest jobs.

Some fifty of Bedford's Polish community come from well-educated or professional backgrounds. For many of them, their jobs in Britain meant changing better for worse. Yet they have accepted their new roles without complaint. They would not wish to show ingratitude to the country which gave them refuge.

Such people felt increasingly the need for a cultural centre of Polish life in Bedford, something more than a social club as represented by the Club Polski. Some money was collected, an old house bought, and the Polish House (Dom Polski) was founded in 1960. The objects were 'To establish, maintain, and manage an institute for Polish citizens in Bedford and/or elsewhere, to serve as a religious, social and cultural centre and meeting-place for such persons.' A Polish school was inaugurated, giving Saturday classes in language, history, culture and religion. Some fifty children now attend, divided into three groups according to age. Small numbers take advanced courses in Polish for 'O' and 'A'

Level examinations. Choir and dance groups also meet there, as do the Polish Youth Club, with some sixty members, and Polish scout, guide and brownie groups.

This development has brought its difficulties. Relations between House and Club have often been tense, Club suspecting House of competition and middle-class pretension, House decrying Club for being no more than a drinking-place. In essence, the divisions have been those of class.

Against this background, the Bedford Polish Joint Council, under the chairmanship of Jan Stefanowicz, was founded in March 1967, partly to present Poland to the local world, partly to bring about unity within its own community. To reconcile differences and to create a local Polish centre for concerts, dances, and social and community activities of all kinds is now among the first of its aims. At all costs, the idea of Poland must be kept alive and inviolate.

'I like very much Great Britain. I love Poland.' For most Poles in exile, this is the heart of the matter. They are proud of their record of good citizenship and of their loyalty to Britain. 'You will find no one more loyal to Britain than us . . . much more, we think, than some of your Commonwealth citizens.' Above all, however, is their wish to preserve a sense of Polish identity. Given that Soviet control of Poland persists, they know there is little hope of return and that in the second generation connections with Poland will surely grow more tenuous. 'To love something or someone, you must see it: it is physical: the exception is love of God.' They realise their children will not be Polish in a full cultural sense and they say to them, 'At the very least, we want you not forget. . . .'

So they transmit and preserve the language and culture of the motherland in the Polish school, in the youth groups, and by an annual celebration of events both from Polish history and from their own experience. These range from ceremonies for the national day recalling the liberal constitution of 1791 to remembrance of Monte Cassino in May 1944.

Outstanding were the wealth of religious and cultural ceremonies to mark the millenium of Christianity in Poland in 1966. At this time, the Polish Council sought advice from Alderman Turner, a former mayor of Bedford, to commission a reproduction of our Lady of Czestochowa. After some inquiries, Alderman Turner – a gifted amateur painter, a noted collector, and local historian – himself took on the task. His lovely copy can now be seen in the

Catholic Church in Midland Road, Bedford. 'It gave me more pleasure than anything I did in my life.'

For the Poles, unlike the Latvians and Ukrainians, at least a measure of physical connection has been preserved. This is directly related to the measure of independence enjoyed by Poland after the Gomulka régime came to power in 1956. The first Pole from Bedford returned in 1958, others followed. For most, the experience was deeply disturbing, their minds and senses a constant confusion of images from the present and the past. Even to hear people speaking Polish in the streets was for many an overwhelming experience. 'When I crossed the border, I cried. I took earth from my mother's grave to scatter on my garden in Bedford.'

For some, even more sadly, there was no connection. 'I had no feelings at all. To me, it was just another country. I had been in so many countries, after all, and Poland was so much altered from what it was I could not recognise it. The people were strangers to me.'

There are others who fear to confront their image of Poland with contemporary reality. 'Every year, I prepare to go back to Poland for holiday. And then I do not go . . . I would be afraid.'

Those who now go regularly to Poland for a holiday can best perhaps put their own country in focus. 'After the first time, it was easier. Now we have gone several times, we can see things much more as they are. We go now simply to see our own people. That is great pleasure to us.'

For many children born in Bedford of Polish parents, visits to Poland have created a sense of living connection: and for no one more than G., a girl of twelve: 'The atmosphere, it's terrific, really. . . . They haven't got much in material terms compared with the comfort we have, but they use anywhere for a study and they work really hard. . . . And then, in the mountains, when you wake in the mornings, the air! You just have to get up early, and everywhere there is singing and movement. . . . My parents, they don't want to go back until Poland is free. I wouldn't mind going back tomorrow. . . .'

In Bedford, meanwhile, after school she helps to organise a group for Polish dancing and runs a troop of thirteen Polish guides that she herself founded. Her elder brother runs the Polish scouts, her mother the brownies. When G. went to register the Polish guides at a youth association, she was asked, 'Who is the leader?'

'I am.'

'Yes, but who is the organiser? Who tells you what to do and so on?'

'I do.'

A little girl like an arrow, her loyalties and purpose daunting but undeviating, her joy and energy affronting all concepts of integration.

Fewer children of Polish parents share her feelings than she would like to think. Some are divided in consciousness and loyalties, but most, though they feel the pull of Poland on holiday, know that, in essence, they are English. 'Motherland is where you are born.' Few, however, would wish to deny their upbringing, especially where both parents are Polish. And that upbringing will lead them to preserve not only many Polish ways but also many aspects of traditional European culture – patterns of religious belief, the respect for family authority, and the habits of courtesy that often seem to them crudely and unthinkingly abandoned in contemporary England.

Like most other immigrant groups, among younger and older people, Poles find the norms of contemporary Britain by no means ideal, though they are usually too polite to make this explicit. To many British people, on the other hand, the sins of the immigrants are measured by the extent to which their ways of life differ or deviate from British norms, though if questioned few people could give a coherent account of what these are. Most Poles feel that certain attitudes and standards of behaviour have changed out of all recognition since first they came here: and some have now been here for thirty years. Many go further when pressed – they are courteous people – and admit, with regret, that qualities which they admired in the British during the war years seem now to have fallen into temporary or permanent desuetude. 'Might it not be that we can best serve you, not by imitating you or by integration, but simply by enacting our own ways?'

'We feel part of your country but we keep our own way of life.' Again and again, one returns to sentiments of this kind. With other immigrant groups the Poles have little connection and from one group in particular, the Ukrainians, they are deeply divided by the experiences of war. Some men in Bedford have seen for themselves how Germans spurred Ukrainians to commit atrocities on Polish people. One saw a saintly woman and her daughter of his village mutilated and hacked to pieces. Another's grandmother was forked to death with a muck-fork against a barn door. 'It is Christian to forgive. Difficult to forget.' Bitterness inevitably stays with them, though there is no open hostility and several Ukrainians come to drink, with many other nationalities, in the Polish Club. There is even one West Indian member of the club, although in general Poles have scant regard for immigrants from the Commonwealth.

They act as good citizens, they feel as Poles. Yet, if the chance came and if Poland were once more free, how many of the 500 Poles in Bedford would go back? After twenty years or more, many have settled family lives, well-paid jobs, their own houses and cars. Even those who still work in the brickfields or on building sites have skilled jobs of one kind or another; and even those who live in lodging-houses have grown used to their comforts. They are also free of fear of political repression or retribution. The children are growing up, are passing examinations, and are developing their own expectations of life in Britain; given all the circumstances most would be content to continue living in peace where they are.

Those most likely to return are the people with skills and education to fit them for a professional post in Poland; also a few only of the young people, together with the older people whose roots were deepest in Poland, who have found it most difficult to settle in England, who are tired now and who wish, above all, to die on their own soil. 'Over the age of fifty-five, one begins to spend more time remembering the past. Memories come back with increasing force. For me, my ties with Poland grow stronger every day.'

In the event, perhaps not more than one in five would return. Most would be content to keep up the connection during holidays from time to time, and by attending the annual Polish ceremonies in Bedford.

On stage during the commemoration of Monte Cassino, a group of Polish girls are dancing a polonaise. There are few boys of their age in this Bedford community, so that girls have also to take the parts of cavaliers. They are wearing perfect reproductions of period dress in pastel shades, lovingly made by hand at home. They bow, curtsy, and begin their movements. The dance is all charm, grace, elegance, courtesy. Nostalgia haunts the faces of Polish ladies about me. '*Ah, monsieur, on dansait à Varsovie il y avait une fois. Hélas!*'

> *Je me souviens*
> *Des jours anciens*
> *Et je pleure.*

3
Latvia

AT 1 June 1969 there were 176 native-born Latvians (151 men and 25 women) living in Bedford. All are over the age of 40. Eighty-nine of them are single, including 4 women, and 87 are married. Of these, 21 are married to Latvians and 45 to other nationalities: 27 of the wives are English. Their children number 80, 23 of Latvian parents and 57 of mixed marriages. All the children are under 20. Twenty-three of the families are childless, 9 Latvian and 14 mixed marriages.

Just under fifty people from the other Baltic States, Lithuania and Estonia, also live in Bedford. It is appropriate to group the three countries together for, despite the diversity of language and customs, their cultural histories share common themes; and what J. Hampden Jackson wrote so perceptively of Estonia is true also of Lithuania and Latvia: 'Here can be seen the working of a bacillus which was strong enough to survive seven centuries of domination by an alien race; strong enough to outlive German landlords and Russian governors; strong enough to withstand, at the end of the First World War, first a Bolshevik invasion, then a German invasion, then Bolshevik invasion again; and strong enough to establish a Republic and to maintain it through the trials of the last twenty-two years.'

This was written at the outbreak of war. Since then Estonia, Lithuania and Latvia have endured yet another Russian occupation, another German invasion, and a further Russian occupation that has now lasted a quarter of a century. Their names no longer figure in geography books as the names of separate countries. Yet they *are*. Their people endure.

They are very small countries. In 1939, Estonia, with an area of 18,300 square miles, had a population of 1·2 million: Latvia, of 20,100 square miles, 2 million: and Lithuania, of 23,000 square miles, 2·9 million. The basic unit of the economic and social order was the small farm, and landownership had long been regarded not so much as a source of profit as a way of life: strong, well-ordered, deep-rooted.

For all three countries, there was a brief moment of independence, the period between the world wars. Then, following the 1939 non-aggression pact between Nazi Germany and the Soviet Union, the governments of the Baltic States were each presented with a Soviet demand for military bases in their territories. Pretexts were subsequently made for Soviet troops to occupy the three countries. Soviet republics were proclaimed, and these were 'kindly admitted' as integral parts of the USSR. Mass arrests followed. In Latvia alone, 6,000 people received long-term sentences for alleged anti-Soviet activities, and a further 1,488 were executed. Large-scale deportations also took place, and on 14 June 1941 34,250 people, including 4,000 children, were taken to the Soviet Union. Most were sent to an area north of the Arctic circle, where many perished in labour camps. The German invasion that followed was felt at first as a relief, a liberation, though disillusionment came quickly. And, later again, the Russian army came back.

The mood of the times is beautifully rendered in a short story, 'The Dove', by Knuts Lesins, one of the most sensitive and perceptive of modern Latvian writers. A Latvian, uprooted by the war, blown hither and thither, at last finds for himself a deserted farm. Around him the Germans are taking what they can, preparing to retreat. Soon the Russians will arrive. He refuses to leave. Compelled by suddenly awakened love, he begins to put the house in order. He knows that for safety he should leave; but for one night it is his farm. He belongs to it, it to him. And when the Russians come, he confronts them: 'What did you come here for, scum? To capture doves . . . ?' Inevitably they strike him down, violently: yet the total mood of the story is of achievement, fulfilment, even of peace.

The qualities of Lesins's stories are those of the Latvian people, that 'strong, resisting, quiet, and at the same time sensitive character' of which Lesins himself speaks in his introduction to the volume of short stories called *The Wine of Eternity*.[1]

The same quietist temper, lack of animus, capacity for endurance characterise also the Latvian immigrants of Bedford.

[1] Knuts Lesins, *The Wine of Eternity* (University of Minnesota Press, 1957). The translations of the story 'The Dove' and the folk song (see below, p. 55) are by Ruth Speirs.

I was born in 1922. When I was a boy, we had a little farm near Riga, not far from the sea. About twenty acres of land, with few cows and pigs, and we grew ourselves potatoes and corn. And I remember cutting the trees and going fishing. My father was often at sea. When the Russians came in 1940, it was in June, his ship was in South America. He had to return. The Russians put pressure on families for men to return. So he took ship and came back to Vladivostok and from there was sent back to Latvia.

Soon the Russians took many people away: on one day, about 35,000 people, mostly the educated people. Ulmanis, the Prime Minister, he died in Siberia, with many others. It was so bad with the Russians, I cannot describe. Many people living in woods. And when the Germans came in Riga, it was in summer time, in 1941, they came out of the woods. In a way, they looked at Germans then like liberators.

Then Germans recruited Latvians to fight Russians. My brother, he was younger than me, eighteen, he volunteered for army. He was one who liked adventure always. Later they had call up, and I joined army in 1943. We got sent straight out to Russia. We had couple of months' training there and afterwards we were in lines against Russians. I still remember loudspeakers along the Russian lines. Of course they knew which places were Latvian units. 'Give up and you will be treated right, otherwise you will know consequences.' We ignore these things. We have seen Russian treatment.

Well, we move about. Once we spend week in cattle wagon. Forty people in one wagon. No meals. We had to make our own coffee, get food as we could. Of course the straw was full of lice. Then, in May 1944, I got wounded. I remember there was few of us on patrol, walking in long grass, and suddenly noise of machine gun, and I feel something hit my leg like piece of wood. I fall down. They sent me out then and I was in hospital, still in Russia, and I knew my brother was near this place. I was lying on table and my brother walk in and I say, 'Don't worry. It is clean shot through leg. I shall go for couple of months' holiday.'

When I get out of hospital, Russians had advanced into my country and my unit was then in Latvia and I wanted to get back again. Then I was in convalescence near Danzig. People there told me I was lucky to get wounded. Just after, Russians overrun the unit, kill all but a few. Well, I couldn't get back, was moving round in Pomerania. That was last time I heard of my brother. He was commanding a little unit and he was wounded and they brought him out. Then I found out a thing puzzled me. He was shot in Germany in a camp near Danzig. That was October. I

ask what sort of camp it was and why he was shot. I have never
been able to understand. . . .

So then the Russians were coming, and everyone was running
away. Women and children screaming. Nothing to do. On coast,
town was full of people running away. We couldn't get anywhere.
Cut off. So we started to pull everything off uniforms. And the
Russians start to come in, and to shoot people, not just soldiers,
but old people, women and children. And everywhere dead
horses. People trying every way to get out in boats. Bigger ships
could not come in, only little ships. I remember there was old
lady left to die, screaming. No one to help her. Left to herself.
We were lucky. We get out on little ship and then to big ship. . . .
That town, Kolberg, you know, was really nice little town. . . .
There was no water in town. Canals full of dead people. You had
to make coffee from sea water. But there was lot of wine.

So we came to Lübeck, just after English air raid. All the
town destroyed. We met old Latvian and he had wife, child and
house there. When he came back he found big hole, and all was
gone. Another Latvian we see wandering round, he had been
taken into Russian army. Latvian fighting against Latvian. . . .
By this time we know everything is going to end. Sometimes we
had to kill horses to eat.

Came May 1945, we learned Americans not far away, and
then we were prisoners of Americans. Again, a new experience.
Of course, they didn't have much time to look after us, and at
night we put out own guards. There were many people let out
then from political camps and we were frightened. We still had
lot of schnapps, though . . . Americans used to drink with us.
No barbed wires round us. No need. Nowhere to run. Just to
wait, hope for best.

Then they send us on train near Hamburg. We find ourselves
behind barbed wires, with Canadian unit. There we had to
throw everything we had into ditch. I was very sorry. I had all
the time kept photos and things from home. So after, all we had
was what we had on, and all the soldiers were looking what they
could take. . . . Of course, food was very scarce. I was lucky.
Once I had tin of fat that was skimmed off food for soldiers. And
we took up nettles. So we could eat, spoonfuls nettles with
grease. And you had little piece bread each day. That was worth
10 cigarettes. Old type wedding ring on finger for packet of
tobacco. Was all like that. Just to keep on. Lucky it was summer
time.

Then news to move us, to Friesland, near Holland. By then,
few thousand of us Latvians all together. No barbed wires. We
were put in cows' stalls. Of course, everybody starving. But it

was August. There was corn, potatoes, peas and beans. We start stealing this food. And there was sugar beet, we were making Latvian gin, exchanging for cigarettes, and at night stealing animals. Then came winter. We slept together to keep warm, stole wood from fences to burn. One night we went to find chicken. Go in through window, open door, grab chicken, break neck, take sack of potatoes. Then back. About midnight, chopping chicken, cleaning pot. Yes, I remember. Nicest stew I taste for long time.

Then I heard Russians put pressures on English to give up Latvians. But they would not. But they said they could not help much. We did not have passports. We did not have civilian clothes. I made own cap and trousers from army blankets. Someone knew sewing. He told us how. And I had document but no photo. So I took photo of friend for my document. No one ask too many questions. With documents, we came on train to Oldenburg, then to village near Hanover. It was made refugee village. It was place where British airmen parachuted, and they had all been shot. So when they found out, they sent the people out, and it was made refugee village. We were there about couple of weeks. Food was good. We live like lords, making own whisky, selling on black market, why not? . . .

Then to Hanover. Accu Camp. DP camp. This was in 1946. I was there about year. We got out sometimes, try to repair houses, get a few marks. One man in my room was from concentration camp. Sometimes he came with others, from Dachau, Belsen and other camps, and they were telling experiences. Then we begin to realise, to understand. When Americans find them, they were hardly alive, they were so weak. The suffering, really, the suffering. . . .

In 1947, we find out English taking people. Of course, everybody for it, to find work. Everybody was excited. We went to coast, we had to wait two weeks. Everywhere full of refugees, sleeping in cellars, under the rubble. Then at last we went on boat. We had meal. Nothing much, but nice and clean. Tables set. And we had five shillings for cigarettes and razor blades. All different. You cannot imagine how we felt.

So we landed at Hull, a little transit camp, and then by train near Cambridge. I think we had five shillings a week. Someone found place near Cambridge with fresh smoked kippers and bakery selling bread, and we used to go there and come back with bread and kippers. . . .

It was June. It was strawberry time. So first job was to pick strawberries. You could make up to ten shillings a day. By the evening, your fingers were sore. After we went to jam factory, picking plums. So now we could afford to go to pub and taste English beer. . . .

Now we must make choice of place to work. Steel, cotton mills, coal mines or agriculture. I like fresh air, so I decide agriculture. I was sent Ely camp. Many nationalities there. Ukrainians, Poles, Hungarians, all kinds. Sleep dozen in a room. It was harvesting time. The first job was potato picking. Round Ely it was very light soil. I remember, first day, how the back aches, and the wind blows, and I fell on knees and thought it would be better to be in coal mines. Next morning, so stiff I could not move.

Of course, we couldn't spend much there. Big difficulty was going to town. If somebody speaks English, at least a dozen following. Hardest part was language. Simply language. I was at Ely more than a year. One day I cut hand very bad. Then for first time I was in kitchen. Chef was Latvian. He told many thing. . . . First, how to peel potatoes. That was first training. . . .

Then, after three years, we were, like . . . free. I went first to sugar beet factory at Bury St Edmunds. After to brickyards in Bedford for eighteen months. I remember first night on night shift at brickworks. It was wet. It was hard. We were staying in Kempston Hardwick hostel and we couldn't rest in daytime. I was eight months on night shift, trying to earn little money. I was really fed up. I thought I had to do something. One friend wrote me from Canada to go there, but I like to stay in England because it is near Europe. I think this is where I belong. Those first years, we were always hoping to go back to our own country. . . .

Then they were short of help in kitchen, so I go there as kitchen porter, doing cleaning jobs, peeling potatoes, until I hear of another job, in this place, where I am now. I wanted to get away from hostel, specially to improve English, so I came here in 1952. Very good head chef then. Good discipline. Clean. So he set me on and taught me and I tried my best and after a while he said to me why don't you settle down and do something in the kitchen? That was first time I think of it as career. . . .

Today he is a head chef of deserved reputation. He has worked for seventeen years in one place. He has roots in England now:

Since the war I do not hear anything of my family. Now I feel like English. But when I go to social evenings with Latvians, I feel like Latvian again. My wife is Irish. My children are English. They all like it here. I would be very happy to go back to Latvia, just for holiday . . . but you would not get visa. You frightened to go. And sometimes I see people begin to think of home, they do not know where they are. I try to put it out of my mind.

Sometimes I think of myself, with big beard, walking in my own country. And no one recognises me, not even my own brother. Stranger in my own country. . . . You don't hear of many people going back. One important thing to me, you know, that is freedom. . . .

By July 1948, there were about 300 Latvians living in the Bedford area and 98 per cent of them were employed in the brick industry. Most were farm boys, although there were also several professional men and university students. The brickyards, with utter impartiality, made labourers of them all.

At first, life in the brickyard hostels seemed almost a continuation of that in the camps: a life in limbo, waiting for the giant convulsions of war to die down, the national structure of life to be reasserted. For the time being, they could only wait, continuing to live as separate people thrown together by chance, aiming simply to make what money they could, to carry on as best they could, living from day to day.

Slowly, they began to sort themselves into groups. Some turned inwards towards their own people, their own kind, seeking security against past, present, and future: brutal memories of war and personal loss, crowded conditions of communal living, the demands of coping in an alien land among people of an alien tongue.

Others looked outwards, impatient of the hostels and their ways, eager to explore the possibilities of the new country, to make their own way. These stronger spirits turned their minds to learning English, to seeking lodgings in town. Here, their task was long and painful, as it had been for the Poles. They, too, encountered deep local fears of the foreigner. Sometimes, in the streets, they were laughed at for their strange speech, their alien mien. Looking for lodgings, they met at local doors suspicion, antipathy, rejection.

A common pattern developed in their search for lodgings. One of them, at last, would get his feet under a Bedford table; confidence would be created in that house; a friend would be admitted and confidence would grow; so, finally, a lodging-house would become a Latvian house, as another might become Polish or Ukrainian.

As with the Poles, the next step was to get property of their own, either as individuals or as a group. Again, there was suspicion to overcome, this time from the banks and building societies; and the search to find wives was beset with even greater difficulties. There were few Latvian girls except in London and few local girls were willing to give them time or consideration. To be a labourer was bad enough: to be a foreigner, worse. To be both together was almost unforgivable in local eyes.

Few found a welcome in Bedford at any level; and most rarely among the middle classes. Such friendship as they got came mainly from British fellow-workers met at pubs or football matches. One Latvian speaks with great warmth of the kindness of an English upper-class family who visited him in hospital during a serious illness and later took him to their own house for convalescence.

After his recovery, he met a Latvian girl who visited him regularly in Bedford before becoming his wife. 'It took me one year to think if I should marry my husband because he was living in Bedford.' She spoke without desire to cast aspersions or to give offence. It was the simple truth – and a wholly representative judgment on the friendlessness of the town. It is clear that, at every turn, the exiles found barriers: of nationality, language, culture, class and economic circumstance.

As EVWs, Latvians had to work three years as indentured labourers before they were 'freed'. By this time, the early fifties, political relationships between East and West had deteriorated to a seemingly implacable condition of cold war. Soviet control of Eastern Europe had tightened and for the people of the Baltic States, integral parts of the Soviet Union, hopes for freedom and independence had become hopelessly remote. It was time for the Latvians of Bedford to take stock, to face the bitter realisation that there was no way back, at least not for a very long time. They would have to dig in where they were, carry on as best they could, or seek opportunities elsewhere, perhaps even farther away from their own country.

To stay where they were could well mean carrying on as labourers, living in crowded hostels or bare lodging-houses, with little life they could call their own. For the older men, for those physically and mentally ill-equipped for work in the brickyards, for those borne down by harsh experience or personal loss during the war, this burden of realisation was especially hard to bear.

For some the burdens were too great. Several committed suicide. Others were broken in mind or retreated permanently from reality. One man still finds peace only in a mental hospital. He works helpfully there. From time to time, he has tried to leave. As soon as he is out of the gates, he begins to shudder uncontrollably. He has to go back.

Many of the solitary men – even today, half the Latvians in Bedford are single men – took to hard drinking. Some became alcoholics. The compassionate licensee of a pub used by a group of Latvians, and by other immigrants, says:

> The Latvians are the saddest of all. Despairing drinkers. They'll drink for days on end. All heavy drinking. And come Sunday morning early, seven o'clock, they will be knocking me up for more. No matter what . . . but never any violence. Never trouble. And no matter how drunk they are, they wouldn't dream to swear in front of me. Those Latvians are gentlemen to the death. Some of them, I think, died really in the war. They saw too much. And they know they cannot go back. They have accepted that they will die here. In that state, some people turn to religion, some turn to drink. . . . Those Latvians are the most lost of all. I have one, he is deaf and dumb. He doesn't want a hearing aid, he doesn't want to know anything any more. He just cut himself off. And now he has drunk himself out. He is waiting to die.

After they had finished their statutory terms of labour as EVWs, many Latvians sought life elsewhere. Some, including most of the highly educated, emigrated to Canada. A number went to Corby, where jobs and accommodation were easy to find. The majority soldiered on in Bedford, learning new trades, improving their material lot, making their own community.

Of the 176 native-born Latvians that remain in Bedford today, five are self-employed, five working in trades they had before the war, and many – since almost all of them come from farming backgrounds – have learnt new skills in several spheres of life. (Of the sixty-two who still work in the brickyards, most are in skilled trades.) In great part, their skills are practical, and no Latvians are employed in commercial enterprises.

The question of how far these exiles should or can preserve themselves as Latvians brings from them widely differing responses. Some, like B., have from early days seen the central task as that of making a new life in a new country. When he says, 'We cannot look backwards,' B. does not speak lightly. He remembers his roots vividly, as most Latvians do. In particular, he recalls with deep respect and affection his father's kindness, understanding, unwavering Lutheran principles, and the old man's words of resolution at the age of eighty in the face of Russian invasion. 'I am old. If I move, I should be lost. I shall stay here. I do not mind if I die here. I would prefer to die among the things I know.' Eighteen months later, his father died in a Siberian labour camp. His sister spent eight and a half years there. An uncle died also in Siberia and one of his two brothers was killed in the war.

Although the past is graven upon him, B. has seen no point in dwelling upon it or in it. From the beginning, he struck out on his own. Disliking the communal life of the hostel, he spent seven or eight months seeking accommodation in Bedford. At last, he found a place with other Latvians in a boarding-house. He lived there for five and a half years. He remembers that the Englishman who lived in the house next door on one side did not once throughout that time answer his 'good morning', though the people on the other side did at least answer his greeting daily.

At the brickworks, he worked first as a smudger, a man who supplies coal for the kiln-burners, then he taught himself the job of kiln-burner and, after a period as relief man, this became his regular job. He worked shift work seven days a week. He saved as industriously as he worked. Now he works in the brick company laboratories. He is happily married to an English wife, with a pleasant home and two sons at Bedford schools. The children have interest in things Latvian, although they do not speak the language. He does not force their interest. 'There is no question now of going back. In any case, there is now in Latvia a completely new generation. There, I would be a complete stranger, far more a stranger than I am here.' Here is his place now, where his family is. Here he belongs.

A sense of Latvian identity is naturally preserved most fully among the twenty-one all-Latvian families. A. met his wife in Germany while in a DP camp. She came to England to be married in 1951. Latvian is the common language of their household and their five children therefore speak both Latvian and English. The youngest child, a girl of four, still tends to mix the two languages. It is clear she will not be entirely fluent in English until she goes to school. Every week, the children attend a Latvian social evening, with classes in traditional Latvian dancing. The eldest son, now seventeen, attends meetings for Latvian adults. In such ways, a sense of cultural continuity is 'preserved, although it has little of the nationalistic intensity that one finds among some Serbs or Ukrainians.

Latvians are not people to delude themselves. Most recognise that, as time passes, as they themselves grow older, roots in Bedford grow deeper, their children's needs develop, and the dream of freedom and independence for their own country continues to lie cold, so their will to preserve their identity also inevitably weakens.

They have their own club meetings regularly and their own library of some 1,300 books. A Latvian Lutheran minister comes regularly to Bedford for services in the Moravian church. Apart from the dancing classes for young people, there are lively and energetic displays of Latvian songs and dances on occasions such as the annual celebration of their independence day (1918) each November. There are also fortnightly classes for the children in the language, history, and culture of Latvia. Their object is not simply to teach formally, but to try to create a sense of Latvian being in the imagination of the children.

For all this, they recognise they are losing ground. Nothing can overcome the barrier of physical separation. The children, for the most part, think of Latvia as a dreamland; some are not even sure where it is on the map. Without the sustenance of real, physical knowledge, it would be impossible for these children to conceive of their identity as other than English.

Here is the root of the difference between Latvians and Ukrainians on the one hand, the Poles and Yugoslavs of Bedford on the other. The latter can keep close human connections with their own countries. Some return regularly for holidays. Not only can the Latvians not do so, they have found that even to write home may endanger relatives. Human movement between Bedford and Latvia has been confined to one man who returned home from Bedford and three old Latvian people who came to join their families here some four years ago. Even this very limited movement has created difficulty. One of the old Latvians, a still vigorous lady of 76, wants only to return to Latvia. She comes from a deeply rooted way of life that is inflexible to change. Here, she has nothing in common with anyone outside her family. She speaks no English, has no friends, and hates the climate. She looked at me implacably while I drank tea with milk and sugar. She does not like English tea. For her son, the situation is deeply disturbing. 'It was very difficult to get the Russians to let her out. I do not know how we shall get them to take her back, but every day she says she must go back. We shall have to try what we can.'

No doubt of it, they are tenacious people. Stickers in every way.

One group of single men lived together in a brickyard hostel for twenty years until it closed down in the mid-sixties: then, they rented two adjoining houses in town so that their pattern of communal life could continue undisturbed. Once a Latvian buys a house, moreover, he wants to keep it. It is notable that very few of them – two or three at most – have resold houses bought in Bedford. A house is to have and to hold, and if their identity as a community wavers for lack of the homeland's sustaining soil, their temper as a people continues unalloyed. One sees it in the life of home and family, in the respect for family authority, in the neatness and order of their houses.

For Latvians, it is a hard fate to be cut off from their roots. Yet, even if some despair, they do not complain of their lot nor do they have much sympathy for others who complain, least of all for the waves of immigrants who came after them. Experience has hardened them, made many distrustful, suspicious, inward-looking. 'We, too, do not stretch out our hand any more. Somebody might cut it off.'

To the world, they are quiet, industrious, undemonstrative people. Their currents of emotion run deep, often dark. I watched a group of them lately listen to a fellow-countryman telling how he was taken on 14 June 1941 for many years in a Siberian labour camp. Theirs was the silence of intense concentration. The man's face was graven with suffering. As he talked, it became quick with intelligence and humour. I remembered the folk song that Knuts Lesins quotes in one of his stories:

> In the coffin where I shall lie soon,
> Pidiralla, pidiralla,
> I will spit at the ceiling and whistle a tune,
> Pidiridirallala.

4
Ukraine

AT the time of writing, 155 native-born Ukrainians live in Bedford, and they have 119 English-born children. Of 86 Ukrainian families, 22 are from marriages between Ukrainian men and women. The remainder are from marriages between Ukrainian men and foreign women, 34 of them British, 19 Italian, 4 German, 2 Austrian, 2 Polish, 1 Swiss, 1 Spanish and 1 Greek. There are also 47 single men, though this number includes a few forced to part from wives in the Ukraine. In Bedford, they own 79 private properties, together with a hall purchased communally for use as their church, and premises similarly purchased as a community centre. As a community, no other national group in Bedford is more single in purpose and being.

You may see community in their faces; their common background and their common hardships. And when they speak of the Ukraine, you may glimpse their common purpose: to keep Ukraine alive within themselves.

Even more than the Baltic states, the Ukraine has a submerged history, of constant foreign domination and of division. Its rich, black earth, its reputation as a granary, made it always a tempting prize for surrounding peoples. The Ukrainians of Bedford are imbued with a sense of their distinct identity as a people, their long and distinct cultural history. Yet only for the briefest moments in history has the Ukraine had distinct political existence.

From the ninth to the twelfth century there had been an independent nation with its capital in Kyiv; but not until the middle of the seventeenth century did anything resembling a Ukrainian state emerge. In 1654, the elected Hetman, or leader, of the Ukrainians, Bohdan Khmelnytsky, made a treaty with the Russian Tsar – the Treaty of Pereyaslav – aimed at defining relations between their two states. The terms, to say the least, were ambiguous. It was never clear whether Ukraine was to be the ally, or the vassal, of Moscow. In practice, Ukraine preserved independence until Peter the Great abolished the hetmanate. Division followed in the eighteenth century, the east under Russia, the western region of Galicia under Austrian rule. Galicia was allowed far greater freedom. It was here that Ukrainian national consciousness developed most strongly; and differences of temper between east and west were further emphasised by differences of religion. Most western Ukrainians belonged to the Greek Catholic Church, while most easterners were Russian Orthodox in their faith.

National consciousness grew more intense in the nineteenth century. It was given impetus by a literature rooted for the first time in the speech of the people. Its focus was the great national poet, Taras Shevchenko. In his poetry and in his life he became spokesman and symbol of his people. Born in serfdom, he spent long, harsh years in exile for his radical views and for his vision of a free Ukraine. Broken in health, he died in his forties. He has become a legend: in every sense, a poet of his people. In many Ukrainian houses his portrait is garlanded on a wall,[1] and there can be few houses where his poetry does not evoke profound response, not least among the exiles of Bedford:

> When I die, then make my grave
> High on an ancient mound,
> In my beloved Ukraine,
> In steppeland without bound:
> Whence one may see wide-skirted wheatland,
> Dnipro's steep-cliffed shore,
> There whence one may hear the blustering
> River wildly roar. . . .[2]

At the end of the First World War, there was again a brief moment of recognition for the Ukraine. Then eastern Ukraine was incorporated as a socialist republic into the Soviet Union, and in 1923 western Ukraine was made part of a recreated Poland. This was the immediate background of the exiles.

I was born in western Ukraine near Lviv. We lived on a small-holding, a little farm with a couple of cows. Family, there was five of us. When the war started, we thought who will come. We had had enough of the Poles. The Germans would be bad. The Russians would be very bad.

---

[1] See Plate 6.
[2] Taras Shevchenko, *Song Out of Darkness* (Selected poems translated by Vera Rich).

Well, first we had Russians for two years. What a life. No
clothing or shoes in shops. Little food. No freedom. And every
week, in every tenth house, a meeting for Russian propaganda.
We had to go, had to listen. My father told me: 'Beware. Do not
believe all you hear. Think what they have done in eastern
Ukraine. People murdered. Churches destroyed. Above all, the
famine they made here to destroy the people.'

The famine of 1932–3 leaves indelible marks on the Ukrainian
consciousness. Long traditions of peasant ownership created deep resentment and opposition to Soviet policies of collectivisation. In consequence, Stalin set out to destroy their 'nationalist deviationism'.
Leaders and intellectuals were murdered; millions of Ukrainians
sent to exile in labour camps, and a great famine manufactured
in this richest of lands. In *The God that Failed*, Arthur Koestler
wrote: 'I saw the ravages of the famine of 1932–3 in the Ukraine:
hordes of families in rags begging at the railway stations, the
women lifting up to the compartment window their starving brats
which, with drumstick limbs, big cadaverous heads and puffed
bellies, looked like embryos out of alcohol bottles; the old men
with frostbitten toes sticking out of torn slippers. . . .' Some 6
millions starved to death within a year. Across the frontier, their
fellow Ukrainians were powerless to help.

In 1939, they too experienced terror, so that, as in the Baltic
states, the coming of the Germans seemed at first like liberation.
On 30 June 1941, the organisation of Ukrainian nationalists proclaimed an independent Ukraine and a provisional government.
Their hopes were soon shattered. The leaders were taken into
concentration camps in Germany; others arrested or killed. Soon
it was clear that one form of oppression had been replaced by
another.

At this time I was fifteen or sixteen years old. The feeling
against the Germans was very strong. They showed great
cruelty. Many people were sent to forced labour, and when the
Ukrainian underground stopped trains going back into Germany, and let the people free, many were shot as reprisals.

From that time, resistance increased. An insurgent army was
formed, fighting first against the Germans, later against the
Russians, wreaking vengeance on both sides. Among its victims
were Lutze, commander-in-chief of Nazi S.A. troops, and the
Soviet Marshal, Vatutin. It was a resistance that continued active

until its leader, General Shukhevich, or Taras Cuprinka, as he was known, was killed in 1950.

At the end of 1942, the tide of war turned; and with Russians advancing, the Ukrainians took stock what to do:

To wait for the Russians or go back with the Germans? For many, it seemed that at least with the Germans, there was a chance of escape to the West. So, in 1944, I went to Germany to join the Ukrainian division. We were trained there, then sent to Czechoslovakia to fight the Communist underground movement. Some tried to escape there back to the Ukraine, and for a fortnight the Germans took away all our weapons. Then again we were given weapons and sent to Yugoslavia.

At last we heard that Hitler was dead. That Germany had surrendered. We were then twenty kilometres from the Russians and seventy-five kilometres from the British. We ran as fast as we could. Soviet tanks were behind us. We came to the British just in time. So we gave up our arms.

There were many other routes to exile and Bedford. N. was working on a smallholding when the Germans came in 1941.

Bad situation for girls and boys. Germans wanted people for work camps. Look all places to capture them: in church, on station, in road. Even take mother from child in street. Later they have card from her in Germany.

At this time, well, I am making politics. Gestapo looking for me. Head man of village come one day and say 'You are in danger. Suspect. Better to go yourself to Germany, voluntary, otherwise you go to concentration camp.'

They take me to Cracow, in Poland. Many people there taken into empty school, holding them five or six weeks. From there sent transport to Germany. Stalag 3. Many French, American, English officers in next camp. They throw chocolate, cigarettes over wall to us. Dangerous because Germans shooting. Six or eight weeks there, just waiting. Lights on all night. Germans watching us.

Then we go on train. People waiting for us to come out from train. Farmers look to see which look strong for good workers. Feel muscles. Like choosing slaves. Then shaved heads, so we are everywhere recognised. Could not run away. Walk ten kilometres to farm. No food. And in the morning, very early, work. No eight hour working day. At harvest time, work all day, sunrise to sunset. Little food. Sleeping on concrete. Work always hard, hard. Aching back and many boils. One time on back nineteen boils. But still work. No two three days on club.

'Well,' they say, 'you must carry "P" or "OST" sign, to show if you Pole or Russian.' I say: 'No, no, I am not Pole or Russian. Ukrainian.' Refuse to carry sign. So must go to court. After that, they let me go little more free. But still work, work.

When invasion of France, very bad time. Gestapo beat many people. Face beaten black blue because they find I have little knife. Then farmers begin to change, look to see what workers think about Hitler and so on. Not speak themselves, they frightened for Gestapo. Just look to see. Yes, they frightened. Start to be little better to workers. All that time, 1942 to 1945, I don't buy not one shirt. No new shoes or clothes. Wood shoes only for foreign workers.

Finish war, and more horrible than before. Before, afraid just for police and Gestapo. Now American troops, Russian prisoners, foreign workers, all with guns. Everywhere robbing and shooting, you don't know who friend or enemy. All round you – fear.

Americans collect many people in camps. First of all, many sent home, mostly east Ukrainians, because Russian subjects. That was terrible. People not want to go. Many suicide. Throw themselves from high buildings or from transport. People desperate. Then Americans stop mass deportations. Let people choose. Start screening. Let forty, fifty people at a time in big room. Raise right hand, swear to tell the truth. Then fill in form. Nationality. Subject. . . . What is this? Ukrainian? Not possible. Just Pole or Russian. 'No, no,' I say, 'I am Ukrainian.' Then big trouble. American MPs come in, and everyone shouting. . . .

Well, in 1947, they ask DPs in English zone if they want to go England; 1948, same in American zone. All young people want to go England. So at last begin three-month journey, Munich to Cambridge. All mixed up together, no one know which which. Russians put down 'Ukrainian' so not to go back. Some Ukrainians put down as Poles. I have 'Pole' on my card, so I cross it out and write 'Ukrainian'. When we come to England, Polish interpreter say: 'He is not Ukrainian. He is Pole.' I say, 'How can you put for horse, cow?'

We told we have choice of three jobs. Agriculture, coalmine, brickyard. But at Cambridge, they say, 'All up to thirty-five go to coalmine.' Many say no, not want to go. Stay there six weeks, and very good food. Very good. After, they stamp card for farm work. . . . Later, after contract finish, come to Bedford for brickyard. Kempston Hardwick hostel.

Those who became prisoners-of-war took a longer route to Kempston Hardwick. With thousands of other Ukrainians, they spent nearly two years in a camp near Rimini, on the Adriatic coast of Italy.

Afterwards, they told us we go to England. There were stories of fog and rain. And when I came to England, I had three words only, 'water', 'knife' and 'eat'. At first we spent one year and a half in a POW camp at Mildenhall in Suffolk, working on agricultural land. We had eighteen shillings a week, nine shillings in real money, nine shillings in camp money. In 1948, we were discharged with £30 for clothes and for what else we wanted. Then we were classed as 'Displaced Persons'.

We did not speak English, so we had to keep together. We went first to a sugar beet factory at Bury St Edmunds, then to Sudbury and Snettisham. Everywhere we lived in camps. I had a little book of English, and when it happened I had 'flu, two weeks in such a way, I learned all the little book by heart. In Snettisham we also had English lessons from interpreters. I learned very much from the pictures. The Picturedrome – that was my best teacher. You listen. You watch people move. You make connections, what they say and what they do. You begin to learn.

Then you go for a walk. You pass someone, and you say, in English for the first time, 'Good afternoon'. In my country, if you go by anybody, you have to greet them. In England, they turn away. Don't answer. That hits you. You feel very bad. You think they don't like you. Then you think more. Perhaps it is because they think you were in German army. Then you understand that in England they do not make such greetings. You learn to be careful, what to do, what not to do. In Italy, back in POW camp, they used to say 'Do not speak to English woman unless she smiles at you. Otherwise, trouble.'

Then we were told the camps would be ended. We were given three choices of work. Coalmine, brickyard, sewage farm. I chose brickyard. In 1950, I came to Kempston Hardwick hostel.

The hostel could take five or six hundred men at a time. In the twenty years after the war, thousands of paths crossed there, people of all kinds thrown together. There they paused in their exile, took stock, sorted themselves, making groups with their own kind. And when the men went out together, it was almost always in those groups. 'Move along! Move along!' they were often told by police distrustful of knots of men in the streets, men who clearly did not belong, who were often shouting out to each other in greeting or in drink. Where else could they go but the pub at the week's end? The hostel was scanty in comforts, few places in Bedford were welcoming. Soon the braver spirits had thoughts of another life.

In 1951 I left the hostel. From the beginning it was hard to find rooms. We would look at the board in the arcade in Bedford. Go to a house. They would look at us. Then they shut the door. It was all like this. After a long time, we found a house where was living a Ukrainian man and wife. At first the English lady would not accept single men, but the married friends guaranteed us. Like this, after a while, there were a few places which would take Ukrainians.

So, after perhaps ten years of being cast adrift, being moved on, making do, they began to think of their own place, of marriage, of making a home. At first there were few chances with local girls for these foreign men, coming strange and rough into an insulated world – and not only foreigners, but labourers too.

The Ukrainians often searched further afield than Bedford. They knew Ukrainian women had come to work in the cotton mills of the north and in Scotland. Some travelled to meet each other. A few men and women had even met before, in the DP camps of Germany. E. had been seventeen in 1942 when the Germans took her from the Ukraine for farm work in Bavaria. She met her husband in a nearby camp in 1947. After parting for their journeys to Britain, they wrote to each other from Scotland and Bedford. And when she could not get release from her job to join him, he came to Scotland to marry her. In Bedford she worked as a nurse in the hospital, he in the brickyard. They went from house to house together, but for almost a year could find no place to live.[1]

So upset all that time. He came to see me in the hospital, but not supposed to come in. I would say to matron, 'Can my husband come into sitting room, just for talking.' And at the men's hostel, women not supposed to go into rooms. We could only talk little time in the canteen.

The Ukrainians lived as they had always lived, abstemiously; saved, became slowly respectable in the town's and the girls' eyes. Fifteen or more years later, those early days seem a world away. Many of the men are married now, with children, property,

[1] Her present home is shown in Plate 6.

a home. But, by the same token, the gulf between Bedford and the Ukraine has grown that much wider.

Some know the families they have left behind have had to endure suffering of a kind unknown in the cocoon of contemporary Britain. B.'s parents were deported to Kazakhstan. In 1956, after seven years in a labour camp, they were freed. Back in the Ukraine, they could find no place for themselves nor jobs on collective farms. So they returned for some years to Karaganda, and now live in old age near the Black Sea, the father doing odd jobs on a collective farm. With them lives their other son, working now as a joiner after eight years in a concentration camp. Like B. himself, he had been a member of the Ukrainian liberation movement.

Despite their tenuous connections with the homeland, the Ukrainians of Bedford have not lost hope of return. They see in Czechoslovakia, Poland, even in the Soviet Union itself, signs of a loosening of bonds, perhaps of a crumbling of empire. 'We always live with hope: that there will be one day our country will be free. And then a lot of us will go back home. That is our hope.'

The intent to return is strongest in families where husband and wife are both Ukrainians. The passing years, of course, take their toll of this intent, not so much by sapping their will, as by strengthening English roots and commitments. The aspirations and needs of the second generation have a central place here; and not least in importance are that generation's problems of identity.

J. is seventeen. His parents are both Ukrainian. At school he is studying mathematics, physics and chemistry for A Level.

Years ago, I felt more English than Ukrainian. When I went to school, all my friends were English. Then, when I was about twelve or thirteen, I started to turn back towards my parents. I began to find, in many ways, that to be Ukrainian, there was much more interest, more meaning, like. Now I'm proud to say I am Ukrainian. Anyway, if I said I'm British, my name would give me away. It's more honest just to say 'I'm Ukrainian'. And I've found out, over the years, that with the British, if you say, 'I'm Jaroslav Madylus' straight out, then they accept you. But if you're, well, apologetic, or you try to hide that you're Ukrainian, or you cover it up, then they're not so keen on being friends. When I first went to grammar school, you know, they'd laugh at me. Some used to call me 'wog'. I suppose they didn't know a better word. Just joking it was with most of them. In the end, I told them: 'Look, my parents came here because they're political refugees. Because they've lost their own country. My mum and dad couldn't go back now, or if they did, maybe they'd never come back. Perhaps it would be the same for me, unless I had a proper British passport.'

Now I know what I am, that I'm Ukrainian, I no longer have to worry. I feel at ease. This girl I went out with last night, I said my name, and she burst out laughing. She said, 'You any relation to Engelbert Humperdinck?' We got on great. I think you gain so much from having, like, two ways of life. Here, in this house, this room, it's all Ukraine – [cushions and chair covers beautifully embroidered by his mother; pictures of saints, of cossacks and of Ukrainian leaders murdered by the NKVD; a carving of the Virgin Mary and a Ukrainian doll in national dress] outside, it's all England.[1] It gives you a chance to compare, to choose what you think best. You know, I wish it was possible to have lots of parents of all different countries. British, Ukrainian, Italian, West Indian, the lot. Then you would know every way of life. You could choose the best of each.

If the chance came to return, his parents would go back, and he would follow after he had finished his education. He has no doubts. Many other Ukrainian boys and girls are far less certain, both of their identity and their intent. Children of mixed marriages, in particular, feel that since they have been born here what else could they be but English? Some cannot imagine how they would live elsewhere. They may read or write Ukrainian, they may like – even love – Ukrainian things, but at root they are English. With the Ukraine, there is no real connection. They are English in instinct, values, tastes – fish and chips ever preferred to varenyky.

In general, it is the mother's way that prevails, her language, her way of life that determines direction in her children's lives, the extent to which they take part in Ukrainian activities. Most mothers agree to their children learning the Ukrainian language, and about twenty-five now attend Saturday afternoon language classes at the community centre. Some are less willing for their children to join the folklore groups, the dancing or the youth orchestra, of which J. is the leader. And, predictably, their attitude to the Ukrainian Catholic church in Bedford depends largely on the nature and strength of their own religious feelings.

For the Bedford Ukrainians, at least of the first generation, their religion is a primary bond, a natural part of their consciousness as a people. 'People who live with nature, they are more religious than city people, because they are always near God on their farms.' So

[1] See Plates 5 and 6.

re in this house it's all Ukraine — outside it's all England

Jaroslav Madylus study-
g for his A Levels. (See
. 63–4) Between the
otographs of the
rainian political mar-
s is the emblem of
ee Ukraine

6. Mrs Emilia Slobodian
(see p. 62) in tradi-
tional Sunday dress
embroidering tradi-
tional patterns. Above
her is the national
poet Taras Shev-
chenko

7. A Serb wedding ceremony
8. A rehearsal for Slovenian dancing in Bedford

says their priest, Father H., for most of his people are the sons of smallholders, and even those who have some other trade or profession – shoemaker, electrician, teacher – come from a way of life rooted in the land. Even after twenty-five years of Soviet domination, he says, every letter from the Ukraine still begins in the traditional way – 'Glory be to Jesus Christ'.

Their church in Bedford is a converted hall, bought in 1958 and opened in 1959. Father H. himself is an exile. 'Go somewhere and hide yourself,' his parents had said as the Russians advanced towards them in 1943, and he had left his seminary to complete his studies in Rome. There he was ordained, and now he serves some 550 parishioners in fifteen places from Northampton to Peterborough. Sometimes he feels he lives in a car – his petrol expenses for March 1969 were £22 18s 4d – but the value of his mission is clear, not only to the Ukrainians as individual souls, but in helping them to preserve their identity as Ukrainians.

It is on the matter of identity that Ukrainians are touchiest. The Home Office, it seems, like other British institutions, clings to the assumptions of 1939. The Ukraine is therefore without recognised political identity. In consequence, many of the people stay stateless. If they can't be Ukrainian, they will be nothing. There are discussions, arguments: to take British nationality, might this be a betrayal of their being? Might this compromise their identity? After their priest became a British national, he came back and asked 'Am I different now? Do I not think and feel just as I did before?' I don't doubt the people listened, nodding, taking the point – and clung to their doubts. Ukrainians are not people to shift easily.

This need to insist on their identity gives them an added edge in making their tightly knit, intensely active community. The house they purchased as a centre in 1962 gave this community focus and added impetus. Each week there is a busy programme of meetings and community activities. The Association of Ukrainians in Great Britain has a local branch membership of 94, the Association of Ukrainian Former Combatants 31, the Association of Ukrainian Women 13, and the Ukrainian Youth Association 44. There are also celebrations of anniversaries of national importance, from that of the poet Shevchenko to those of their political martyrs, Petlura, Konovalets and Bandera. At such times you may hear their fine choir; and they are justly proud of the choir's successes at Bedford's yearly music festivals. In 1969, alas, nine of the 23-man

c

choir were on night shift during the festival, and they were forced to withdraw their entry.

As this fact suggests, many Ukrainians still work in the brick-yards. Immediate reasons are that many have only limited English, and, since most were boys when the war came, few had education beyond the age of fourteen. In the DP camps, it was general that most of the older people, including the intellectuals, opted for the United States. The younger, more active men chose Britain. But it is not these things alone that hold them in their modest situations. It is also a matter of temperament and experience. They are not by nature high flyers. When they are content, they stick. Born to a modest way of life, they have suffered much and have learned, often bitterly, not to expect too much. They have learned to accept, to eschew ambition; above all, perhaps, to shun the light. In many ways, they feel consciously different from the immigrants who came later to Bedford: 'They came here to earn money to have a better life. We came here to save our life. We just want to live our life.' In brief, their aims are simply to live in peace and to preserve themselves.

With most other peoples of Bedford, their relations are amiable but not close. Though Slavs by race, they feel little kinship with the western Slavs, the Poles, or with the southern Slavs, the Serbs and Slovenes. With the Poles, in particular, there are too many ancient causes for enmity. 'Lvov is Polish,' say the Poles. 'Lviv is Ukrainian,' they answer. In Bedford, of course, historical differ-ences are tempered by a sense of their common suffering and their common domination – a sense shared with the Yugoslavs and with the people of the Baltic States. They are closest, perhaps, to the Latvians, also a people of smallholders, rooted in the land: a people also accustomed to take a little bag of soil with them when they quit the land, so that it may be buried with them. And beyond that, the Latvians accord them what the Poles do not, a recognition of Ukraine as a separate political entity. That, for them, is the heart of the matter: Ukraine as a living, independent fact.

Their attitude to the later immigrants, the Italians, West Indians, Pakistanis and Indians, is one of reservation. They classify them as those who came for money, people of different purposes and being. As for the British concern over immigrant problems, they would have been more impressed if it had come twenty years earlier. When the Bedford International Friendship Association was formed in the mid-sixties, for instance, their reservations were tinged with a certain irony. The best thing for any people, for any community, they said flatly, was to learn to help themselves.

In those times, after the war, there was no one to help us. Why did we have to wait twenty years before anyone thought of the problem? These people must organise themselves. Self-help. We got our own church. No one gave us a penny. We got our own centre. They have to help themselves. It is best for them so.

Their lack of sympathy points particularly against the West Indians. Many, they feel, 'hate English'. This offends the Ukrainians. Like all the Slav and Baltic peoples of Bedford, they have their own reservations about British policies, particularly after Yalta; yet there is also a deep sense of obligation to, even affection for, the country that gave them asylum, and a deep respect, at least for the England that was, if not so much for the England that is.

For contemporary Britain, they have diminishing regard. That is one sentiment which unites immigrants of all kinds and conditions. In general, their reactions to the permissive society are those of shock and repudiation. Discipline, order, authority: these are words often found on the lips of the first generation immigrants, and surprisingly often among young people of the second generation. There are constant condemnations of British laxity in morals and authority, the weakness of parents and teachers. Many confess they are sad to see the country of 1940 in the guise of 1969. Their feelings, no doubt, stiffen their resolve to preserve themselves.

Time will weaken this resolution as it will weaken their connections with their homeland. Yet still the Ukrainians preserve themselves with pride, industry, devotion. Who can doubt it when their choir sings, and you watch faces on which suffering is written together with power to endure. All stand for Shevchenko's *Testament*. There is an elegiac note of tenors, and, at the last, bass voices in swelling resolution:

> Make my grave there – and arise,
> Sundering your chains,
> Bless your freedom with the blood
> Of Foemen's evil veins!
> Then in that great family,
> A family new and free,
> Do not forget – with good intent,
> Speak quietly of me.

5
Yugoslavia

SERBIA

THE last act of Milovan Djilas's novel *Montenegro* is imbued with a tragic sense of man's inevitable march to a destiny of conflict to the death with his fellows: 'Bull butts against bull in the place where the cattle mass and shall not man against man?' The spurs of action are, on the one hand, the violent, idealistic nature of the Serbian protagonists, on the other the promptings of a political agent – opportunist and manipulator – for whom the human conflict may serve a turn. The end is senseless carnage – 'A woman, the Moslem Fata, shouted into the darkness: "This is the end of Montenegro; the Montenegrin chiefs have butchered each other".'

Talking to the Yugoslavs of Bedford, Djilas's symbolic vision possesses the mind: 'There were unresolved political conflicts, there were acts of violence, attempted murders, conspiracies, imprisonments, escapes from the country, and wanderings in foreign lands.' Though the southern Slav people have made up a single country since the end of the First World War, the main ethnic groups – Serbs, Croats and Slovenes – differ greatly in national character, traditions and aspirations. Religion–Orthodox, Catholic, and Muslim – also divides them; and to this may be added deep social and political divisions. Even in notions of government, centralist ideas war with concepts of federal organisation.

In Bedford today, there are some 400 Serbs and some 60–70 Slovenes. The Serbs, the largest ethnic group of Yugoslavia, have long been fiercely proud of their distinct Serbian heritage. In mediaeval times they were the only southern Slav people to achieve independent political existence. Their zenith of power was marked by the coronation of Stephen Dusan on Easter Day 1346 as emperor of the Serbs, Croats, Bulgarians and Albanians. Later, after nearly five centuries of Turkish rule, two Serb uprisings in the early nineteenth century restored their country as an independent kingdom. The first, between 1804 and 1813, was under George Petrovic, better known as Black George or Kara George, from his black hair. 'He was one of those wild, elemental natures so often found among the savage peasants of the Balkans, cruel yet heroic, wild yet generous.'[1] The bravery and purpose of himself and his people allowed them to regain control of much of Serbia, only to lose it again through intrigues and dissensions in their own ranks. By a second rising (1815–17) under Milos Obrenovic, Serbia achieved autonomy and Milos was elected as hereditary prince of his country. Serb national feeling developed with rapid intensity, though the murder of Kara George in 1817 led to a long and bitter blood-feud between the two ruling families which dominated Serbian political life throughout the century. It was characteristic of the insensate hatreds and feuds that so indelibly mark Serbian history.

The Serbs took the lead in helping to create the new independent kingdom of Serbs, Croats and Slovenes in 1918, and they pressed for a centralised state under the Serbian dynasty with its capital in Belgrade. In this they were challenged by the Croats, mainly Catholic in religion where the Serbs were Orthodox, who feared and resented Serbian domination and advocated a federal structure of government, giving autonomy to the various regions. The first fruits of the new state were bitter antagonisms, corruption, and a political atmosphere charged with violence. This exploded in 1928 with the murder of the Croat leader Radic, his brother, and another Croat deputy, in the National Assembly; and in 1934 with the assassination of King Alexander in Marseilles by an agent of the exiled Croat Fascist leader, Pavelic.

After the German occupation of April 1941, this same Pavelic became ruler of the newly proclaimed independent state of Croatia. There followed a reign of terror as vile as anything in modern history, against Serbian Orthodox Christians, Jews, and Muslims. Between 1941 and 1945, there were exterminated 750,000 Serbs, 60,000 Jews, and 26,000 gipsies. The account is sickening: of eyes, tongues, genitals, and hearts torn from living flesh; of women raped and hacked to pieces; of children impaled upon stakes. Most monstrous of all is the picture of Ante Pavelic showing an Italian visitor a gift from his followers, the Ustase – a basket containing 40 lb. of Serbian eyes. Hate proliferated, leaving permanent scars.

[1] H. W. V. Temperley, *History of Serbia* (London, 1917).

Some in Bedford have seen such things first-hand. One man saw Orthodox Serbs crowded into their own church and there burnt alive. In his own village, some 3,000 people were knifed to death by the Ustase and their bodies thrown into three great holes. The late summer of 1941 was hot. The bodies, swelling and putrefying, pushed back the light cover of soil, revealing horror. One woman, as a young girl, saw her family cut to pieces, was forced to serve the murderers, and then escaped while they were drunk.

The Germans knew Serbia was a tougher nut than Croatia. The partition of Serbian lands in 1941 reduced it considerably in size and for the rump a puppet 'Government of National Consolidation' was founded under General Nedic, former war minister. Although Serbs, in general, were opposed to the Germans, the new government made appeal both to Serbian nationalist feeling and to anti-Croat and anti-Communist sentiments; and these motives led men now living in Bedford to join Nedic organisations. Among these were the militia or State Guard, special security battalions organised by the Serbian Fascist leader, Ljotic, and the Chetniks of Kosta Pecanac. These Chetniks derived their name from the bands of guerrillas founded originally to fight the Turks. The Germans, of course, in Serbia as in Croatia, did everything possible to manipulate patriotic and religious feelings and associations, in order to create internal hatred and division.

The official Chetnik organisation was quite distinct from the Chetnik groups which crystallised round Draza Mihailovic to form the first organised resistance to German occupation. Many of Bedford's Yugoslavs served with Mihailovic, a pious and patriotic Serbian officer loyal to the Crown, and opposed alike to Germans, Croats, and Communists. This fact was the vital flaw in his – and their – standpoints. He and his Chetniks opposed themselves to forces themselves opposed to each other. This led them, first, to make brave and determined resistance to the Germans. Later, after the occupation of Russia in June 1941 and the formation of a Communist resistance organisation, they came also into conflict with Tito's Partisans. Thereafter, a policy of expediency prevailed, local Chetnik leaders at times making accommodations with the Germans against the Partisans.

Who was enemy, who was friend? To whom was a man's first loyalty due? For many Serbs in Bedford today, the tragedy was that the highest motives of idealism and patriotism often led them only to political and military confusion, and served only to extend chaos and suffering in their homeland. In the belief that communism was a more permanent, more dangerous enemy than Nazism, many Serbs who had begun by fighting the Germans came at last to side with the Germans against Communists. This was only partly a matter of Mihailovic's own policies. It also derived a good deal from the will and the situation of his local Chetnik commanders.

Some Chetnik groups were also dominated by strong separatist feelings. One group based on Dalmatia still maintains an identity quite distinct from that of other Chetnik groups in Bedford twenty-five years later. It had formed originally to fight the Italians after the partition of 1941, whereby Italy was granted the Dalmatian coast, southern Slovenia, and military control of Montenegro. Subsequently, the men fought with equal zeal against Germans, Croats and Communists. On one side of the coin was pride and patriotism: on the other, hate and dissension.

Finally, Mihailovic came to direct his forces as much or more against the Partisans as against the Germans. In so doing, he gradually alienated allied support. And among the southern Slav peoples themselves, his Serbian, royalist sympathies made a far more limited appeal than Tito's 'Death to Fascism. Freedom to the people.' In early 1944, Churchill recognised Tito as leader of Yugoslav resistance, and in August 1944 the young King Peter, in exile, followed suit. This alone was a bitter and confusing blow to Serbian patriots who had identified Mihailovic with the royal cause: and new conflicts and loyalties were thus added to the political, religious, regional and organisational conflicts already existing.

In Bedford today, they rage on. So many brave men, so much hatred and division. 'If only there were as much intelligence as there is heroism, as much unity as there is quarrelling.'[1]

Following Tito's visit to the Soviet Union in September 1944, the Red Army joined the Partisans in Yugoslavia to recapture Belgrade on 20 October. Thereafter, the Mihailovic forces fell back in front of their advance, three divisions finally withdrawing into Italy, two divisions to Klagenfurt in Austria. As opponents of the recognised Yugoslav resistance army, their status was uncertain. The men were gathered in camps and required to hand in their arms. They were virtually prisoners. For many, it was a bitter ending to their struggles. One man saw three of his companions, in despair, lie down over hand-grenades and pull out the pins.

[1] Milovan Djilas, *Montenegro* (London, 1964).

Pressures from Tito's side for the return of Mihailovic's military leaders also bred fear and resentment. In some camps there were emotional scenes as soldiers gathered to protect their leaders. In other places, they wept as leaders left them to go back to their deaths.

Most terrible of all was the fate of many Chetniks and other Yugoslavs who had retreated into Austria. On guarantee of safe conduct, they handed in their arms and were put aboard trains for Italy. As the trains passed through Yugoslav border country, they were halted by Partisans, the men taken out, divided into groups, and most over the age of eighteen were massacred in cold blood, many machine-gunned over open graves. As a few survivors came back to Klagenfurt, there was panic to stop more trains departing, though some men chose to leave on trains already arranged so that they might die with their comrades. For the Chetnik refugees, the cup of wormwood spilled over.

Most were sent to camps in southern Italy, treated as prisoners-of-war rather than as allies, though not always closely confined. To their resentment was added suspicion that Titoist agents were infiltrating their ranks to stir up conflict. The murder of Tito's consul in Naples was almost certainly an act of revenge. Later, the men were sent to POW camps in Germany as 'voluntarily surrendered enemy personnel'. Again, there were requests from the new Yugoslav Government for the extradition of Mihailovic's officers.

One such was M., a regular officer before he became a Chetnik leader. 'In guerrilla warfare, rank does not count. Counts man. You follow man, not rank.' He who had fought bravely and with pride for his country, now suffered the humiliation of questions by British officers on Tito's behalf. He and others were privately advised to get clear of their camp as best and as quick as they could. So, in the chaos of post-war Germany, many collected again in DP camps and came eventually to England as EVWs.

On arrival in England, M. and many others were questioned as to their background, education, and skills. Among intellectuals and professional men, hopes were raised of employment suiting their talents. In the end, the questions proved meaningless. All were disposed to work as labourers on farms, in mines, or in heavy industry. Thus, a brain surgeon who had served the British forces in Italy became a farm labourer, a lawyer a brickworker, like M. himself, who was well-educated and spoke five languages.

Some 66,000 Yugoslavs came to Britain in such ways, about 800 of them to Bedford, mainly for work in the brickfields. They soon gained a reputation as good workers. Most were country people, small farmers from frugal and hardworking backgrounds, hardened by recent experiences, although, as in other refugee groups, the older people and those unaccustomed to physical labour found it difficult to adjust to the tough demands of work in the brickfields and of making a new life in a new country.

The essential difference between Yugoslavs and other post-war Europeans is that their country is not controlled by the Soviet union. Although political fears still prevent most from returning home, even for a holiday, there has been a considerable movement of people, mainly in family groups, between this country and their own. Thus, while there are few, if any, Poles, Latvians or Ukrainians in Bedford between the ages of twenty and forty, there are a number of young Yugoslavs between twenty and thirty.

S.'s father came here as a brickworks labourer in 1947. S. and his three brothers were brought up in Yugoslavia by the mother. He remembers, as a child, the older people sitting down together at Christmas and family occasions, talking of the good old days and crying as they talked. The family were denied rations and other benefits because the father was in England. Then, in 1956, his mother unsuccessfully applied for the whole family to join the father in Bedford.

By this time, S. had completed the first two years of a four-year university course in architecture. Tremendous efforts by the whole family were needed to support him. The cost of his education to his mother was almost equal to her wages and they were kept going largely by money sent from Bedford. S. was disturbed and divided in mind; on the one hand conscious of being a burden on the family, on the other wishing to join in the full range of student activities. While the family application to leave Yugoslavia was under consideration, he left university and worked for a while as a village postmaster. Later he joined a youth group working on a new motorway. A second application to leave Yugoslavia was successful and in 1958 the family travelled to England.

On the way from Dover to London, I would have gone back. The flat countryside, the backs of houses, the tiny gardens and yards all dirty and depressing. In Yugoslavia, at least there are open fields, rivers, animals. You felt nature alive round you. I had romantic dreams, though, of continuing studies at

C2

Cambridge, where I imagined my father would keep me. Then I found he was not rich at all, that he worked very hard in the brickyards. My dreams collapsed. I went with him to the brickyards and I worked there for two years.

Everyone, of course, told me all about British life. I knew nothing. I could speak very little. 'All English workers are so bad and slow. You will soon recognise them. They do so little!' Then, all about the unwritten laws. 'You can lean on a shovel, doing nothing. That is all right. But do not put it down. Do not go away from it. That means trouble. And keep away from drink and women. The English girls are not good girls. . . .'

Well, I looked around for these famous English workers, and one day I saw this man – a big, red-faced man, shouting at everyone, doing nothing at all. My father was working close by. I went to him. I said, 'Yes, I see exactly what you mean about English workers. That man there. . . .' My father looked. He said, 'Why, you fool, that is a Yugoslav.' And, of course, I did go out with English girls. Sometimes when I should have been at English classes, I would slip away to take an English girl to the pictures.

After several years, S. began work in an architect's office, studying for professional examinations in his spare time. He has recently become an associate in a firm of local architects. One brother is a manager of a garage, another the manager of a small works, another a charge-hand. Like most younger men, S. has adapted quickly and intelligently to English life and language. At the other end of the scale are the older men who came in 1947, some of whom have no more words of English than they have years of life in this country, and who are often set fast in their traditional ways of life and their traditional political loyalties.

The gulf between younger and older Yugoslavs in Bedford is not merely to be expressed in terms of differences between the generations. To many Serbs who left their country at the war's end, confined by conservative traditions and hostility to communism, everything and everyone associated with the homeland since Tito came to power has the smack of communism about them. Distrust comes to them as naturally as the air they breathe. In Bedford today, one may even hear Mihailovic criticised as unpatriotic on the sole ground that he had discussions for joint action with Tito in 1941. Small wonder that young people of the families that came from Yugoslavia in the fifties are not free from suspicion, and the less ready the younger men are to accept the narrow, intense loyalties of the older people, the more suspect they are.

Political distrust and divisions intrude even into their religion, the one possible unifying force in a Serbian community. Suspicion breeds that the centre of the Serbian Orthodox faith in Belgrade may itself be tainted by communist influence; and this leads some to renounce the authority of the patriarch in Belgrade in favour of the so-called American patriarch. After the First World War, a North American diocese ruled over by a bishop was created for Yugoslav immigrants. In recent years, this has taken added dignity upon itself to make a centre for Serbian orthodoxy free of any possible suspicion of communist influence. More than ten per cent of Bedford's Yugoslavs now look to this authority.

While such divisions persist, the chances of creating a true community of Serbs in Bedford are slim. Some ten years ago, attempts were made under the auspices of the Church to found a committee to promote social and cultural organisation. The first tasks were to see that the interests of all political factions were adequately represented. Arguments were long and passionate, punctuated by threats of withdrawal by this group or that. Finally, during 1962 and 1963, a number of activities were launched. A successful drama club has performed in recent years to other Yugo-slav communities in London, Manchester, Birmingham, and Corby. Folk-dancing and choir groups also sustained themselves for a while, though the dancing group failed gradually as girls fell out on getting married.

In 1963–4, a Yugoslav school was founded, at first with a teacher from Oxford, later with a teacher from the local community. Some thirty children were divided into two groups according to age, for ten hours' teaching a month in Yugoslav language and history. Recitals of music and poetry were also given for national festivals, although not infrequently these were attended by argu-ments as to whether poems in favour of King Peter or Draza Mihailovic should be recited, and the organisers found it increas-ingly difficult to resist pressures for the children to recite poems of past bloodshed and conflict.

The clash of factions finally broke the committee and closed the school. When the time came to dispose of the school's assets, divisions were so extreme that there was even a suggestion for a table housed in the school to be cut in half. Not until 1968 did the school reopen and, although at present continuing, there are some differences as to whose needs it should serve and in what ways. In particular, should the younger children be taught Serbo-Croat for the sake of the community or English to help them to cope more readily in English schools?

There is a saying in Yugoslavia, 'God help us if the Serbs unite.' Intelligence and energy abound among them. Traditions of Serbian culture strongly persist, and not least the traditions of family responsibilities and obligations: 'If I were to let anyone in my family go to an old people's home, I would be an outcast. It is more than duty. It is pride.' In their family lives, love and authority go hand-in-hand. Serbs have no sense that these impulses are in any way opposed, and are certain that both must be present for the family to have full meaning.

Their family life thus has a strength and richness of relationship which they feel is waning in contemporary English society. The household gods have had a central place in Yugoslav life since pre-Christian times and families today still have their household saints and keep their slava – their annual family days. Family bonds and family hospitality in this way continue to have the force of religious sanctions.

Thus, I have been given hospitality by a Serbian family even while obviously suspected of being a police spy. Suspicion and fear continue to condition too many good people. There are fears of informers and fears of Titoist agents infiltrating their ranks to foment conflict. Such fears have been reinforced in mid-1969 with the murder of several Yugoslav emigrés in Europe. 'They are damaging us from day to day. But we are fighting. . . .'

There are some – particularly the more educated – who stand apart from the factions. Others would wish to do so but are chained to their comrades by past loyalties. Their great tragedy is a distrust of their own people, even of those who serve their faith. 'All this plotting is going on in the darkness of eclipse. There is whispering on all sides. We know nothing, we can do nothing. The Serbs begin to split into pieces: but who can split his own soul?'[1]

SLOVENIA

Among the Slovenes, one breathes a different, calmer air. Though exiles, they are people at peace. Though Slav by origin, they seem by nature more akin to Austrians than to Serbs.

Slovenes have lived in the valleys of the eastern Alps since the sixth century. They are country people, many living on small

[1] Milovan Djilas, *Montenegro.*

farms. Some 1½ million live in their homeland, about ½ million in the bordering countries of Austria, Italy and Hungary, and a further ½ million in the rest of the world, mainly the Americas. There are now about 600 Slovenes in England, over 10 per cent of them in Bedford.

From the end of the eighteenth century, national consciousness among the Slovenes, as among many European peoples, grew rapidly. Under French rule, the Slovene language was encouraged in the schools, and the country's organisation and material conditions were vastly improved. When the area was returned to Austria after the Congress of Vienna, German influence and language once more prevailed, though constantly resisted. By 1914, however, Slovenes controlled the local government of Carniola and Ljubljana was Slovene.

Unencumbered by the conflicts of Serbs and Croats, and in close touch with the ways and means of Central Europe, Slovenes developed their economic and cultural organisations with speed and efficiency. To this, their religion gave added impetus, for Catholic clergy took a leading part in the national movement, in developing the co-operatives which did much to build up Slovene economy, and in establishing effective traditions of Slovene education. The Slovenes showed themselves, in brief, a practical, competent and devout people. By the time they came to take their place in the kingdom of the Serbs, Croats and Slovenes, they were generally better educated and better off than their Slav neighbours.

Following the German occupation, northern Slovenia came under German control, Italy receiving Ljubljana and southern Slovenia, and Hungary a small area to the east. The partition divided R. from his parents; they were in a German zone, he was studying in Ljubljana. The difference between life in the two zones was very great.

In the north, German rule was efficient and utterly ruthless. A thorough de-nationalisation was attempted. No Slovene schools were allowed. Indeed, the language was utterly forbidden. The Slovene educated classes were almost wiped out. Doctors, lawyers, priests – especially priests – were killed, ejected into Serbia or Croatia, or deported to the Reich. In the southern zone, the Italians were much more genial and less competent masters. They began by promising to respect Slovene culture. The University of Ljubljana and the Slovene

schools continued to function. The Slovene newspapers were
not suspended. Slovenes were not taken for the army. The clergy
were treated with respect.[1]

As resistance to the occupying powers increased, Italian attitudes
inevitably hardened. In 1943, R. found that he could not gain
admission to the university unless he joined the Fascist Party. He
abandoned his hopes for study. In the northern zone, his mother
was shot by Partisans. 'I tried to get a job. At labour exchange they
sent me to work on a building-site as a labourer. Italian soldiers
with guns watching us. After few hours, hands bleeding. After first
day, I did not go back.'

Later in the year, he joined the police; he also joined a Chetnik
underground movement, and used his job to distribute illegal
literature. Since the Germans had taken control of the whole
country after the fall of Italy, he was in constant danger. His
superior was caught and sent to Dachau. There was danger, too,
from Communists who had also infiltrated the ranks of the police.
In Slovenia as in Serbia, although to a lesser degree, there was the
same bitter round of hostilities between Germans, Chetniks, and
Partisans: the same tragic misalliances for the best national and
religious motives.

R. left Ljubljana on the evening of 8 May 1945, just before the
town was taken by Partisans. He crossed the border to Klagenfurt
and there, by lucky chance, fell ill, thus avoiding the trains which
took thousands of fellow Slovenes to their death at the hands of
Partisans. After some years in DP camps in Austria, he came to the
brickfields in Bedford in 1949 as a EVW. He lived in the Coronation hostel until he married his Slovene wife in 1951. After forced
labour in Germany, she had been a servant with the British
occupation forces and then with an officer's family in London.

The couple had little money and used much of what they had to
send parcels home to their families in Slovenia. Like most of their
kind, they worked without respite. At first, they felt keenly the
force of British insularity and the constant allusions to 'bloody
foreigners'. Then they came gradually to realise that what they
endured was not so much active hostility as traditional habits of
mind and traditional forms of words. And, with the coming of the
Italians, British antipathies were transferred from the post-war
Europeans to the Italians, just as, with the coming of the West

---

[1] 'Dacius', *Yugoslavia* (London, 1945).

Indians, they were transferred away from the Italians. 'Dislike is always most towards the lastcomers and the least familiar.'

Z. stayed on in Slovenia after the war's end. A farmer's son, born near Maribor in the north, he had attended an agricultural college and, at the time of the German attack, was training as a reserve officer with a 75mm gun battery. After capture, he was sent to a stalag in Germany and set to work on a dairy-farm. The farmer, an old soldier of the First World War, gave him understanding and extra rations. Z. escaped back to Slovenia, only to be called up for the German Army in 1943. Determined not to fight for the Germans, he enlisted for fear of reprisals against his family, and deserted later in the year. Back in Slovenia, sick with heart trouble, he went into hiding and was looked after in secret by his sister. His brother was killed on the Russian front.

At the end of the war, he came under suspicion by the Communist Party. Threatened with death, he declared, 'I was not traitor born. I will not traitor die.' He wanted only to keep clear of politics and to live in peace. In 1946, he married, settled on his own small farm of forty acres, and was given a position on his local council. At that time the Tito government, in attempts to enforce collective agricultural policies, was making impossible demands on local farmers and smallholders. Almost all production went directly to the state, leaving little for local people, and many farmers were forced to buy corn back from the state at exorbitant prices. Protests, disturbances and organised resistance quickly developed. Z. himself became involved in that resistance. In October 1947 there were waves of arrests.

I was still free, but I knew my days were numbered. There was young daughter, only three months old. Wife still suffering from birth. Along the frontier, mines and swift river. I said I would give myself up, but my wife said, 'You have to resist or be killed.' On November 8, I went to a meeting of local officials. All day, I was expecting they must come for me. When I came home, very tired, I called for a glass of wine. Then my wife saw men outside at the gate, some way from the house. My wife went out to meet the leader. I pushed baby's pram into a corner. Then, as they came up to the back door, I went out of the front door, quickly away into the trees.

That evening, I came back to fetch wife and daughter. It was impossible. My wife came out on to the balcony, with child crying. She made me signal not to come to the house. Men were inside, waiting. So, after a few days' hiding, I went across the river. Battling for my life there a good hour against the stream. I did love my wife and child too much to give up life. Then I found a log of wood fixed between rocks in the stream and stopped there to get strength. I had with me half-bottle brandy. I remembered they say brandy acts soon but not long. I drink brandy. Wait ten minutes, then cross rest of river into Austria.

In 1948 he came to the brickfields in Bedford. In the intervening time, his wife was several times questioned, a guard kept on house and village, and a price put on Z.'s head. Then he heard that his wife was to stand trial. To clear her of suspicion of shielding him, he wrote to say he was now in England. 'We decided to love each other whatever the situation.'

In 1947, she was tried and sentenced to 2½ years' hard labour. For 1½ years she worked sixteen hours a day, first carrying concrete: then, when her health became poor, on a state farm. The little girl was looked after by his family. In 1950, Yugoslavia accepted aid from the Western powers and, although no strings were officially attached, amnesty was given to some 11,000 political prisoners on New Year's Eve 1951. S.'s wife went free at this time, although her applications for a passport to leave Yugoslavia were six times refused, and it was not until 1964 that she and her daughter were able to join her husband in Bedford. They had been apart sixteen years. Although Z. still works in the brickfields, they now have a small farm.

From the beginning, the Slovenes in England cleaved together. The Slovene Association was founded in London in 1949 and in that year, R. wrote the Christmas play performed by them in Clapham South underground station shelter. As the London Association declined in force, the community in Bedford developed on its own account. In 1962, a Slovene Cultural Association was founded here. The members, sixty or seventy, including children, found rooms to meet as and where they could, avoiding church halls if possible because they like to drink where they meet. Over the years drinking habits have been changing from wine to beer. Since 1968, the small active community has used an old hut behind the Catholic club for meetings. Several times a year, too, the priest who serves all Slovenes in Britain visits them for services in their own language in the Catholic church.

Hard work and self-help characterise the Slovene community in Bedford. In the early days, a number took more than one job to make savings, and one old lady worked both as a hospital cleaner and at washing-up in a hotel. They live frugal and abstemious lives, pooling money to make first payments on houses for newly married fellow countrymen.

From the conflicts of the Serbs they keep clear, although, like the Serbs, they put great emphasis on family life and festivals. It is at Christmas and on family occasions that they feel most acutely the separation from their homeland. And, like the Serbs and other immigrant groups, they are made sad and anxious by the failing of family life in British society and by the growth of a permissive moral climate. 'With my daughter growing up, at times I feel desperate.'

The Slovenes are kind, modest, hospitable and stable people, making in Bedford a small, strong, self-regulating community. With local people they live in peace, respected for their hard-working respectable qualities. And, withal, they preserve their own identity as Slovenes.

Nowhere is that better demonstrated than in the ways they preserve the traditions of Slovene songs and dances: and the measure of their strength and unity is that at times of cultural festivals half the community – more than thirty people – take the stage to sing and dance in colourful costumes they themselves have made. At such times they show how, in Bedford, Slovenia lives on.

6
Italy

TEN per cent of the population of Bedford – some 7,000 people – are Italians: 51 per cent of them are men, 49 per cent women; 30 per cent are under 14, 22 per cent between the ages of 14 and 29, 44 per cent between the ages of 30 and 64, 4 per cent over 65. They have created a settled pattern of family life in Bedford and have a high rate of natural increase.

To know these immigrants, one must know something, at least, of the places from which they came. The great majority are from southern Italy, a world for long utterly distinct from the affluent, industrial north – in effect, a separate nation. Thirty per cent are from Campania, 15 per cent from Calabria, 15 per cent from Abruzzo, many from the areas such as Carlo Levi[1] describes, where, according to local legend, Christ never came – 'that land without comfort or solace, where the peasant lives out his motionless civilisation on barren ground in remote poverty, and in the presence of death.'

Twenty-five per cent are from Sicily, the 'irredeemable' land of Giuseppe di Lampedusa,[2] 'aridly undulating to the horizon in hillock after hillock, comfortless and irrational with no limits that the mind can grasp, conceived apparently in a delirious moment of creation.' No one conveys more finely than Lampedusa such a living sense of this age-old, insular world, 'this violence of landscape, this cruelty of climate, this continual tension in everything.'

Until very recent years, the history of the south has been that of a static way of life, fated under foreign domination, absentee landlords, and its own nature to poverty and neglect. For centuries its people worked with primitive techniques a rocky, unrewarding soil: for centuries they lived in isolated villages where poor houses clustered close against the hostile land, condemned to ill-health

[1] Carlo Levi, *Christ Stopped at Eboli* (London, 1948).
[2] Giuseppe di Lampedusa, *The Leopard* (London, 1960).

and ignorance. Small wonder that apathy, resignation, fatalism ruled the land.

For many in such a world, emigration became the one way out, the one way to a real possibility of life, both in economic and human terms. In *The Times* supplement on southern Italy (3 February 1969), Carlo Levi emphasised that 'Mass emigration is not a free choice, but a necessity, an obligatory and violent solution caused by general economic policy, unemployment, or insufficient employment (an old ailment of the south).' So, for many southern communities, emigration has become a tradition; and over the last hundred years, some 24 million Italians have left their land. Initially, the people sought new opportunities mainly in the United States. Latterly, the movement has been rather to other European countries. There are now about 200,000 Italians in Great Britain.

In the mass emigration to Bedford since 1951, the local brick industry was the prime mover. Following negotiations with British and Italian ministries of labour, Naples was made the centre of recruitment and local brick company representatives travelled out to select their men. The first batch of Italians arrived in Bedford on 31 May 1951.

Like their predecessors from Central Europe, they were housed, first of all, in brickyard hostels. Kempston Hardwick was given yet another pronunciation. Many sought a place in town. They could put up with hostel living conditions – they were accustomed to bare comforts – but few could stand the food. 'All that potato and stuff. I didn't know how to eat it. I mashed it all up together.' Above all, they wanted to live in their own way among their own people. By this, they meant not so much the Italians as people of their own district or village. Many could not write Italian and were unaccustomed to speaking it. Almost invariably, they spoke their own dialect. So, they cleaved to their own kind, and, though it was desperately difficult to find a place to live in Bedford, even in the lodging-houses they contrived to keep up their former associations. In one room, four men lived a year together. Two were from Busso near Campobasso, two from another district. Throughout the year they lived wholly in pairs, even preparing their food and eating apart, sticking to their own speech and to their own ways.

In the face of an alien people of alien habits and tongue, they needed their own kind. Security was more important than comfort. In Bedford they felt bewildered, at a loss among these cold, northern, undemonstrative people. 'Not friendly to you, you don't know what

they think.' They held the local people half in repugnance, half
in awe. The best thing was to keep away from them: do your work;
keep to your own people. If you came from districts round
Campobasso, Avellino or Agrigento in Sicily, there was no shortage
of your own kind.

So long as they could be together, they accepted without
protest the overcrowded living conditions that were forced upon
them. They were, in any case, used to poor living conditions;
and habits of acceptance and thrift had been bred in them over
centuries. Cheapness, too, was also valued over comfort. For most,
the aim was simply to scrimp and save enough money for the day
their wives and families could join them here.

From the beginning, then, the Italians clung together. Bedford
was horrified by the loud speech, the violent gesticulations, the
pungent cooking smells, the noise of radios at full volume, particularly in the summer months, when Italians spilled out of their
crowded houses to conduct a communal life on the streets.
Through open windows, the radios continued at full blast. What to
Italians were normal acts of human interchange were to the people
of Bedford acts of indecent exposure. 'These people . . . noisy . . .
smelly . . . undisciplined . . . these people making the town a slum. . . .'

Their displeasure grew as men from southern Italy in increasing
numbers responded to the brick industry's tune, and as their
families came to join them here. In the area west of the town
centre, Italians seemed to pullulate: the streets seethed and vibrated
with their presence. And in the shops there was resentment at
Italians wanting to taste, touch, smell and exercise judgement, as
they did in their own markets at home. How could one accustom
Italian women to the impersonal, dehumanised shopping habits
of people who put packages between themselves and reality?

Yet, if there was displeasure, there was little conflict. The
Italians took pains not to upset the natives, to avoid friction or
even commitment, whether in the face of housing authorities or
the trade unions. Again, fear of authority and bureaucracy was
bred in them – they wanted only to live in peace.

In recent years, I have heard Bedfordians instance the peace
between Italians and the local community as proof of how fully
and harmoniously Italians have been integrated into the life of the
town. It is a charming delusion. Peace there is, certainly, but it
derives from the simple fact that, from the start, Italians have led
their own life in their own way, quite separate from the people

of Bedford. It is the peace of apartheid rather than that of inte-gration: at best, the peace of co-existence. Proof of the pudding is that most native-born Italians, after fifteen years or more in Bedford, still have only rudimentary English.

Their prime object has always been to make money. Neither the men nor the women have ever been choosy in seeking jobs, and at almost everything they have done they have worked hard and well. *Soldi. Soldi.* Work and save. In town, native-born Italians have rarely been seen in the usual public places. Few frequent pubs, and if they want to drink they will do it at home, drinking wine they have made themselves, with soft vermouth and liqueurs for special occasions, or for visitors. They rarely go to the cinema. Apart from the expense, few understand the language. Eating out is a luxury foreign to their natures. Is it not revealing that, in a community of 7,000 Italians, every attempt to open an Italian restaurant in Bedford has failed? They live, in brief, tight, self-contained lives, frugal and industrious. They are peasants to the death.

These southern Italians make a community almost entirely within their own families or among people of their own district. Some districts of southern Italy have been virtually stripped of all able-bodied people by the movement of emigration. In St Angelo, near Agrigento, or Busso, near Campobasso, few are left except the very young and the old; and even they now are coming to join their families abroad. There are some 200 people in Bedford from St Angelo. Some had land of their own in the village but it gave poor return and a man might well have to travel $1\frac{1}{2}$ miles by horse to get to his plot of olive trees. In Bedford, the old ways of life continue: the traditions of mutual help in times of illness, the celebration of christenings, or the mourning of death.

From Busso there is an even larger community in Bedford, with many members of individual families. G., a young man from Busso employed at the Cranfield College of Aeronautics, for instance, has eighteen close relatives in Bedford: his married sister's family of five, a cousin's family of five, one uncle's family of six, and another uncle's family of two. His father, mother, two sisters and a brother live together in the United States. He is soon to marry a girl from Busso whom he met in England.

G. was a late arrival. 'It was the twenty-fifth September when I landed on the English ground and I was really surprised to find all the people originally from Busso, it was like being at home again.' Indeed, although the homes of his relatives have English exteriors, the interiors – spotlessly clean, with formal furniture and cocktail cabinets in the front rooms, and religious pictures on the wall – are Italian: and the way of life – the food, the speech, the welcome and the kindness – is all Busso.

Church and consulate have helped to keep them a self-contained community. The Italian Catholic mission run by the Scalabrini missionaries has been active in Bedford since 1954 and its present director, Father Vico, has been here since 1958. These missionaries take their name from Giovanni Battista Scalabrini (1839–1905), bishop of Piacenza, known as the 'Father of the Emigrants' after he had founded the Congregation of Missionaries for the Italian emigrants in 1887. There are now some 700 Scalabrini missionaries working in fifteen countries. And Pope Pius XII has said, 'The Apostolate among the emigrants is the most necessary in our time and the cause nearest to our heart.'

The initial tasks of the Scalabrini brothers in Bedford were essentially practical. Since virtually no immigrants had much command of English, they had to act as interpreters in every sphere of life and to do almost everything for the immigrants in their relationships with authority – sorting out housing or police problems, filling in income tax returns and birth and death certificates, making out applications for jobs, and so on.

Today, the role of the missionaries as interpreters has virtually ended. Most Italian families have enough English to cope with everyday needs and their English-speaking children help out when required. Special problems are dealt with by the resident Italian vice-consul and members of his helpful staff. The missionaries can thus give more time now to their pastoral activities, although still deeply involved in practical affairs.

A remarkable achievement was the building of the Italian church, consecrated on 28 March 1965 and dedicated to Sta Francesca Cabrini, who devoted her life (1850–1917) to the service of emigrants and was canonised in 1917. Money devoted to the shrine of Sta Francesca Cabrini in Rhode Island, USA, was given for the building, and contributions also raised locally. Beautifully built, its interior is plain, distinctive, and harmonious.

Other activities of the Scalabrini brothers include the production of a fortnightly newspaper, *La Voce Degli Italiani*, with a country-wide circulation, and the running of an *asilo* or day-nursery, staffed by the working sisters of the Holy Ghost of Nazareth. The *asilo* was opened in 1961. It takes fifty children (the majority

Italian, but with children of many other nationalities) on weekdays from 7 a.m. to 6 p.m., at a fee of 35s a week including midday meals. Conditions are excellent, the nursery is kept impeccably clean, and the children's wash-basins and toilets are the most charming I have ever seen.

The 'Circolo Leonardo da Vinci' is the somewhat grandiose name for a small social club originally started as a private business but taken over by the Scalabrini brothers after it had gone bankrupt. Inside, there is a bar and reception facilities; outside, a bocce court next to the railway. On warm evenings, it is agreeable to play or watch while trains pass, West Indians stand smiling at the gate, and Neapolitan voices are thick and quick with the passion of the game.

For those who prefer the atmosphere of a working men's club – or may not like the 'priest club' – there is a private Italian club with some three hundred members. To watch the men playing cards there, to listen to the explosions of dialect, is to realise how completely the ways of life of southern Italian villages have been put down whole in Bedford, with hardly a button awry. To this world, Bedford is entirely irrelevant: the notion of integration an absurdity.

One other club, the Italian Cultural Circle, was formed in Bedford in May 1969, though its impulse was political (and in some measure anti-clerical) rather than cultural. Despite the great number of Italians in Bedford, there is none of that vivid feeling for national culture and folklore which one finds among the other European groups. Nature in southern Italy is neither benign nor romantic, but harsh, forbidding, primitive, to be shunned rather than celebrated. Christ, one remembers again, stopped at Eboli.

The Italian virtues are practical, down-to-earth. Their industry has won appreciation wherever they work: 65 per cent in manual occupations, 23 per cent in semi-skilled jobs, 20 per cent in services, 1 per cent in business. They have created in Bedford a law-abiding and ordered community. Their efforts to work and save have been unstinting. 'Italian man, he comes for money. He don't care how hard he work, as long as he get money. He used to working hard. Look at Italian people's hands.[1] See if he got corns. He used to working hard on farms in Italy.' J., the speaker, was Bedford's first Italian immigrant. Born in a village near Naples, conscripted into the Italian Army in 1939, captured in North Africa, he arrived

[1] See Plate 9.

in England as a POW in 1942. He worked on a farm near Bedford
for six years and began work in the brickyards in 1950. Although
married and rearing a family, he worked all hours and saved hard
enough to open the first Italian café in Bedford in 1955. From
then on, one was sure of a decent cup of coffee in town. He works
still with the same thrift and drive. He is proud that, in 1962, he
was able to buy his own farm and now has eighty-two head of
cattle: proud of his sons' studying at the local technical college to
improve their lot as he has done. Here are the characteristic Italian
qualities that have won the respect of Bedford. These, and the
spotless cleanliness of their houses and shops, an irresistible
recommendation to British natives. Cleanliness, after all, is next
to godliness.

There are now some two dozen Italian businesses in Bedford,
mainly cafés, hairdressers, ice-cream distributors, and retail and
wholesale food stores. This business success has been founded,
in the main, on peasant qualities of undeviating purpose and
grinding hard work. What is astonishing is that it has also been
built on such limited English. D., for example, came to work in
the brickyards with his father in 1954. After the required four
years of service, he set up his own shoe business. Now he has one
business in Bedford, another in Luton. His father has a small ice-
cream business. His wife, who came over eight months after her
husband, has a hairdressing saloon. After fifteen years, D.'s father
speaks just a few words of English. D. and his wife have enough
only for simple conversation – 'but enough for business'. The
mother, who lives with them, speaks virtually no English at all,
though she does the family shopping with the same peasant efficiency as at home. 'She don't know no English words. But she know
shopping. Eh, Mama, you know when it say cut price, eh? And
she go back. She argue if the price ain't right. Mama, she know,
eh?' Everyone rocks with laughter. The old lady grins hugely with
delight.

So business is good. Now most of the clients are English.
Relationships have been slowly established. 'After about five to
six years, some start to say "Good morning".' Now, the family
feels its roots are in Bedford. 'Nice to go back for Ferragosto. But
we stay here. It take twenty years to build a business, so we stay
here. If we went back to Italy, we would be emigrating.'

Though many are confined to manual and semi-skilled work, the
Italians of Bedford prosper. In most families, the wife goes to

work as well as her husband, she commonly at Meltis or Texas Instruments, he in the brickyards. Most families have their own bank account and own their own homes. Many also have property in Italy. The foreign exchange counter clerk of one bank in Bedford estimates that Italians send back some £2,000 a week through his desk.

To all appearances, the Italians of Bedford have 'made it'. They are established and accepted. Bedford has been converted by their qualities. Many Bedfordians only regret that, after the crisis in local housing[1] in the late fifties, the borough council put an embargo on further recruitment of Italian labour by the brick companies. Since that time, immigration has been no more than a steady trickle. In all sections of local society the Italians are frankly preferred to West Indians and Asians. 'If we only had more of them, less of the other sort. . . .' The wheel has indeed gone about.

Just as the Italian community seems fully established and accepted, it moves towards crisis. You may sniff its nature in almost any Italian household. There is the original immigrant and his wife, perhaps fortyish now, in their own house. They speak English with difficulty: after fifteen years, just enough to get by. Mama, who lives with them, speaks next to no English. Their children habitually think and speak in English.

G. is ten. She was born in England. She has visited Italy on holiday. 'Rome was nice. Didn't like Busso and all those country places. Nothing to do there. Italy was nice for a holiday. Wouldn't want to live there.' A. is eight. She felt much the same as G. when her parents took her to Sicily. 'I liked the big town, Palermo, but not St Angelo. It's so old-fashioned. When I saw horses doing plop-plops in the middle of the road, that is what I didn't like. It seemed dirty.'

These little girls are Bedford born. Their accents and their attitudes are Bedford born. They looked at Italy as tourists, interested but not belonging. In essence, they *are* Bedfordians.

What this gulf means one sees more explicitly in homes where the children are older. P. has two sons, aged twenty and eighteen. They have been in Bedford thirteen years, educated at local schools and the local technical college. In almost everything they prefer British ways of life to Italian ones, even British food to Italian food. 'All that carbohydrate. Stands to reason, it's no good to you.' They see little rhyme or reason in the traditions of the Italian

[1] See Chapter 12 (Housing).

family. 'Parents, they say "Why don't you find yourself a nice
Italian girl?" "How can I find one?" I say. "They don't let them
out." English families, they tell you what is right and wrong, and
they leave you to make up your own mind. Italian families, they
tell you to do what they say.'

They are big lads and clearly past caring what their parents
think. When father voices a warning on women who make up or on
women who smoke, they can hardly be bothered to listen. Parents
and sons, inhabiting the same house, live in two utterly different
worlds. As they discussed the matter of two Italian girls who had
recently run away from home with West Indians, I began to
realise how brutal, implacable perhaps, the conflict is. After the
father had spoken of 'Disgrace ... dishonour ... disaster ...' I
asked the sons what they thought of the girls.

'Bloody good luck to them.'

Two ways of life, two modes of consciousness, stood in total
opposition.

The world of the first generation is the static world of southern
Italy. Its intense feeling for the primacy of the family group, its
religious respect for the authority of the father, its seclusion and
control of unmarried women, its devotion to the Church: all have
the force of permanent, unquestioned values. Here is Europe at its
most traditional and inflexible. In Sicily, in particular, it is not long
since brothers were held accountable for their sister's honour and
might avenge its violation with death.

These southern Italians brought their culture – their way of
life – to Bedford, lock, stock and barrel. Few had much schooling.
Few had moved around to see other people and places, and the less
they knew of other things, other places, and other standards, the
more tightly they cleaved to their own ways.

Most of their children in Bedford were born here or brought here
at an early age. Many have now gone through the whole cycle of
education in Bedford, absorbing new habits of mind from that
education, and new ways of thinking and feeling from daily interchange with their contemporaries in and out of school. They have
been shaped, above all, by their daily environment, by the sights,
sounds, tastes, touches, smells, values, attitudes, desires and aspirations of a swiftly changing, urban culture. The longer they have
known this environment, the less they have known the environment of southern Italy, the more completely they have been made
Bedfordians.

The two worlds implicitly deny each other. Inevitably, the young people who inhabit both worlds are divided in consciousness. As children, they learnt to move between these worlds with relative ease. As they grew older, the divisions became to them increasingly explicit. As they developed as individuals, with new needs and aspirations, they came to feel the conflict almost as a conflict of physical forces. The tensions now are explosive.

The girls, traditionally so closely confined by the family, experience these tensions more deeply than the boys. Rival values and loyalties war constantly within them, particularly in girls who have left school and are working among British girls of their own age. L., for example, is a typist.

Well, you know, you go to work and someone says 'I went out with my boy-friend last night.' Went to a dance or went out somewhere. When they ask: 'What did you do?' I have to say I stayed in, helped my mum, watched the telly, did the washing-up. Italian parents, they are more particular than the British. If you are late home from work, 'What were you doing?' When you want to go out, 'Where are you going?' They expect you to do what they say. Sometimes it's difficult. You want to go out somewhere and your mum says you will have to ask your dad. Women have no say. Dad's the authority. Well, perhaps he comes back tired from the brickworks. Just wants to sit down and watch telly. Perhaps he can't be bothered to talk about it. He just says, 'I am your father. You will do this or that. No argument. Finish.' Maybe, now and then, they will let you go to the Italian youth club. That is all right, more or less, although they have their doubts about that. Anywhere else is not all right.

It is not always all right with me. You see your English friends from school or from work doing all those things you can't do. Well, I don't like to argue with my parents. I wouldn't want to do anything to hurt them. I know how bad they would feel if I did. But when it comes to marriage, that will be something different. Who I marry will be my own business. I don't know if I will fall in love with an Italian or an English boy. But whoever it is, it'll be me who will have to live with him for the rest of my life, not them. So it will have to be my choice then.

Where there is understanding in the family, a bridge may be made between the two worlds. Where tradition attempts to make a rational compromise with reality, it may be preserved. Where it remains quite inflexible, it may be rejected in brutal and extreme ways. If a break comes about, it may be total and dramatic, and family relationships may be completely severed. So far, only a few Italian girls have run away from home, but it seems inevitable that more will do so.

Among young Italian men, rejection of their backgrounds is more overt. Those who have passed all their conscious life in England see Italy in the image of their parents, identifying it with backwardness, illiteracy and ignorance. Often, the force with which they reject it is what impels them towards the society of their British contemporaries. They need to belong. In proportion to that need they become vulnerable, both to local group pressures and the socio-commercial pressures of British culture as a whole.

Among young people in our society, group pressures upon the individual are already intense. A fear of not belonging, of not being 'with it', increasingly dominates individual consciousness. What the group demands, the individual is ever more quick to obey; and where demands are trivial or unworthy, dangers are greatest. It is group demands rather than individual needs which first spur many young people to the use of drugs, for instance. Those who refuse are 'chicken'; they don't belong. It is no coincidence that several Italian boys have recently come on to hard drugs in Bedford. At the recent trial of an English boy and an Italian boy who had been found fixing themselves with heroin in the Market Square public lavatories, 'social reasons' were given as the cause of the Italian's addiction.

Inevitably, the desire to belong makes these young people more vulnerable. So, also, the young Italian becomes whetted by consumer appetites his parents have never known. He is attracted by the will-o'-the-wisps of a commercially based culture utterly distinct from that of southern Italy; a culture which puts value on change rather than permanence. There is perhaps a certain irony that the desire to break the bonds of traditional values and family orthodoxies, the desire to be distinct as an individual, may lead young Italians to orthodoxies of a different kind, where traditional social and moral codes yield places to new kinds of social and commercial direction, impelling them towards the material objects, the modes of dress, the forms of words, that contemporary fashions – ever more imperiously – decree.

Can there be meaningful dialogue between Italian immigrants and their children, between peasant Italy and suburban England? Is the gulf absolute? Can a sense of Italian continuity be in any measure preserved? Church and consulate are certainly both concerned that awareness of Italy, of its language, and of the dignity and meaning of its cultural achievement, is preserved among the children of local immigrants. After-school classes in Italian in history, geography, and culture are arranged for all Italian children over nine for four hours a week. The ends are also practical. Such courses enable a child returning to Italy to take his place there in the Italian school system. Pupils can go on, if they wish, to take Italian secondary school certificates and British 'O' Level examinations in Italian.

For many immigrant children, to learn Italian is like learning a new language, for at home their parents speak dialect. This points to one danger in the scheme. The children's sense of Italian achievement and tradition may remain academic, quite disconnected from home where the language of that achievement is not even in use.

From the tensions between generations has come one achievement of real promise. In the mid-sixties, two Italian boys and two Italian girls made a survey among local families which led to the founding in 1966 of an Italian youth club. Families accepted the idea, and later the fact, because the club was established on holy ground, on the premises of the Italian church, and under the aegis of Father Vico.

There are now 120 members between the ages of thirteen and twenty-one: 60 per cent are Italian, 40 per cent of other nationalities. No other youth club in Bedford[1] is so genuinely cosmopolitan. Here, at one table, Italian, English, Egyptian and Maltese boys and girls chat animatedly together over cokes. There, boys are playing chess, draughts, cards or dominoes. There are also groups playing darts and table-tennis. The record-player at full blast reminds you that you are in an Italian youth club. All around is a sense of warmth and community, of activity balanced between casualness and control.

This is more than a youth club. It is the one institution which makes a bridge between the world of the Italian parents and the world of contemporary Bedford. For many young Italians – in particular the girls, whose home lives may be at times an anguish of tension – it offers refuge and release. The boys have greater independence and, as they gain education, parents more willingly come to terms with their ideas. For the girls, the situation often seems hopeless. Many escape parental control only by contrivance

[1] See also Chapter 15.

and pretext. The youth club may well be the only place they can go with their parents' approval. Here they meet normality and understanding. And sometimes a boy with a car will come in and take a group of girls out for the forbidden pleasure of a drive in youth club time, so that their parents won't know.

V., the chairman of the club and one of its founders, was two and a half when he came to England. 'If I went back to Italy, I'd be lost now. England is my country. I don't mean I want to rush out and die for it. If I had to die for something, I'd rather it was the flag of a united Europe. But I belong here.' He attended a local secondary modern school, battled with his parents for a chance to stay on after 'O' Levels, and is now studying law, with hopes of qualifying as a solicitor. Most of his friends seek more practical forms of employment: jobs in engineering or in mechanical and craft trades.

V. sees the founding of the youth club as the first of a series of radical changes in the Italian community. 'I feel there will be a series of crises. Girls going off the rails, living around with people, and so on. Then, after this has happened a few times, parents will begin to realise they have to come to terms if they don't want such things to continue. So, gradually, understanding and freedom will come.'

The club aims consciously to help young Italians 'integrate' with the life of Bedford. It is a testament to V.'s balance and perception of mind that, despite the reaction of Italian youth against the authority of their parents, he does not identify 'integration' with 'absorption', nor seek a complete abandonment of Italian values.

The English have a lot to learn from the Italians in terms of family discipline and unity. Often, you will find that English girls going out with Italian boys change their attitudes to their own families. They begin to realise it is important for the family to keep together. And if they ask an Italian boy whom he wants to marry, he will say he wants to marry someone who will respect him, his family, and what they stand for. First of all, those English parents didn't like their daughters going out with foreigners. They'd tell the Italian boys to clear off. Now, they are beginning to find out they are not so bad, that they are more respectful, the feeling is beginning to break down.

Father Vico moves unobtrusively about the club, playing draughts here, chatting there. Total acceptance makes his presence almost unnoticed. Yet his is the key function of all. He, above all, acting for the Church, may be able in some measure to reconcile the generations, ensure continuity.

No purpose is more vital for the Italian community of Bedford: and in human terms it must often be thankless. At root, it is the task of making a meaningful dialogue between the Church and contemporary society. This inevitably involves challenge to many cherished and obstructive elements of tradition. Father Vico's obvious concern for the predicament of the youth, and the help he has given them, has already incurred bitter criticism from the more inflexible of his faith. Their hostility is reinforced by objections to other aspects of his work, such as his attempts to restrain the traditional pomp and extravagance of the ceremonies of death.

Father Vico is aware that the time for utterly unquestioning faith is passing: that if the new generation in Bedford is to preserve its faith, it will do so increasingly as a matter of conscious choice. At the present time, he says, 'How deep young people are in religion is a question mark.' Some are searching, idealistic, fervent. Some seem as indifferent as the children of English society, where the process of de-Christianisation has been taking place over generations. One thing is clear. If the young people come to faith or continue in faith, it must be in greater consciousness of its meaning.

The task of making a bridge of understanding between the generations is, therefore, bound up with that of creating some measure of continuity in faith and values. The Italian community in Bedford is fortunate that Father Vico brings to that task such sensitive qualities of perception and understanding, allied to a firm grasp of contemporary realities.

Few young men will go back to live in Italy. They are as deterred by an immediate prospect of military service there as they are attracted by education and apprentice training facilities in England. Their roots in England will quickly grow deeper as they develop their own patterns of living. Many will marry English girls, with whom already they have more in common than with the sheltered Italian girls.

As a whole, the children of the immigrants will remain an equivocal generation, divided people. There will be no unambiguous identity until the third generation which, if it so chooses, will pass as English. In that generation, no doubt, some will make sentimental journeys to Italy to rediscover their roots.

Even among the first generation, the traditional emigrant myth loses force. In former days, an emigrant could expect to return to a world virtually identical to the one he had left. In foreign parts, he could cherish a wholly possible dream of returning, cigar in hand, to flaunt awhile his new-found opulence, patronise his less enterprising fellows; above all, to invest his savings in a choice piece of land.

The dream is no longer tenable. Over the last twenty years, southern Italy may well have changed more than in the previous two thousand. Industrial civilisation has ventured into regions which, in the legends, Christ never trod. Since the time when most emigrants left for Bedford, the modern world – its television services, road and transport systems, development projects, schools – has come to their former doorstep. Their villages, even the people that they left behind, have been involved in processes of change they themselves have not known. They return to find themselves no longer at ease, for no longer can they slip naturally back into place. It is no longer *their* place. In their absence, the old order of things – *their* order – has been at least modified: in places, transformed. The world, inexorably, has passed them by. Is it not remarkable that of those who returned to southern Italy after the brickyard redundancies of 1967, most were back in Bedford within a year?

In essence, then, the Italian immigrants in Bedford are detribalised people: to use jargon, 'deculturated'. Their roots in southern Italy are withering and in no sense have they attempted transplant to the soil of English culture. In Bedford, their commitment has been merely economic. Here they do not – will not – belong in any real or cultural sense of the word; certainly, not in the way their children will belong. They are, in this real sense, people in slow process of becoming extinct.

The old emigrant myth persists, of course. Even the traditional notion persists of money sent back for land and property, though the drive to work and save for the day of return may no longer be quite so intense. By this time, a family may well have bought its own house, the children may already be earning. The women, in particular, no longer have quite the same urgency of purpose in going out to work. They are getting older, settling down. One day, no doubt, the time will come, but for the foreseeable future, at any rate, they will stay where they are. Bedford, at least, has the great virtue of allowing them to live in their own way with minimal interference: and British people, at least, have the great virtue of

9. A woman from South Italy

10. West Indians at the Bible Way Pentecostal Church

11. A Sikh engagement ceremony (see pp. 121–2).

minding their own business. On this score, naturally, there are reservations. 'Mind business is good. But British people too much apart. Too cold. Very nice, very good people. But not *simpatico*.'

About the other peoples of Bedford, they have greater reservations. In particular, they have little love for the immigrants who arrived after them. They are proud, after all, to have dignified the name of immigrant, to have won respect and acceptance in Bedford by hard work, self-discipline, and obedience to law. They thus resent being classified with people who, they feel, often compromise the name and status of immigrants. West Indians and Pakistanis, especially, attract their antagonism; and this antagonism is often acted out by their children in local schools. 'Indian people is nice people. Clean. Most work good. Jamaican people not so good. Not work hard. Difficult people. Pakistani people; don't like. Stink. All got funny smell, specially on hot day. And very poor people. No good for work.'

There is little more sympathy among the younger, more educated Italians. 'You can't have much sympathy for people who don't help themselves. Most of them, so far, haven't done much to help themselves. And many of the coloureds – the West Indians, I mean – they are the most prejudiced people I've ever met.'

Finally, Bedford remains a place to live at peace, where each family and each community can live in a condition of co-existence. One makes, of course, certain accommodations. Even the older Italians have learnt to gesticulate less in the streets and to use the volume controls on their radios. But here one can live one's way of life essentially undisturbed.

It is now for holidays that most families return to Italy. In August, Busso swarms with people from Bedford, noting with vivid interest the changes in the village. Many of these changes – the new petrol station, the new houses along the road – derive from money earned in Bedford. At such times as these, the village is all animation. At the end of the holidays, by contrast, it seems deserted. The last voices echo in darkening streets. '*A riverderci. All'anno prossimo. Tante belle cose. Salutatemi la gente di Bedford. Ciao. Ciao.*'

D

7
West Indies

THE term 'West Indies' comprehends islands of great diversity set in an arc of 1,500 miles in the Caribbean Sea. Physically, they range from the wet, mountainous forest of Dominica to the flat, dry strand and dazzling beaches of Anguilla: culturally, from the exaggerated Britishness of Barbados to the Afro-French ambience of St Lucia: economically, from the sugar plantations of St Kitts to the seafaring of Carriacou. Racially, they have brought together Africans, Indians, Europeans, Syrians, Chinese and even, among others, Caribs themselves, many of these bloods profoundly intermingled.

To this diverse life, there is one common factor: the plantation consciousness – the characteristic attitudes to life framed by the colonial plantation system. Each island people bears its mark in greater or in less degree.

As the supply of European indentured labour became inadequate for the development of the islands by the colonial powers, the slave trade from Africa began. Uprooted from his own close-webbed community, cut off from his own culture and language, the Negro slave came to the colonial plantation as an isolated individual. And where his African tribal and family culture had made for community with his fellows, the plantation culture tended only to divide man from man, each for himself competing for the planter's favours. Status on the plantation was signified by closeness of relationship to the planter, and the most successful were not so much those of intrinsic worth as the pliant, the flexible, those who could work the system best. The race went often to the most cunning, the fly-boy or girl who could best beguile, or con, the master; and such a character is celebrated throughout West Indian folk legends, tales and songs, from the Anansi stories of Jamaica to the calypsoes of Trinidad.

In the close, highly personalised, inward-looking plantation community, the weeds of intrigue and dissension flourished. The values of truth and plain dealing and such concepts as 'a fair day's work for a fair day's pay' had little relevance in a society where rewards derived largely from the personal whims of the planter, and where casual plunder, from breadfruit, water coco, mango or avocado tree became a law of nature.

Such a system enshrined the norms, standards and values of the planter. In the Negro slave, it engendered self-contempt, reducing him to an isolated and imitative man, deprived of cultural identity and polarised upon a 'white' quasi-European culture. Though he might love or hate it, reject it or embrace it, his consciousness remained dominated by it. Was it not inevitable that from such soil – common to the Antilles and to the mainlands of the Americas – should later spring extreme theories of race hatred and movements such as Black Power?

'*Peau noir, masque blanc.*' The old Martiniquan saying sums up as well as any the central predicament of West Indian man: a man in cultural limbo, cut off from African roots and commanded by the standards of a 'white' culture to whose activities and privileges he was granted only very limited access. In religion, for example, slaves were long denied the rights of communicants in the established Christian churches, nor were they admitted to marriage ceremonies. Since each slave was a commodity of monetary value, there was thought to be little point in placing Christian restrictions upon their fecund breeding habits. One set of consequences has been the continued prevalence of common law relationships, loose family structures and an illegitimacy rate of 70 per cent in the West Indian islands. (In some islands the Anglican Church still holds separate baptism services for legitimate and illegitimate children.) Further consequences were that many slaves turned away from the established religions, either towards fundamentalist sects more congenial in atmosphere and emotional tone, or to their own religions of the woods, grafts of African and European knowledge. In some islands, official and unofficial religions co-existed. Though St Lucia is 92 per cent Catholic, for instance, obeah beliefs and practices still pervade its whole fabric of life.

In such a society, privilege became endemic: and not the least of West Indian tragedies in modern times has been the extent to which the new political and commercial ruling classes have perpetuated rather than challenged that ruling characteristic. In social terms, it means such things as the continuing valuation of light skin over dark, with its attendant rage to marry 'light', a continuing preference for expatriate whisky over native rum, and, in its most absurd form, spectacles such as that of a quadroon blackballing a pureblooded Chinese doctor for membership of a 'white' tennis club.

In the plantation society, few outside the planter class could have much sense of belonging. Since it was not their land, the slaves had no more pride in it than in themselves. Consequently, there are in the islands few traces of real peasant traditions, with their characteristic pride of land and craft and their characteristic values of thrift and industry. For most, the plantation was a place of unrewarding, irregular and degrading work in poor living conditions. People were thrust hugger-mugger together in the simplest shacks where dirty and insanitary conditions, malnutrition and high infant mortality rates all came to be regarded as inevitable conditions of life. In a number of islands, it is still common for one-third of all deaths to be of children under one year, for most children to be infested with worms, for poor feeding and sanitary habits and their consequences, inertia, to be endemic; and, withal, a severe shortage of trained medical staff.

For the mass of the people, the plantation was somewhere to escape from. It is hardly surprising that in the islands today so few trained men are willing to make careers in agriculture and that the movement of emigration to Britain is overwhelmingly towards city life. Under the pressures of the colonial system, education itself has become not so much a great potential for social revaluations and economic development as an escape route, either to occupations of acknowledged status and privilege, or simply to other countries. Once emancipated from the constrictions of his own society, there is little to tempt the emigrant home again; and most West Indian islands today suffer both from a lack of trained men where they most need them – in health, agriculture and education services – and from an embarrassment of riches in status occupations such as that of lawyer.

The plantation consciousness most fully pervaded life in the islands where the plantation economy was most firmly established. The rigid class-colour stratification of Jamaican society, its inward-looking attitudes and the malaise of its new middle class 'deliberately avoiding identification with the black majority yet never really accepted by the white élite it seeks to be'[1] are all

[1] Gordon K. Lewis, *The Growth of the Modern West Indies* (London, 1968).

evidence of its indelible mark on the life of that island. Trinidad, by contrast, with only a brief history of slavery, has been far less affected, though it has been profoundly influenced by the nineteenth-century system of Indian indentured labour as Jamaica has not.

It is in St Kitts that the plantation economy has persisted most strongly, dominated life most completely; and here the plantation consciousness is in purest culture, Bradshaw[1] its personification, its type man. Standing in contrast is Anguilla, where the plantation economy fell early into desuetude, and where circumstance and environment have helped to fashion an outward-looking, self-reliant people, seamen and travellers.

For the most part, the islands stood in virtual isolation from one another. Each had its own jealously guarded umbilical connection with the mother country, but between them was little evidence either of movement of people or of understanding: unfruitful soil for federation to root. (Even while West Indian politicians were so furiously denouncing the first British restrictions on commonwealth immigrants in 1962, they would allow no freedom of movement to the people of other West Indian islands). The Second World War served in some measure to create new horizons, as West Indian volunteers came to serve with British forces and American bases and servicemen were established in some West Indian islands. Their heritage was one of fresh attitudes, good airfields and, in Trinidad, a measure of political tension. After the war, this new consciousness of the outside world interacted with new economic pressures within islands woefully lacking in job opportunities to induce more and more people to look further to fare better.

West Indians first appeared in Bedford in 1955. Italian labour being scarce at the time, local firms had to look beyond the immediate vicinity of Bedford for the labour they needed. The personnel manager of the Britannia Iron and Steel Works found a West Indian community in Ipswich with a number of unemployed, interviewed some forty men there, and recruited twelve. They arrived in Bedford in high summer: a plumage of bright colours. Bedford stared. Traffic stopped. Workers at the factory crowded to see the sight.

Two houses were commissioned to house the men, but the plan of two men to a room soon went up in smoke as news of jobs and

[1] Chief minister of St Kitts-Nevis at the time of writing.

housing travelled back to Ipswich and produced a new crop of West Indians. D. was among them.

> In Barbados I didn't feel I was progressing. For nine years I had a good job in the electric company, but I had two children, and didn't feel I could give them the education I wanted for them. Then a friend came back from America. He said: 'You think you all right here. But you wasting your time in this island.' Up till then I hadn't thought of emigration. But this sowed the seed of discontent. Then a friend who had a job in Ipswich wrote to me and tell me to come and I thought, well, I will take a chance. I was in Ipswich two weeks without a job and then I heard the man from Britannia coming to look for men. Man, I had a rough old job there, in that old foundry. Ten and a half years I was there. Work? I did work more in one day at Britannia than in one whole week in Barbados. And then all crowded together, three or four to a room. People say: 'Those West Indians, they make bad housing conditions!' How could we help crowding together? Every day we look in the Arcade at the notices for rooms. 'English Only.' 'English Only,' they say. I remember when my wife coming from Barbados. I was living in a tiny room, just a bed and chair, no room for a table. £3 a week. I saw this notice of a room, went to this house. The woman say 'Is taken.' But the next week, the notice still there. Then a friend of mine went. He was lighter colour than me. The woman say 'Is taken.' But as he went away, there was a Pole there. He say to the woman: 'You know that room not taken. Why don't you let him take it?' So they called him back. And after a while, the woman say to him: 'You know any more coloured men would like a room here?'

Local reluctance to accept them as lodgers made their needs for accommodation more desperate; and both their needs and their ignorance of British society were widely exploited. Rooms could be found, mortgages could be arranged, but as a special favour, you understand, not a word to anyone. And at a special price. The needs of some were so great they were ready to take anything on virtually any terms, even to pay for their house several hundred pounds more than its value. The late fifties and early sixties were in Bedford a fruitful field for exploitation.

In 1969, the movement of West Indians to Bedford is complete. Of some 2,000 living in the town, rather more than half – say, 1,100 – are from Jamaica, rather more than 400 from Barbados; from Grenada and the Grenadines, about 250, at least a hundred of them from the tiny island of Carriacou; about 100 from Nevis; rather fewer from St Kitts; no more than a score from Antigua, from Trinidad and from Montserrat: a sprinkling of others.

They came with glowing expectations. Some had made their image of Britain from that of the plantation houses in their own islands. There they saw a life of ease, plenty and privilege without physical labour. (They ignored the reverse of the coin: the enervating round of whisky drinking, bridge and adultery; the cultural void.) Their school books, their empire readers, had given them consonant images of a Great Britain who was the pride of nations, the source of light, and *their* mother country.

Between the colonial image and British realities, they found an abyss. H. is from Trinidad:

> When I was a boy, I thought of England as a land of golden streets, silver alleys, diamond mountains. Well, of course, it was not like that – but when all said and done, it was not what we expected. You know, when an Englishman came to the West Indies, whoever he was, whatever he did, he got the best of treatment. We didn't even get recognition here.

V., a nurse from Nevis, came to join her daughter here in 1960:

> It was so shocking to me. From what I had heard, I really thought everyone had servants. And when I saw everyone rushing about with their baskets to the market, I thought, are these the servants? Then my daughter tell me, everyone here serving themselves. And I remember the smoke coming out of their mouths, and thinking, are they all smoking? Then I find smoke coming out of my own mouth. That was November cold. In the Bible, we had read about snow, but never realised what cold is.

T. had been a church social worker in Jamaica. He came to England in 1957 both to seek advancement and to learn more of the great Christian country which was *his* heritage:

> I thought that when I came here, I would be walking on gold. I found indifference and apathy to religion. I came to realise that for most people in Britain, religion is more and more dissociated from everyday life and experience.

During his twelve years here, he has been further shocked by the development of a permissive moral climate:

> To think that the Great, Great Britain we were taught about could admit open homosexuality, drugs, free sexual relationships.

It's like the story of Sodom and Gomorrah. If only Britain could go back fifty years, to what she once was.

They also came as islanders: Jamaicans, Barbadians, Kittitians, or Grenadans. They had been bred to insularity. 'I never thought of myself as West Indian until I came to Britain.' The sentiment is widespread. Few had knowledge or experience of other islands. G. came from Jamaica eleven years ago, just before his tenth birthday. Born in Port Antonio, on the north eastern tip of Jamaica, he had lived only on the east coast and had never been west of Kingston, the capital. Though the son of a schoolteacher, 'I never knew these other islands existed until I came here. Carriacou? I've never heard that name.'

Even today, then, the name of Carriacou, an island to the north of Grenada, is not widely known among Bedford's West Indians. For the sake of convenience, the people of the island accept classification as Grenadans, though in way of life they differ a good deal. And where most people from the larger islands were swept to England on new tides of hope, traditions of emigration were established long back on Carriacou. As in Anguilla, only the sea offers opportunities. Circumstance and environment force most of the men to look elsewhere: to the oilfields of Aruba and Curaçao, or to the canefields of Santo Domingo.

P. came from Carriacou in 1964. His father was a fisherman, like his father before him:

In a small island, you ain't have any experience. Just the same people all the time. Day come, I see you. Night come, I see the same you. Here you meet different people. People talk different things. And people learn. The first day I come here, I say to myself, 'I can't stand this place. All grey and cold weather.' Then I think, I am not poor West Indian boy run back to his small island. Keep telling myself so. First week at work, when I come to bend the back, I couldn't bend. Now is all right, I used to it. No, I ain't have no trouble. With this job on the fork lift truck, always moving around, joking around with everyone. I wouldn't go back now. If I go back to Carriacou, would be just the same. And father and mother dead since I come here. I think, if my grandmother alive, I would go back some time. My mother go away when I was young, and I live with she. She always there. I think sometimes, was she make me what I am. I am like this because of she. In this way, then, she not dead. I have this feeling, she still living. Now, I stay here. I still got a young age in front of me. And life don't make you. You got to make life.

In the early days in Bedford, the insularities were intense:

When I first came here in 1958, the feeling was terrible. At parties, in particular, there was always fear of trouble. You never knew when arguments and fights would spark off. When I was in the hospital, they all used to talk of small island people. I never said nothing. Well, the people in the hospital used to say my reports were very good, and one day, this nurse she say 'That Nurse V., she could really do something. She from J.' 'Not me,' I say, 'I from small island. Nevis. And I proud of it.'

These divisive forces have never been far from the surface. In December 1966, insular feeling sparked off an incident that became the flashpoint for the murder of a Nevisian by a Barbadian. The murdered man's girl friend subsequently stated: 'Last night R. came to stay with me in my flat, which is on the bottom floor. When I got up this morning I spoke to J., who lives just along the corridor. When I went back to my room R. was mad because I had spoken to the woman, and he punched me in the mouth and busted my lip. He said I wasn't to speak to her because she came from a large island and we, meaning me and him, came from a small island. When R. hit me, I screamed and cried and then a knock came on the door and Mr G. came in.' This man called the police. A dispute followed, and next day, Mr G. stabbed her lover to death. After the stabbing, he went back home and was peaceably eating his lunch when the police arrived to arrest him.

'It's quietened down now, and there's far more mixing. Even mixed marriages between Jamaicans and Barbadians, those most at loggerheads. Ten years ago, that would have been impossible. Everyone kept to his own kind.' Certainly in Bedford's West Indian Club today, inter-island feeling is more often than not a matter for jokes.

'Why don't you take a West Indian drink?'

'Do you have a Mount Gay?' I asked.[1]

A Barbadian hugged himself with laughter.

'Eh, eh, he doan't want that Jamaica. He know what good rum is. Barbados.'

It is a tenuous harmony. The divisive forces in West Indian life are deeply planted, and Bedford's West Indians are still subject to the pressures from their native islands. A vicious article in the *Jamaican Weekly Gleaner* (17 September 1969) on the 'fiasco of

[1] Mount Gay is a Barbados rum. Most Jamaican varieties are sweeter.

Gary Sobers', the West Indian cricket captain, for example, quickly creates bitter controversy, reopens old wounds: 'I was mad. I told this Jamaica feller, I said they should have printed that article on toilet paper so it could be used for some useful purpose. . . .' The same Barbadian, protesting against a Jamaican neighbour's noisy party, meets the ancient sneer: 'You all Barbadians got white hearts. You think you white men.'

West Indian problems of relationships are more complex than those of any other national group in Bedford. Most foreigners coming to this country know what will confront them: that they will find a gap between the ways of British society and those of their own society. They either accept that gap or they take steps to bridge it. The West Indian, however, comes in perfect confidence that he is *not* a foreigner, that he *is* British. He comes as to a promised land which is the centre of his own culture, assuming that he will slip easily and naturally into its ways of life, fully integrated, completely at home. But he finds himself without full recognition: British and not British, or rather, quasi-British, off-centred in culture, condemned to a twilight world as a man from Martinique or Guadeloupe never is in metropolitan France. The Martiniquan comes to France as a full citizen, *un français – tout à fait*, no doubt of it. The West Indian in Britain is relegated to the fringes of acceptance: 'We who love the queen, reverence the constitution, who sing 'Rule Britannia' at the drop of a hat, find ourselves classified for the most part as foreigners, treated no better, and often worse, than Italians – often simply as wogs or niggers.' The shock is cruel, the realisation bitter. The strains and stresses of everyday relationships become intense, difficult far beyond those of any other immigrant group. The wonder is that the ensuing resentments have not turned further into hate.

History has taught the West Indian to learn quickly, to accept and adapt. Yet many suffer greatly after arrival:

The second day I was here, I went to a post office and stood at a counter writing an airmail letter. A young English boy, seven perhaps, came and looked at me. He stood a long time there, scrutinising me. Then he went back and pulled at his mother's skirt. He said: 'Look at that black woman there. Writing.' You could tell from his voice how surprised he was that a black woman was able to write. I felt my eyes fill with tears. God, those first few months, I thought Britain the most terrible place on earth. I used to cry every night.

Even after many years, each day can bring her new stress:

> Going into a shop in uniform, usually they treat you well, serve you quick. Without a uniform, if they don't know you, you're often overlooked or pushed to the back of the queue. The English are very class conscious. They'll accept you as nurse or doctor or whatever, but rarely just as a West Indian.

The cultural dilemma of the West Indian, then, is that of a man without cultural identity. If he does not belong in a British culture, he belongs nowhere. He has no other sense of being, as the Italian has, the Indian or the Pole. He cannot stand apart, as they can if they so wish. He is condemned to aspire where he is rarely allowed to belong; to remain dependent on the British way of life, yet not fully part of it. From this dilemma he takes far more hurt, suffers far more disappointments, than from overt acts of racial discrimination. And to this dilemma, the costly apparatus of the Race Relations Board is largely irrelevant.

In this context, it is natural that West Indians should have sought to establish identity as 'coloured people' and to make common cause with those also commonly identified as 'coloured', the Asians. Numerous organisations within our society, from committees for commonwealth immigrants to the Black Power movement, have done much in recent years, consciously or unconsciously, to encourage this and to bolster a sense of common identity. Few of Bedford's West Indians find it sustaining fare: 'They asked me, one time at the works, to be a shop steward. They said it would be useful for someone to represent the coloured workers. I said no, I wouldn't do it. I didn't want to be involved in policies I didn't agree with. And in any case, there's no unity among coloured people. Indians will never act as "coloureds", nor even recognise themselves as coloured. And where a West Indian, when he thinks an Englishman is wrong, will make a commotion, Asians never protest in the open. Just mutter among themselves. No, I wouldn't do it.'

'What do you mean by "coloureds", then?'

'Well, I guess' – he shrugged and smiled – 'just West Indians.'

H. has as much experience as any in Bedford in making relationships between different peoples: as a leading member of the Bedford International Friendship Association, as an organiser of dances, talks and other meetings and as one involved in Church affairs.

I've spent a lot of time trying to mingle people of different countries together. But let me put it on the table. They want to stay with their own people, and there's too little effort to make it otherwise. Though most West Indians come here as strong churchgoers, for instance, the Church has done little to bring them in. I am an Anglican, and one time, tried myself to bring a whole group of West Indians into the Church. They found only a cold shoulder, and after a couple of weeks, most of them went away. The Church proposed to set up a committee – always a committee – to look into such problems, but the committee never really existed. If I were going to Church for the people, I would never go at all. On the other hand, I personally have never met racial discrimination in Bedford.

There seems general agreement that in this respect, 'Bedford is second to none'. Yet while cases of overt discrimination have been few, there are numerous complaints of petty discriminations: that in the allocation of council houses, West Indians are being pushed towards the areas of poorer housing; in employment, towards poorer jobs. D., with perhaps the longest experience of the town, quotes a graver case some five years back at his place of employment, of a West Indian sacked after he and an English woman serving tea at the works had been swearing at each other. Since there was doubt as to whether the West Indian had started the swearing, the management agreed to reinstate him. At this, English workers threatened to strike, and in consequence, the man was not taken on again. 'At that time, there was real tension. You could feel it in the atmosphere. It was really bad. I felt disgusted with it all, ready to leave.'

The majority of complaints are of discriminatory practices by building societies, insurance companies and banks in such matters as raising loans and mortgages, purchasing houses, and fixing insurance rates. A local pastor estimates that up to a quarter of all West Indians here have complaints of this kind. The local institutions, for their part, admit to no more than natural caution following histories of irregular payments and bad debts. Is their caution excessive? Have some West Indians been unnecessarily penalised for the sins of others? On the other hand, how far are these the complaints of people rubbed raw by their cultural predicament, made excessively thin-skinned, over-suspicious, prone not only to take offence but to look for it? The realities are infinitely complex and clearly impossible to unravel. What is clear, at least, is that West Indians' difficulties in raising loans and mortgages have only served to drive them further into the grasping hands of exploitation.

If West Indians are often quick to take offence, they are equally ready to appreciate help; and they speak with particular enthusiasm of borough council aid in founding a West Indian club. The council leased a building to the West Indian Association and spent some £3,000 in putting it in order. The West Indians themselves raised money from dances and parties, and spent £600 on further improvements. Opened on 5 April 1969, the club now has 140 members, including a number of English people. So far, it caters mainly for the younger West Indian men, with regular dances, and its own music group, the Groovers, but attempts are being made to build up other activities, including a youth movement.

G. is a leader of the youth group. With his mother, brother and sister, he came here from Jamaica in 1959. After leaving school, he was first a trainee, then an apprentice, in a local firm; and has lately returned from a month's 'Outward Bound' course in Scotland.

> At this moment, there are about forty boys in the youth club. There are teams for tennis and dominoes, and another forming for table tennis. When we have parties, we have about sixty boys and girls, but so far there's not much for the girls to do otherwise. The main trouble is discipline, to get people to behave properly, to respect things. It's difficult sometimes.

The creation of community is an uphill task. The plantation society created a race of disparate individuals, so that in Bedford today, West Indians number among the most intelligent and the most ignorant; the most virtuous and most base. Some of their houses are as spruce and immaculate as any in town: others are disordered and neglected. Of no local national group is it more difficult to generalise, and no other group has fewer common standards.

Without the framework of a strong and distinctive common culture, West Indians lack the close-knit family and community ties which give the local Indian community its unity, its capacity for self-regulation, and its concerted drive. The West Indian family is often loose in structure. It is common for parents to travel separately to different lands and for children to be left with female relatives, often with the grandmother. It may happen that by the time a child comes to join one or more of his parents in England, he hardly knows them. He may even find that a parent has found a new partner.

This is not to say that West Indian family life is poor in quality. The 'sweetheart life' of common law relationships is often long-lasting and profound, while love and affection for children and old people are salient characteristics of island life. Many of Bedford's West Indians are deeply shocked by the decreasing concern for old people in British society as human responsibilities are shed upon the state. 'In Barbados, when my great-grandmother was very ill, my mother stayed home from work, and I helped her, and we looked after her until she died. Here many old people just seem to be pushed out and forgot about.'

Where Indians seek education and advancement as a community, West Indians seek them as individuals. In one West Indian home there is the strongest encouragement for the children's studies and aspirations: in another, apathy and inertia. Even in the drive of individual families to better their material lot, West Indians are often less single in purpose than Indians. Many of the women, for instance, are divided over whether to persist in earning or to let the babies keep coming. Where Indian women in Bedford at the present time are turning quickly to contraceptive devices, West Indian women are tending to hold back. Since fertility has long and fundamental value in West Indian societies, many West Indians view restriction through primordial fears of denying life. And just as the principle is feared as unnatural, the devices are feared as harmful.

Those who fare best are, for the most part, those who have made most effort to adjust to local ways of life: 'You got to adjust to it. When you come, you have to realise that you may have to accept a job not necessarily to your liking, and people's behaviour not always to your liking.' 'But if you go against them, it makes no sense for you.' 'Those who are prepared to give and take, they are okay.'

In general, it seems that the most successful in settling and making their way in Bedford are the people with better educational backgrounds – notably Barbadians, though the intense, even caricatural 'Britishness' of Barbados is also a factor here. 'Some people, on the other hand, can live here for years and know nothing of the society in which they live. Just living as if they still living in Kingston, Jamaica. All they can think is big car.' Certainly a number of Jamaicans in Bedford are poor in literacy and educational standards; and it is among such people that resentment and poor living conditions are most commonly found. Here again, an added factor in their difficulties is the profound class-colour tension bred within Jamaican society itself.

Most West Indians recognise that the coin of 'adjustment' is two-sided, and that advances such as those in housing standards and marriage customs are balanced by failings induced by the permissiveness of contemporary British society and its prevailing climate of apathy towards religion.

When we first came here, we went to Church. Most of us were brought up in Church, and my wife and I, we met there. In Barbados, on Christmas mornings, everybody – Anglicans, Methodists, whatever they are – they all go. Here you scarcely realise it is Christmas. Everyone stays at home just to eat and drink. Now I don't go any more. I don't really know why. Perhaps it's because you get used to working some Sundays, and you get out of the habit. Then there are families visiting from other towns on Sundays. In the end, you become like English.

'If you talk about religion at work, they laugh at you.' 'About religion, English don't want to know.' Yet though many yield to English ways, most are steadfast and devout in preserving their faith, notably those who belong to one of Bedford's four West Indian evangelical churches: the Pilgrim Holiness, the Church of God in Christ, the Church of God of Prophecy and the Bible Way Pentecostal Church. To the activities of these churches gather the modest and devout people most representative of Bedford's West Indians.

The Bible Way Pentecostal Church has sixty-two parishioners, though attendance at services is often greater, drawing people mainly from Jamaica, Barbados, Nevis and St Kitts. A substantial number of them give almost every night to the work of the church: to services, Bible readings, choir practices and activities for the young. And the Pentecostal youth movement not only gives teachings in the scriptures, but provides classes in history, geography, handicraft and knitting, as well as organising visits and parties.

On Sunday night, the church hall is crowded. The pastor and his assistants sit on a low platform flanked by a lectern on one side, by a choir on the other. The women of the choir are in black hats, white blouses and black skirts; the men behind in dark suits. Another choir group of boys and girls – the girls in white hats – are seated to one side of the room, opposite the piano and in front of a congregation of some sixty men, women and children. Among these are five or six English people.

It is an atmosphere of joy and devotion, of vivid exhortation and confession. A speaker repeats a phrase – 'I want to go home to that land' – and the choir begins to sing, at first almost casually, then slowly building a concerted melody and rhythm, and swaying with it, defining and sharpening it, rocking with it, till people in the congregation too begin to stand and rock with them, and suddenly on the platform and among the mass of people, there are guitars and accordions and tambourines all making percussive, hypnotic rhythm until more and more bodies are standing, shaking, moving, and next to me a man is dancing on one spot, his body held tense in exultation, eyes closed, face streaming with sweat, hands clapping like pistol shots, and a woman twisting and turning with her hands to heaven, and all, all now are seized by sound until their bodies are become their hymn, and faith is found, is found. Praise Him. Praise Him.

The song stops abruptly. People return to their seats. Some are led or half-carried. Some are still in trance. The body of the man beside me jerks convulsively. He is racked with sobs, and mutters words as if they were wrung from him. 'Speak, speak. Speak, my Lord. . . . *Chantez le bas.* . . . Ho, Ho, Hallelujah! Ho!' *Chantez le bas?* How should he know this phrase? Had he lived in a French island, Haiti or St Lucia, or had he been in Louisiana? 'All I know is Jamaica. But understand that when the spirit moves, the Lord speaks through you in known and unknown voices.'

An English Evangelist speaks: 'It is nice to be home. . . . These past weeks, I have visited people in many different churches. . . . They were thrilled when they heard there was in this town people of another colour who were more diligent than the inhabitants in carrying out the message of the Lord. . . . ' Then the slow chant of 'Jesus took my burden in answer to my prayer' over an imperative percussion of tambourines and guitars, and finally the message of the pastor, culminating in a complex rhythmic exchange between speech and responses.

'The sun black as sackcloth, the moon turn to blood.' *'Praise Him.'*

'And the day's going to come. . . .' *'Um! Um!'*

'I say the day's going to come.' '*Hallelujah!*'

'The earth going to dance like a drunken man.' '*Yes. Lord!*'

'So why not come? I say, why not come?'

And at the last come three men and a girl to kneel before the platform and to accept Christ. The first is an Englishman. A young Jamaican places his hands on the Englishman's bent head and closes his eyes in prayer.

The pity is that the reputation of local West Indians is too often made not in the image of these humble and devoted people but in that of a comparatively few layabouts and drifters. 'Too many of my people are living on immoral earnings and the welfare state, in pubs and in betting shops. Twenty-five or more of them I know. . . . Come Friday nights, they are stopping you in the streets, asking for freeness.'

Such people gather in particular houses and pubs.

Regulars and casuals, about 100 girls come from all around here, most of them prostitutes or whores. Many are black men's women. When they start off, maybe they're just bored, and they go to a dance with West Indians. West Indians really love dancing. They're not like us, all stiff and self-conscious. They really relax, dancing. Joyous. And when they dance slow dances, close, the girls love it, they're excited. And then maybe they get invited to a party and take a drink and a spliff[1] or perhaps somebody gives them a drug without them knowing. When they wake up, they find they've been humped, and then it's too late. They're black women. And there's no return. In the beginning, of course, the men pet and pamper them. Dress them up. West Indians love finery. For the girls it's exciting, having someone care for you, look after you, not letting anyone touch you, ready to fight for you. Next thing, the girls are on the streets, keeping them. Doing anything they want.

S. is a prostitute who lives with a West Indian.

Sometimes they make you feel as if they really care for you. Sometimes, as if they just use you. They'll do what they want as long as they want. They won't care about you – you know, as if you were a slave to a master. Some, I think, hate us for being white. It's as if they were getting their own back for all the past. Small island people are the best people. Jamaicans the worst. They're the ones who cause the troubles, make the fights. God knows, some of them are crafty. Like X., one of those who organises the parties. At one time there were four West Indians

[1] A cannabis cigarette.

used to run a party each every week-end in town. Then other parties started, making competition. X., he used to organise fights and disturbances outside these other parties, so no one would go, and he destroyed their trade. He ran girls, too. There are several hundred girls now living hereabouts with West Indians, I reckon. It's hard to say why. Of course, there's the story that coloured men are bigger sexually. Well, I've been with men of all kinds. Some so big they near tore you apart. Some so small it was a crying shame. But when it comes to different races, God made all men equal.

Many of those who bring notoriety and disrepute to Bedford are from out of town; floaters organising girls to do business in different places. For the big week-end parties organised for profit, there are often numbers from the bigger centres of West Indian population – Birmingham, Leicester, London; even from as far afield as Huddersfield, where a good many local West Indians have relatives.

The great majority of local West Indians stand quite distinct from this world. They seek only to make a modest living in peace: and they have not always found it easy to adjust bright hopes to grey realities, and to endure grudged acceptance and petty humiliation. In this, the Race Relations Board gives little help. 'I disagree with the idea of the Race Relations Board. How does it help me? If a man does me hurt, goin' to the Board won't change him in any way.' Some West Indians have given up and gone home in discouragement; and a group of about 200 others have just left, in the summer of 1969, to seek new opportunities in Canada. The majority soldier on, making constant accommodations with English life until gradually they meet acceptance and find places for themselves to put down roots to live their lives more or less in their own way.

More or less. Like H., many of them have some ambiguity of feeling about their stay here. 'I wouldn't say I regret coming to this country, but one day I want to go home. As I said, it was not really what we expected.' The younger people are the most contented, especially those who have established relationships and have come to appreciate the British way of life in local schools. J. came here some five years back. She is now twenty, a punch operator, in her leisure time a devoted church worker, and happy in making her life here. 'I would like to go home, but not to stay. I see things now in a different way, at a different angle.'

The longer these younger people stay in Britain, the harder the return would be. Anyone with experience of life in small islands knows how difficult it may be for a returning emigrant to fit back into those highly personalised, inward-looking, stratified societies: close, constrictive, claustrophobic even. The boy whose departure was strewn with good wishes may well on return meet only suspicion and resentment for his new attitudes and abilities: 'That man, now, who he t'ink he is?' The plantation consciousness is not easily extirpated.

In general, it is the older people, those most firmly rooted in their island life, who most want to return to live their later years, free of the rigours of English climate and English society, among their own kind in their own ways:

> What would I do for ever in a big place, who
> have lived all my life in a small island?
> The same parish holds the cottage I was born in, all
> my family, and the cool churchyard. . . .[1]

For a few, there are special difficulties in going home: 'We Nevisians, we like to be independent and to live up to certain principles. Now we are tied under Mr Bradshaw. We can make no progress until we get help so that our country can be free and prosperous. If man cannot move him, God will move him.'

In the final account, perhaps half of Bedford's West Indians, mainly the younger people, will stay to put down roots. None of them, I think, will be more completely at home than M., with a thriving tailoring business in town (all his employees and 98 per cent of his clientèle are English) and a pleasant home in a residential quarter: 'When I first came to this house, they said look out, you going to be the only coloured man in the area. Within two days, there was the vicar inviting me to church and the neighbours making us cups of tea. In the summer I can hardly go outside but the kids next door are asking if they can cut the lawn or prune the roses. Personally, I don't like big town life. London now, it gives me headaches. Bedford has this quiet way of life – well, it suits me.'

'If you get him away for a holiday, after a week or so he's always wanting to get back. You may get him out of Bedford, but you'll never get Bedford out of him,' says his wife.

'Well, man, you know; Bedford – it's me.'

[1] A. L. Hendriks, 'An Old Jamaican Woman Thinks About The Hereafter', *Focus, An Anthology of Contemporary Jamaican Writing*, edited by Edna Manley (Kingston, 1960).

8
India

NEARLY 2,500 Indians live in Bedford at the time of writing. Rather more than 2,000 are from India itself, the great majority – more than 90 per cent – from the northern state of the Punjab. Most of the others are Bengalis. In addition, there are about 300 Indians from East Africa – their numbers are still growing – and many of these families also came originally from the Punjab. About three-quarters of Bedford's Indians are Sikhs, and Sikh Punjabis have long had a reputation as active, self-sufficient, mobile people.

A few came first to England in the thirties, mainly as itinerant small traders. After the Second World War, their numbers quickly increased, particularly after the disturbances which followed the partition of 1947. This division of the Punjab between India and Pakistan led first to brutal atrocities and to the slaughter of some half a million people; subsequently, to the uprooting of millions of Muslims from the East Punjab and of millions of Sikhs and Hindus from the West. 'It is reckoned that about five and a half millions travelled *each way* across the new India–Pakistan border in the Punjab.'[1] The Punjab thus swarmed with homeless, landless people, many of whom were impelled to seek new opportunities in other parts of Asia and in Africa. During the fifties, Britain's needs for industrial workers also began to draw Indians to this country.

B.'s family were among the first to settle in Bedford. A Sikh born in Karachi, the son of a contractor, he was forced by the partition of India to move, first to Jullundur, then to Delhi and Bombay, where he set up in business as a radio engineer. In 1955, he came to England to train as a television engineer, and two years later settled in Bedford to work at this trade. His son attended a local secondary modern school, then took several 'O' Level examinations at Mander, the local technical college, with the intention of joining his father at work. For some time he found apprenticeships hard to come by, but he persisted, and at last became apprenticed

[1] Percival Spear, *Pelican History of India*, vol. 2.

to a local firm. 'By the grace of God, we are now in the right trade.'

Most of the Indians who came to settle in Bedford in the late fifties and during the sixties were from far more modest, agricultural backgrounds. Over a thousand of Bedford's Indians – more than half of them – are of the shoemaker (Athharmis) and the sweeper (Balmikis) classes, known formerly as Untouchables. Although the term 'untouchable' no longer has legal sanction in India, many lived in enclosed and secluded communities outside the villages, often in poor conditions, performing the most menial tasks and with virtually no opportunities for education and advancement. Of the other Indian immigrants in Bedford, almost all are either from the farmer class (Jats) or from the craftsman class (Ramgharhia). The majority of these immigrants also come from particular areas of the Punjab, especially from the districts of Jullundur, Hoshiarpur and Kapurthala; in most cases, they came to join members of their families already established in Bedford. It is small wonder that they have preserved their close-knit sense of community, together with their traditional patterns of family and community life.

These immigrants are quite distinct in background, education and skills from the Indians who have come to Bedford from East Africa. The wave of Kenyan Indians has also been more recent, mainly over the past two years. It is notable that, while at the beginning of 1968 there was only a small handful of Kenyan Indian children in Bedford schools, a year later there were fifty.

Only religion cuts across the barriers of caste and the differences of background. Most of the farmers and craftsmen, a number of the shoemakers and some of the sweepers are Sikhs. The remainder are mainly Hindu, with the exception of some forty Christians. As the dominant religion, Sikhism is a primary factor in the making of the local Indian community. A protestant reaction against the abuses of priesthood, the idolatry, corruption and rigid caste system of orthodox Hinduism, Sikhism was founded by ten spiritual teachers or gurus between 1469 and 1708. They taught that God is one and indivisible, that all people are His children, and that mankind is one equal brotherhood, regardless of race, creed, caste or sex. They condemned what they regarded as the excessive ceremonies, asceticism and divisions of Hinduism, and like the first Protestant teachers in the Christian church strove for direct communion between man and God within the simplest framework of ceremony.

The last of the Sikh *gurus*, Govind Singh, commanded his followers to wear five religious symbols: the *kara* (steel bangle), *kirpan* (the short sword), *kachcha* (shorts), *keshas* (uncut hair), and *kanga* (comb). All men were to bear the name of Singh (the lion), all women that of Kaur (princess). They were to abjure tobacco, alcohol, and every kind of drug that could impair the mind and senses in the search for perfection, the main purpose of man's life. They were also forbidden to trim or cut their hair and beards so that they would the better resemble their Creator.

The outlook and values of Sikhs owe much to the deep roots of their faith in the human condition and in everyday relationships and activities. A Sikh searches for God not by abjuring the world and its ways, but through involvement in them. From this involvement comes a deeper understanding of He who creates and orders the whole pattern of man's activities. 'The Sikh sees God in every thing and in every human being. You name it, He's there. Through his grace, all is discovered.'

In their characteristically practical concern for life, Sikhs look back to the qualities of their gurus, not only spiritual leaders but leaders of their people in every way. Govind Singh was not only saint and mystic, but poet, soldier and statesman; and some of his most famous hymns have a down to earth militancy akin in feeling to such hymns as 'Onward, Christian Soldiers':

> Grant me this favour, Lord,
> That I may never shun good deeds,
> That I shall never fear the enemy in the fight,
> And that I shall bring victory to my side.
> In my mind I have only one desire,
> That I shall ever sing Your praises,
> And that when the time comes,
> I shall die fighting in the midst of battle.

The Sikh place of worship is the *gurdwara* (the place of the teacher). Being poor people of few means, Bedford's Sikhs for a long time had no place of their own and only recently bought an old house at 72 Ford End Road as their gurdwara. A wall on the ground floor has been removed – apart from the central chimneypiece – so as to make one large room for religious services. It is all very simple and bare, the lino floor covered with old blankets and just a few religious pictures and posters on the walls. At the far end of the room, a cloth of gold, red and green weave hangs from the ceiling above an opaque light-shade and beneath this is an improvised altar with a green silk cloth over a yellow cover. Here is placed the holy book (the *Guru Granth Sahib*). In front and to each side of the altar, on the floor, are vases of plastic flowers, and in the middle the space where money and gifts are put by those entering and making their obeisance.

This Sunday morning, it is bitterly cold. It is early yet and only a few men and boys are present, seated on the floor against the right-hand wall. They courteously make room for me. A senior member of the Sikh community is seated at the altar, while the people chant, one man playing a small harmonium, another beating a small drum. A boy clashes two rods of tiny cymbals together. Most are poorly dressed and in the space in front of the altar there are, as yet, only a few coppers and bags of sugar and semolina. Several old men are grouped round a small oil heater by the chimneypiece, warming their hands. Another harmonium player joins the group of men and then a new drummer with two drums of his own on which he beats more complex and intricate rhythms. Then a woman and a girl come in and sit against the wall opposite the men, and they are followed by an old woman who kneels and stretches out her hands to the oil heater.

People come thick and fast now. The collection mounts, for many of the later arrivals are well-dressed and have an air of prosperity. There is a division of sexes to either side of the room but no social divisions, for within the gurdwara in the sight of God all men are equal. All are seated on the floor together. The old man acting as the priest leaves the altar and another takes his place. He follows the chanting and the music with fixed attention, nodding approval to the rhythmic patterns of the drums, slowly waving from side to side the *chohar*, a whisk of pure white hair from the tail of the cow of the Himalayas, which lives by the holy places of the Sikhs among those mountains, its handle of beautifully decorated silver. And while the reading and the ritual proceeds, young children play at ease together behind the chimney-piece.

Many of the younger men are cleanshaven. 'Beard, no job. No beard, job.' For some, it has been as simple as that. A. came to Bedford nearly six years ago, with an engineering qualification from Delhi. For nine months he made unsuccessful attempts to find a job in a machine shop. Finally, he had to settle for a labouring job in the brickworks. For some time he wrestled with his conscience, then shaved, and immediately found a job as a jack-borer in a local machine shop. Opinion is divided here. For the orthodox, to shave is to lose identity as a Sikh. 'I would not do this in the face of death,' one young man said. Others are more ready to accept such an accommodation with English life where it derives from necessity rather than fashion.

The gurdwara is much more than a temple. It is the centre of communal life, a meeting-place and a shelter for travellers. The service is followed by a *langar* or communal dinner, in which everyone eats together informally and in community.

In strength of community and family ties, Bedford's Indians have much more in common with the Italians than with either their fellow Asians, the Pakistanis, or the 'coloured' group, the West Indians. Like the Italians, they crowded together in lodging-houses on first arriving in Bedford, usually with members of their own family groups. 'Family' here implies the joint family, with its web of aunts, uncles, cousins and nieces, even to the most distant relatives. And, as with the Italians, there has been a great deal of mutual help within these groups to allow individual families to buy or rent their own accommodation. They too are putting down strong roots in Bedford; and, as they make their own homes, so standards of hygiene and cleanliness are rising.

The family structure, and family values and attitudes are of first importance to them. Most Indians were married before they came here, many have a number of close relatives here, and the percentage of children to adults among Indians is higher than that of any other national group in Bedford.[1] If anything, their ties of kinship have been strengthened by their needs to protect themselves and preserve their community in the face of modern industrial society: a world alien, often bewildering to them in language, behaviour, organisation and values; often terrifying in its strains and stresses, noise and bustle. It has been inevitable that many, especially the poorer and least experienced, should often shrink from contact with this grey, harsh world, often feel at a loss in coping with it.

Most Indian immigrants, then, keep closely to their own kind and to their own traditions, as the Italians have done; and there are certain striking resemblances between the two groups in conditions of life, in standards and values, and even in their dilemmas in

[1] See also p. 179.

settling in this country. Both peoples are thrifty and hardworking, their communities inward-looking and self-regulating, dominated by considerations of kinship and by rigid moral codes. Among the Indians, of course, there is an additional factor – that of caste – as a governing force in social relationships, and especially in marriage relationships. Even the younger, more emancipated Indians rarely marry outside their own caste, and the histories of families for three or four generations back are often minutely explored before a marriage contract is made. Making a marriage is a matter too vital to be left to a boy and girl alone. It is a matter for the whole family.

Plate 11 shows the engagement ceremony of the son of a devout family of Sikhs in Bedford. Tirath Singh Bhavra, a local television engineer, has never seen his fiancée, nor will he see her till his wedding day. She lives in Delhi, the daughter of a bank accountant. A long period of negotiation lies behind the moment recorded in the photograph:

> The girl's father came to England for a holiday. He was also looking for a suitable boy for his daughter. By chance he met one of our friends, who told him that we were religious people, and well-known in the Sikh community. This friend brought him to our house for a social visit. He did not let us know at that time what he came for. But talking to us, he came to know about our family, how we think and what we do. After a period of time, the friend told us that he was interested in discussing a marriage arrangement. Then, of course, we began making inquiries about his family. We knew already that it was a very nice, very religious family, and that he was a leader of his community. Each year he takes a pilgrimage of people to Mount Everest, which for us is a holy place. He is a very saintly person. And we think, if the parents are religious people, then surely the children will be the same. So we began to negotiate. First we had to see that the surnames of the father and mother differed from ours, for we must not mix the same bloods together. Then he invited us to come to India to see the girl, or for our relatives in India to do so on our behalf. We knew enough of the family to think this was not necessary, but we arranged to exchange photographs.
>
> Of course, we consult with the boy. We do not wish to be dictators. If he had had objections, we should not have proceeded. Now we are much more flexible than we used to be. Of course, it is not just a matter of the photographs. The

important thing is that boy and family have the feeling of accord in the mind with the other family. We believe that marriages are made in heaven, and that in making this union, we are enacting the pattern of God's will.

The son takes up the story:

The day we received the photographs, I was in Coventry all day. When I got back, and came into the room, my parents had taken my photograph off the mantelpiece and stood hers in its place. I did not know where to turn. My mind went blank. I could not speak because I was shy. My mother said 'Do you like this photo?' 'Yes,' I said. 'But are you sure? Do you really like it?' 'Yes,' I said, 'it's a very nice photograph.' They would have seen from my face if I did not like it.

Both she and I, as Sikhs, are seekers for God. Like moths, we seek His light and to merge with that light. And it is through the world that we come to our Creator. Through human relationships that we achieve salvation. For us, marriage is another, necessary stage of understanding in the search for perfection.

At the engagement ceremony, they asked me to come and sit in the centre between the men and women before the *Guru Granth Sahib*, the holy book. And when I was seated there, her uncle, as the oldest and nearest member of her family in the absence of her parents, came and sat next to me on my left-hand side. First, he touched my head, which is the Sikh sign of love and affection. Then all asked for a towel to be brought, the symbol of the bond. This was placed round my neck and draped in front of me into a fold or bag. Then her uncle placed a dried date (*shhorara*) in my mouth, which I had to eat. This means the contract is made. He placed a ring on my finger and in the bag pieces of coconut and gifts of money. The coconut means a blessing, and the pieces will be kept for the wedding day next year. Then my mother was required to make her gifts of coconut and money,[1] and after this, family and friends all put in their gifts. Our next door neighbour, Mrs Readman, an English lady, she also put a garland of flowers about my neck. As the towel grows heavier, this symbolises the burden of worldly things. At the wedding ceremony itself, I shall share this burden with my wife. We will carry it together. This burden, which the love of God will make as nothing to us.

Throughout life, relationships between the sexes are strictly controlled. The activities of girls are rigidly circumscribed before

[1] Plate 11 shows this moment.

marriage, and the activities of women after marriage almost entirely confined to the home. Deviations from the traditional codes evoke profound disapproval and intense shame. The loss of a girl's virginity, for example, becomes for the family involved a matter of irreparable harm and long-lasting humiliation. In cases such as this, indeed, the whole community shares the sense of ignominy.

As an immigrant community, it has been punctilious in its desire to regulate itself and to prevent any tarnishing of its reputation. Reverence for the order of society, for the authority of the father, and for the institution of marriage, together with the value placed on modesty and restraint in human relationships, have created a strong climate of moral conformity. Illegitimacy is rare. Conversations with local prostitutes suggest that Indians rarely have recourse to their services, while medical statistics confirm that the incidence of venereal disease among Indians is negligible. Their crime rate, like that of the Italians, is also low and mainly confined to a very small lawless minority. The few crimes of violence spring mostly from family or group disputes within the community.

The coin of self-regulation occasionally shows a reverse, stamped by the excessive rigidity of traditional standards. In a recent court case, for example, Indian parents who suspected their daughter of forming an attachment with an Indian boy were found guilty of severely beating her with a plastic curtain rail and locking her up in a room for days together. There is no doubt, too, that at times the community has settled privately affairs that should properly have been settled at law, and that the desire to preserve community reputation has, in several police cases, led to a smoke-screen of false evidence. Distrust between Indians and local authorities has thus sometimes been created from the most praiseworthy motives: and, failing proper advice, there is little doubt that ties of kinship, especially among the least educated, will often continue to take precedence over the requirements of British justice.

At the root of most misunderstandings between Indians and British authority is ignorance and fear. The majority of Indian immigrants are very poor people, with virtually no education, no experience of life outside their own villages, and little or no understanding of British norms. Written communications and notices in Punjabi or Hindi are virtually useless, since many are illiterate even in their own language, and all too few people are working to bridge the gulf in values and modes of organisation between the two communities.[1] It is understandable that when such people are challenged in any way by police, health or tax inspectors, or any other persons in authority, they are often seized by blind fear; they panic and retreat into a stream of frantic, often senseless, denials: 'No, no, no . . . I have not done this. I have not been there. I have never seen the man. I know nothing, nothing, nothing.' It is equally understandable that distrust on the part of the authorities proliferates.

Ignorance and fear live longest among those least in contact with British ways: the women. Most have virtually no English, and for them the strains of coping with everyday problems – how to keep house, feed and clothe the children in a cold climate, shop, deal with tradesmen, health and housing officials, use the medical services, and so on – are often intensely demanding. To give them the fundamental grasp of English language and English organisation that they need is certainly a major task for liaison work in Bedford, though the restricted place of women in Indian society makes it difficult to organise this in an acceptable way. The one likely method, it seems to me, is through teaching by their own people within their own institutions. If so, the logical centre for such work is the gurdwara.

The Indians from Kenya, far more cosmopolitan in outlook, share few of these problems. Most have a knowledge of English, and many of the younger people have been educated in schools on the English model using English as the language of instruction. Besides being better educated they are more sophisticated in work skills and experience of life than the native Punjabis. Most are also considerably better off. Their familiarity with Europeans and with European ways of life, moreover, gives them the confidence that Punjabis often lack, and ensures them a greater measure of acceptance in British society.

Some of these families came originally from the Punjab. K.'s father left there for Kenya in 1949 and found a good job with a contractor. K., his brother and his mother joined the father in 1954. For six months K. attended a private school to learn English, and then attended an English school. His ambitious mother instilled in him ideas of advancement and encouraged his studies.

[1] See Chapter 13, pp.194–6.

K. began to dream of a flamboyant college life, possibly in India. Then his father's fortunes declined and the dreams faded. He decided to come to England to work and study, and in 1961 joined a cousin already living in Bedford.

I arrived at eleven o'clock at night. Imagine. England in my mind had always been something quite lovely. When I arrived, it was dark. I found the house at last. It looked very small. My cousin opened the door. He stood in night clothes. The house too was dark. I found myself sleeping four people to a room. For three months this went on. I was very miserable, in a state of shock. So miserable I did not think of study. So miserable I could not look for work. My money was running out, my health deteriorating. It was winter, too. There were stories of turban people not getting jobs. And I was afraid of refusal. But in the end, I had no alternative. I went out and got a job as a labourer in the brickyards. After a bit, they asked me: 'Why the hell are you working here, speaking English, and with all those 'O' Levels?' Then they began to give me work as an interpreter, and this gave me confidence for the first time. I began to study, and to send money home. I would not have missed the brickyards for anything. It taught me what hard work is, and an understanding of ordinary English people. I made many good friends there. That was my *adjustment*, you might say. Before I came here, I thought that to do manual work was to fail. I had always connected English people with leisure, the old colonial image. I remember that when I got off the plane at Gatwick, this white porter came up to me and said 'Do you want your stuff carried, sir?' I could hardly speak. I didn't know what to say. An Englishman, my porter! All the time he was carrying the cases, all I could think was, what would be the right tip for a white man?

After successfully completing a national certificate course in electrical engineering at Mander College, K. now works as a supervisor in an electronic components firm. Like many of his fellow Kenyan Asians, he is intelligent, adaptable and ambitious. Already the Kenyan Indians are making their mark locally, and in the schools, their children, with their knowledge of English, their cosmopolitan background and their acquaintanceship with books, are impressing teachers with their performance. Kenyan Indians, no doubt, will increasingly come to take up responsible positions in local industrial and commercial life.

With the influx of such people, and as the younger Indians grow up, gain education and become familiar with the British way of life, so dialogue between Indian immigrants and the local society becomes more rational. The younger Indians learn quickly, and no national group in Bedford has greater reverence for education. Enrolment statistics for the 1968-9 session at Mander College, for example, confirm that far more Indians are attending courses, particularly in engineering, commerce and science, than any other Commonwealth immigrants.

How the Indian community in Bedford develops in the future depends a great deal upon the attitudes of these younger people to life in Britain. How do they see the future? What problems have they, and to what do they aspire? How far are they satisfied with their jobs and with their relationships in our society? To what extent do they want to belong?

It seems clear that, though in their acts and in their ways of thinking young Indians constantly have to bridge the gulf between two worlds, they do not, in general, suffer the acute divisions of consciousness of young Italians in Bedford. Though they aspire to advancement in their work and seek accommodation with British ways of life, they rarely react against traditional sources of authority and traditional values within their own society. Though many seek to eliminate outward and visible signs of difference between themselves and the British – in particular, the five Ks of Sikhism – they remain in their values, their respect for patriarchal and religious authority, and even in their responses to the demands of caste, rooted in the past and in their identity as Indians. And, though they may sometimes chafe at the inflexibility of their elders, most young Indians stand firm for traditional concepts of the sanctity of human relationships against the tide of 'free' or 'permissive' relationships within contemporary British society.

> Young people here, we think, have too much freedom. They have no respect for parents, for authority. Young people taking drugs, or having sex in public, these are cheap people, though it is not their fault alone. It is rather the fault of the parents, who have ceased to do their duty. The parents are the first teachers, the first gurus.

The future is glimpsed most accurately, perhaps, among the members of the Young Indian Association. Founded in 1966, this association now has about 180 members between fourteen and thirty who meet regularly in the rooms of the Howard

Congregational Church. Here they can buy soft drinks, play chess, darts or table-tennis, make their own music, organise coach trips, make arrangements for their football, hockey and table-tennis matches, and, most importantly, exchange views and discuss their plans for the future.

Many of these young men are the sons of brickyard labourers. Many, too, are following classes at Mander College for 'O' and 'A' Levels or for craftsman or technician level examinations. They are ambitious, and one in ten of them is convinced that his job does not measure up to his qualifications.

B. is one of the dissatisfied. Now twenty-four, he came to Bedford nearly eight years ago. After attending Mander College for three nights a week over two years, he passed a City and Guilds examination and is now going on to further studies. Although he has experience as a welder, he has been unable to obtain a job in that trade, and at present is working as a labourer. He has doubts as to whether his studies are really worth while, resents what he regards as the degradation of his own position, and also the general rumours of Indians living on the dole. He would prefer any job to the dole, even though, as a recently married man, he thinks he would get nearly as much on the dole as in his present unskilled job. He also resents smears about 'dirty Indians'. 'I have taken English boys to my home and they have been amazed to see how clean it is.' Another cause for dissatisfaction lurks here. 'I have taken English boys many times to my house. They have never invited me to their houses. I do not call that friendship.'

The majority are satisfied, to a greater or lesser degree, with their material lot. Their difficulties now, in 1969, are not so much those of obtaining jobs as of obtaining jobs at a certain level, in particular, those that involve supervisory responsibilities. While it is comparatively easy to gain acceptance among British workers in a technical function, there is a good deal of resentment and resistance against immigrants exercising supervisory or minor managerial functions.

Most of their criticisms of British society are in wider terms than those of job opportunities. D. is twenty. After passing City and Guilds examinations in mechanical engineering, he was apprenticed to a local firm, is proud to have been top apprentice in a group of twenty-four, and thinks Bedford 'the best town in Britain to gain acceptance'. He is shocked, nevertheless, at the ways in which Britain has changed since he came eight years ago:

If you had said then about showing blue films and strip, everyone would have thought you mad. But now it's all changed, it's all corruption. English girls, they seem sex-mad. If they want enjoyment, why don't they get married? England is best country in world for education, but not for other purposes; not for settling down. In fact, I will go home. In a few years, it could get bad, as in South Africa. To stay, you must be treated as a person, as a human being.

Beyond the immediate concern for job opportunities, then, are more complex general problems of relationships in British society. Though the first concern may seem more pressing initially, it is the wider issues which finally prove most wounding. Not only for the younger Indians, but for the better educated Indians in general, the stigma of 'colour' is especially hard to bear. The feelings of C., a trained nurse, are characteristic:

Not until I came to England did I discover 'colour'. I had not heard the word before. Then I found I was called 'coloured'. That was terrible. A bitter shock. I wanted to go home, to get away from it all. In the hospital, West Indian nurses wanted me to associate with them rather than with the English. I did not want to. I found I had much more in common with the English nurses.

Most Indians of Bedford have similar views. Despite the common label of 'colour', they feel little or nothing in common with West Indians, and relationships between the two communities are few. Indeed, all immigrant groups in Bedford stand in virtual isolation to each other.

Among certain of the more successful Indians living locally, there are further problems of relationships. These may be seen pre-eminently among the members of the Asian Society, a consciously elite group of professional people who, some three years ago, formed what is virtually a closed society meeting monthly. Composed essentially of six or seven families, their social relationships are restricted to no more than a hundred other Indians living in Bedford.

Why do we meet separately? From the majority of Indian immigrants in Bedford, the Punjabis from the villages and those that are called Untouchables, we are quite distinct. Separate. We have nothing in common. On the other hand, although we are economically and culturally of equal status to most British

2. The interior of a Bedford lodging-house

13. Ampthill Road Junior School, where there is a high proportion of immigrant children

people, we are still made to feel second-class citizens. We are foreigners and therefore outsiders. The English do not like people who are different from themselves. Even on my bus to [he named a new area of middle-class housing in Bedford where the immigrant population is still negligible] it becomes clear when the bus is crowded that people do not like to sit next to me. Why is this? Is it my appearance? Is it my smell? Is it simply that I am a foreigner?

In brief, this is a group in limbo, cutting itself off from its own people yet not fully accepted by British people of the professional class. Sitting among them, taking tea and sweet biscuits, watching an ageing film of the royal tour of India in the early sixties, with its bowings, scrapings and effusive commentary, I felt once again in a colonial society. The air was heavy with imitations of Empire, social consequence, sterility of purpose.

The members of the Young Indian Association are far more characteristic of the Indian community in temper, views and aspirations. One of the leading members is T. He is of the caste of craftsmen, from a family of blacksmiths who formerly lived in a small town close to Jullundur. In the early fifties his father's poor health brought a fall in trade. In 1954, the father came to England and, in 1958, to work in Bedford. T. joined his father at the beginning of 1962. He was then fifteen, so that he spent only three or four months at school. It was hard going for him. He was the first Indian in his school and spoke little English. Often he was teased, though without bad feeling. Finding it difficult to get a job in Bedford, he went to live with relatives in Birmingham and sought a job there. After two months, he was taken on as a moulder in a foundry, and kept his job for two years until work became slack in the firm and he and other men were put off. He returned to Bedford, and, after several months' fruitless search for semi-skilled work, made do with a job as a cleaner in a local chocolate firm. He rose quickly to be, in succession, packer, machine operator and refiner, and to be responsible for liaison work with Indian employees. In 1967, he returned to India for a holiday, fell ill, and thereby lost his job. After a brief spell as a machine operator in Stevenage, he found a similar job locally and now works as a senior technician in a firm making electronic components.

Tough, practical, adaptable, T. has made his way by hard work and determination.

E

I never had no trouble at work. Never met discrimination. And when I go to the pub I drink with anyone, Indian or English. They come to my home. I go to theirs. I don't have no problems of that kind.

T. puts the same energy into his work for the Young Indian Association, particularly to extend its activities for the greater benefit of the Indian community as a whole. The main aim now of the members is a centre of their own which will act as a focus for community activities and where they can provide classes in Punjabi, Hindi and English, have their own library, their own cultural programmes and their own films.

There is a sore point here. In the early sixties, regular film shows in local cinemas were organised by an Indian Workers' Association in collaboration with a Pakistani association. Some five years ago, after several incidents of violence and of fiddling the finances, local authorities caused the shows to be discontinued. Many Indians now feel strongly that, under guarantees of effective organisation, the film shows should be resumed. Failing that, a community centre of their own would enable them to organise such shows on their own account. Almost certainly they will soon ask the borough council for the same kind of help in finding suitable premises for a centre as has already been given to the Pakistanis and to the West Indians.

The Indians, then, like many other immigrant groups, want to come to terms with English life and organisation, and to 'fit in' as citizens, yet at the same time not betray their own identity. 'The ideal', as one young Indian recently said, 'is not that of integration but of people of all kinds living their own lives in their own ways beneath one roof in mutual tolerance and respect.'

Such young Indians therefore seek to preserve their own ways, not least the structure and values of their family life. With T., his wife and two young children, live his father, his mother and his two brothers:

We are always together. And all the money I earn, that all of us earn, it's all for the family. In England, many people work just for themselves. We work always for the family.

As for the future, I was thinking that one day I might set up a little business of my own. Now I don't know. England is going down and down. Not just money-wise. The government and unions always fighting. Young people and drugs. I switched on the telly the other day; there was this naked girl walking

about and pictures of man and woman naked, having sex. At
the end of it, she just walked away from him – you know, like a
dog. It didn't have no meaning for her, or for him. I think now,
finally, I'll go back to India. Not now, say in ten or fifteen years'
time. Even the poorer Indian people here, yes, they've settled
down, but many of them are sending money back to buy a
little piece of land back home.

So, at the final count, the problems of immigrants living in our
society are not merely to be reckoned in terms of job or colour
discrimination. There are other, more fundamental, problems
which all who live in our society share: problems of quality of
life.

To talk with Bedford's Indians is to be reminded that there are
ways of looking at such problems other than those of the contemporary materialist Western world; issues and purposes other than
those which we habitually focus upon. I remember sitting one
damp Saturday afternoon in the home of a family of devout Sikhs:
'Integration? Is it not more important to unite with God than to
unite with each other?' I could hear the distant roar of sports
watchers over the sets of sports viewers from a world that gives
increasing worship to the images of telly personalities. Was it not
salutary to be reminded of other scales of values? And not least
for my own purposes to come under new light? 'You come to us as
a beggar. And we also are beggars. God is so great, no one can tell
his greatness.'

9
Pakistan

OF late, for reasons purely economic, there has been some movement of Pakistanis away from Bedford. 'Here wages are the same but costs are higher than in other places.' The rising cost of local property, in particular, has spurred a number to look elsewhere: and Peterborough is frequently mentioned as a place which offers employment and lower property prices. This situation, together with further movements of people to and from Pakistan, makes it difficult to estimate with accuracy the number of Pakistanis currently living in Bedford. There are probably not less than a thousand and not more than twelve hundred and fifty.

Rather more than half of these are from East Pakistan, mainly from the district of Sylhet. The remainder – with the exception of about thirty Punjabis from the areas of Lahore and Rawalpindi – are almost all from the district of Mirpur, one of the three districts of Kashmir administered by Pakistan since the country as a whole was created in 1947 as a homeland for Muslims of the Indian subcontinent.

The people of Pakistan are thus united in the faith of Islam that 'there is but one God, Mohammed is his prophet'. The main duties that the faith imposes on its people are those of a pilgrimage to Mecca, of fasting during the month of Ramadan, of giving alms and of making daily prayers. Five daily prayer times are prescribed: before sunrise, after noon, before sunset, after sunset and before midnight. In general, the absence both of a tight-knit Pakistani community in Bedford and of a local mosque acts against the strict observance of religious forms. The pressures of daily work in an industrial society – especially those of shift work in the brickyards – also mean that in practice few make more than three observances a day, many no more than one a day, and most only one a week. The demands of brickyard labour in a cold climate have meant further compromises in the making of Ramadan, though this is not to say that faith is failing. Some fifty local Pakistanis are reckoned to have made their pilgrimage to Mecca on journeys either to or from their native country.

While the Muslim religion is the force of unity among Pakistanis, ordering the whole fabric of their lives, determining their laws, their modes of organisation and even the very nature of their personal relationships, there are considerable differences between the Sylhetis of the East and the Mirpuris of the West in terms of environment, language and even diet.

The Sylhetis of Bedford come from an area of hot, wet, rice-growing plains near to Assam, and they speak a Bengali dialect akin to Assamese. A number were immigrants or refugees from Indian territory at the time of partition, and came to Sylhet as landless agricultural labourers. To earn a living, even for those with land, was often a precarious matter, for a violent tropical climate brought constant flood disasters, and a livelihood could disappear in a day.

In this enervating climate, poverty, poor health, poor housing and ignorance bred together. Ninety-four per cent of those who live in Bedford at the time of writing are illiterate in their own language and in English. Not more than a small handful, less than 1 per cent, speak, read and write English; and only about 5 per cent can read Bengali and speak broken English. They are also poor in health standards, due in some measure to their ignorance of feeding habits suited to life in an English climate; and the conditions of East Pakistani lodging-houses are in general lower than those of any other group in Bedford.[1]

The movement of emigration from this under-privileged, over-populated area began shortly after partition. Its main motive forces were the many Sylhetis who had worked as lascars in the British merchant navy and who returned to their country to give word of Britain as a land of opportunity. 'Up there, they think that England is wonderful, with rivers of milk and honey and streets of gold.'

Some of those who gave the word also lent the money for the first passages. Virtually everyone who has come to England from Sylhet has had his passage arranged for him, by someone of his own kin or village or by professional money-lenders. Some 15 per cent of local Sylhetis have probably been sponsored by these money-lenders, and thus subjected to great exploitation. High prices for arranging true or false passports, rank over-charging for air passages, additional charges for fictitious entry requirements, for

[1] See also pp. 180–2.

aiding families left behind and for bribing real or imagined officials, together with high *monthly* compound interest rates mean that some of these poor people are paying most of their earnings in Bedford directly into the pockets of their sponsors.

Although the movement of emigration from Sylhet began about 1949, it was not until 1957, in response to local labour needs, that the first Sylhetis found their way to Bedford. In the early years, particularly, even local employment was often 'arranged' by sponsors; and since Bedford has enjoyed a condition of virtual full employment since the war, the trade was lucrative. Every Friday, the three main organisers had their collectors outside local works gates to take their pickings from the pay packets of their hapless, ignorant countrymen.

The Mirpuris come from a vastly different environment some 1,300 miles from Sylhet: non-tropical, mountainous, corn-growing. They speak a different language, a dialect of Urdu, and most, too, are physically different, being taller and fairer than the Sylhetis. Yet here also living is precarious for the smallholder or labourer. The average annual rainfall in Mirpur is little more than the fall in one day during a time of flood in Sylhet; the temperature is extreme, unemployment high, and the whole area has a long history of maladministration and neglect.

Emigration thus became equally a tradition in Mirpur as in Sylhet. N. has about fifty members of his family now established in this country – brothers, uncles, nephews and their individual family groups. His brother came first, arriving in England in 1954 and in Bedford in 1957. N. himself came in 1961. Others followed, each in turn helping the others financially. Most now have their own houses. 'I have now been eight or nine years in this country. I am far better off than I could ever hope to be in my own country.' Some of N.'s relatives live in Bedford itself; and many local Mirpuris are bound together by ties of kin.

In general, the level of education among the Mirpuris is higher than that of the people of Sylhet. Speaking Punjabi as well as Urdu, they have a good deal in common with the small group of people from Lahore and Rawalpindi, almost all of whom come from relatively affluent and educated backgrounds, and who are proficient in English as well as their own languages. Taking the West Pakistanis of Bedford as a whole, it is reliably estimated that about 5 per cent can speak, read and write English, about 8–9 per cent can speak English fairly well without being able to write it, and some 16–17 per cent can both understand English and speak a broken form of the language.

It is apparent that virtually all Asians in Bedford are from disputed or border areas of their countries (Kashmir, Sylhet and the Punjab): and for the Pakistanis, this also means some of the poorest areas of their native land. While some, like N.'s family, may have come to settle, most are here simply to improve their lot and earn what they can over a period of say, fifteen to twenty years, so that they may return to their own country to make a better life for themselves. Their commitment to Bedford is thus far less positive, and almost certainly less permanent, than that of the local Indian community. Relatively few have brought their families here (the majority still live in houses in multiple occupation) and few have any connections with the mainstreams of local life. Most are quiet submissive people who want simply to be left in peace to live in their own ways among their own people at minimum standards, to save enough to ensure a better life in their homeland in years to come.

With such aims, they have come inevitably to constitute the hard core of immigrant social problems in Bedford. To housing standards, most of the single men are quite indifferent. Even poor and crowded lodging-houses suffice them. They have no objection to sharing a bed with another man provided the weekly rent is no more than £1. For the sake of cheapness, they live and feed communally. Given their poor general standards of health, such communal living becomes a health hazard in itself; and their standards of communal feeding are often hardly adequate to sustain them for hard physical labour in the brickyards where the majority work.[1]

Lack of family life has also meant regular recourse to prostitutes; and since the prostitutes who serve them – invariably British – are mostly of the lowest grade, the incidence of venereal disease has been relatively high. It has been common practice for girls to be delivered to lodging-houses on pay nights, and to do business with the lodgers in turn. Police have sometimes raided such houses to find a queue of docile men patiently waiting on the stairs or by the bed for their turn to come. Some have not stirred on seeing the police. How could they know that their necessary, often momentary, act was regarded as contrary to law? The dangers of venereal disease have recently been abating, and

[1] See also the chapters on Housing and Health.

far fewer Pakistanis now seek the services of the local VD clinic than they did two or three years ago.[1] This is mainly due to their growing acquaintanceship with prophylactics. It is also, in much smaller measure, related to a slowly growing pattern of family life amongst the Pakistani community.

It is the Mirpuris rather than the Sylhetis who have recently begun to bring over wives and other members of their families, though this is still on a very limited scale compared with the influx of Indian families. In early 1969, there were only fifty-five Pakistani children attending borough schools against a total of nearly 500 Indian children. Most of the Pakistani children were boys of secondary school age, and in fact some forty-five Pakistani 'family' groups in Bedford consist only of father and son: a wage-earner and a potential wage-earner. In some cases, it is probable that when the son has learnt a trade and become established in work, the father will return to his own country and leave the son to carry on.

By contrast, there was not one Pakistani girl of secondary school age attending borough schools in January 1969, and at the time of writing there are still no more than one or two. Pakistani girls are rarely brought to this country, and those who have been, or who have been born in this country, will almost all be sent home before they reach marriageable age, i.e. by the age of twelve or thirteen. Talking recently with two bright little girls of nine from Mirpur, both of whom had lived three years in Bedford, I asked if they would stay in England.

'No, we shall be going home to be married.'

'Are you looking forward to going home?'

'Oh, no, we would like to stay in Bedford.'

Later, at a secondary school, I met a Pakistani girl of $11\frac{1}{2}$ who has lived here for six years: also attractive and like any English schoolgirl in her ways. She too would like to stay, though she knows she must return. For such children, what lies ahead after these years in which they have absorbed, consciously or unconsciously, so much of English ways of thinking and feeling, so much both in terms of consciousness and values? After all this, how will it be to have to fit into a pattern of female seclusion in, say, a Mirpur village? Are not the difficulties of immigrants often far less than those of emigrants returning to their own country?

[1] See VD statistics in Tables 5 and 6 (p. 191).

Pakistani parents also fear to let their girl children follow the paths of local secondary education lest they become infected by the permissive climate and corrupting standards of adult life in this country. A characteristic judgment upon present-day trends in our society is given by D., who first came to Bedford in 1960, returned to Pakistan in 1966, and then came back to Bedford a few months ago:

> I observed very many differences from the England I left three years ago, especially among younger people. Most of them at that time were well-behaved, well-dressed, conventional people. The Englishman has the name throughout Asia of a most conventional man. But now it is changing. Many young people are dressing themselves shabbily and they seem like rebels bent upon destruction. At one time, the English sins were beer and gambling. Now they are sex and drugs. The worst thing, that is drugs. It is very shocking to us.

The gradual influx of wives from Pakistan means that more men are buying their own houses and that living conditions among the Pakistanis are slowly improving. 'Now we are bringing families there is world of difference.' As yet, only a minority experiences this 'world of difference'; and among the largest group, the Sylhetis, there are still not more than thirteen or fourteen families in Bedford.

The coming of the women also brings its own problems. Given their lack of competence in English, their lack of experience and knowledge of English norms, their lack of adequate advisers and their traditions of seclusion, how can they learn to cope with the demands of everyday living in Bedford? 'Main problem, it is that of women. To teach them to shop, feed baby, call doctor.'

The problems of these Pakistani women are generally more complex than those of local Indian women, for they lack the habits of mutual help that are active within the tight-knit Indian community. If the number of Pakistani women continues to grow, there will be a growing case for a fully qualified Asian medical-social worker – a Pakistani if possible – to help advise them in the direction of their daily lives. There could be no better way to help tackle the roots of their community's social problems and to help bring them into the normal fabric of local life.

No local immigrant group suffers more than the Pakistanis from lack of leaders and educated men; and most attempts to promote

E2

community activities have met only temporary success. Film shows in the early sixties brought accusations that some of the organisers had had their hands in the till, and outbreaks of violence at the shows brought about their cessation. More latterly, the Pakistani Cultural Association has failed to develop as was hoped, despite the personal encouragement of Ernest Avison, chief public health inspector for Bedford, and the help given by the local council to create premises for the association to meet. At the time of writing, the building has shattered windows, wears an air of neglect, and arrears of rent are owing.

Difficulties are aggravated by the atmosphere of dissension, intrigue and distrust – further exacerbated by ties of kinship – which dogs so many Pakistani and Indian activities in Bedford. Accusations proliferate: that X is using his position only to line his pockets; that Y does not want to help his people because he profits so much from their ignorance. Nothing is certain except that this general atmosphere can only serve to act against trust becoming established, both among the Pakistanis themselves and between their group and the local authorities. It is so easy for distrust to breed. He who acts as interpreter between his own people and the police, for example, no matter if it be to the benefit of his own people, may well find himself an object of distrust. In this climate, it is not surprising that few Pakistanis able to interpret are willing to do so, or that police distrust lingers on.

There is all too little evidence to allay distrust, and as yet all too few of the more educated Pakistanis are ready to serve their people disinterestedly. Many make charges on their countrymen even for filling in the simplest form, let alone for helping them to apply for jobs or loans, or for advising them on tax matters. Who could be easier prey than these helpless, hapless, utterly dependent people?

Habits of corruption in Pakistan have been quickly translated into Bedford too, and have meant a spate of headaches for the local tax office. False documents and false records of a man's dependants in Pakistan can be readily supplied for the right price, so that it is virtually impossible to determine the rights and wrongs of individual tax claims with certainty. In this situation, the most astute are those who contrive to serve three sets of interests at the same time: the tax office, their own people, and themselves.

The main enemy, however, is ignorance. So few Pakistanis know either what to do or how to do it. Baffled and bewildered by forms and regulations, they are ready to turn to any source of help. Written notices in Urdu and Punjabi in the tax office are of very limited use to these mostly illiterate people, and their own community association is not yet organised to give them the impartial help they require. Yet it is clear that unless officialdom and community association join to give them help, exploitation and evasion will continue their field days.

It remains to be said that a good deal of mutual help is given between Pakistanis without strings attached, and that many have shown themselves very willing to give others financial aid free of interest. The need now is to develop this spirit within a revived community association. If this can be achieved, it will do much to revive the Pakistani community's confidence in itself and to give it new standing both among local people and among other immigrant groups.

To establish good relationships with other peoples and to live in peace are certainly among the first aims of local Pakistanis. They are acquiescent people. They take great pains to avoid giving offence. They rarely make any kind of complaint – except, of course, against the tax office. They are grateful that they have been allowed to slip into place in Bedford with so little fuss, that they have incurred so little local hostility. As for hostility on grounds of colour, their general view is that 'colour prejudice doesn't exist'. Recent experiences lead some to qualify this viewpoint. 'We did not feel anything against us until the first speech of Mr Powell in April 1968. Then there was dislike from many English people after that time. Now it has died down a great deal.'

As Muslims, the issue of colour means very little to them. Islam is a multi-racial community; and since the faith extends throughout the Middle East and into Europe, and Christ is a major prophet of Islam, Pakistanis feel natural affinities with Christianity, Europe, and the Western world. To be identified as 'coloured' is thus both utterly alien and deeply shocking to the Pakistani mind. The term 'coloured person', they feel, is meaningless in defining identity, and issues made in 'colour' terms are thus false issues. The affinities they have with Indians are those not of colour, but of culture. With the West Indians, they feel they have nothing in common; if anything, less than with any other group in Bedford.

What complaints they do make of relationships in Bedford are usually in quite different terms. Educated Pakistanis, for example, sometimes resent traditional native assumptions about ignorant foreigners. 'When they see you, they assume you are a savage. In shops, they start counting on fingers to you. They say, "Me. You. Understand?" Like that. Then you begin to speak more, and when they see that you speak properly, then they are all right with you.' In general, however, they think that their problems of relationships in Bedford are minor ones. 'If you're prepared to work, all right, you're accepted.'

With the great weight of illiteracy and ignorance that it has to bear, and with only a very limited measure of family life, it is inevitable that a Pakistani community is far slower in establishing itself in Bedford than any other immigrant group. It is still, perhaps, too early to speak of 'community', for although many local Pakistanis are joined by ties of kinship, they have not yet developed any strong sense of corporate being. The great majority are single men – the percentage of children to adults among local Pakistanis in houses of multiple occupation is only a tenth of that among local Indians – and their commitment to Bedford has none of the wholeheartedness of the Sikh community. Though a few have recently been bringing wives and sons to Bedford, the overall movement of Pakistanis out of Bedford in the last two years out-weighs the movement in. Redundancy in the brickworks in 1967 and rapidly rising property prices have both served to deter them from commitment and to direct their aspirations elsewhere; and Bedford certainly cannot give them the sense of community that a town like Bradford can give.

On the other hand, for very simple economic reasons, there is little likelihood of a rapid movement of Pakistanis away from Bedford. As long as the brick industry continues to need men, Pakistanis – like Indians – will be knocking at its door. Many, indeed, made aware of labour shortage in the industry, are currently making applications to the brick companies for their relatives to join them here. Given a continuing demand for labour, then, it seems likely that most local Pakistanis will stay where they are, at least for the foreseeable future, and that others may well join them if given work permits to do so.

The longer they stay, the deeper their roots become. Several Pakistani businesses are now firmly established: four retail shops, one restaurant, and another restaurant opened recently. It begins to look as if some Pakistani immigrants will stay, or at least that they will leave their sons to carry on earning here. The birth of a second generation tends to reinforce these roots: 'The children born here will not want to go back. Even we, after ten years in this country, we feel that in Pakistan we are in a strange country. If it is so for us, what will it be for the children going back?'

This remark is almost certainly over-emphatic. A group of ten Pakistani boys at a local secondary school recently discussed with me their intentions for the future. Five were from West Pakistan, three from East Pakistan and two were Muslims from Kenya.[1] The Sylhetis from the east were clearly boys apart. Easily distinguishable by their darker skins and round faces, only one of them could understand and speak English, and none of the West Pakistanis could understand their common tongue, Bengali. All three were here with their fathers only, and all three intended to return to Sylhet within a few years. Of the West Pakistanis, all spoke Urdu, Punjabi and – with one exception – English. Two thought that they would be returning home within a few years. One wanted to stay longer in Bedford to train as a TV engineer before he went back. Only two of the eight who had come from Pakistan itself thought they would settle here. The two Kenya Muslims, of course, had no doubt at all about settling. Already their sights are set high. Religion apart, they are indistinguishable from the Kenya Indians: indeed, their families also came originally from the Punjab, and they share the ability and drive that sets the Kenyan immigrants so much apart.

Finally, then, for the majority of Pakistanis, the family base will remain in their homeland, east or west. They are working and saving for *that*, above all: to better their position at home, to buy a business or a piece of land, or, as some of the men have done already, to purchase a new young wife. (Muslim law permits a maximum of four wives, and where the percentage of women to men is high, as in East Pakistan, it is commonplace for men to have several wives.)

No group in Bedford, moreover, continues more completely in traditional ways, and makes fewer compromises and accommodations with English ways of life. They continue to keep to their own kin and customs, their own languages and food, and to practices such as that of rubbing mustard oils on their bodies[2] Even the habits of walking the streets of Bedford in single file derive directly from the ways in which they used to walk the high, narrow paths between the rice-fields in Sylhet. Such people will change only

[1] Some three Kenya Muslim families are now settled in Bedford.
[2] See pp. 193–4.

very slowly and to a very limited degree: 'The British Raj sat on top of the Indian subcontinent for centuries without changing the fundamental patterns of culture. Bedford, then, isn't likely to change them all that much. Might it be that Asian culture is indestructible?'

PART II

Immigrants in the Community

10

Employment

ENGLAND MY ENGLAND

I come to England poor and broke
Go on dole see labour bloke
Fill in forms have lots of chatters
Kind man give me lots of akkers
Thank him much and then he say
'Come next week and get more pay
You come here we make you wealthy.
Doctor too to make you healthy'
Six months on dole got plenty money
Get red meat to fill my tummy
Send for friends from Pakistan
Tell them come as quick as can
Plenty of us on the dole
Lovely suit and big bank roll
National Assistance is a boon
All dark men on it soon
They come here in rags and tatters
Go down dole and get some akkers
They come with me we live together
One bad thing – the bloody weather
One day white man come inside
Ask me if we wash in Tide
I say 'Yes we wash in tide
Too damn cold to wash out tide'
All get nicely settled down
Fine big house in busy town
Fourteen families living up
Fourteen families living down
All are paying nice big rent
More in garden live in tent
Soon I send for wife and kids
They won't have to live in digs
Six months later big bank roll
Still on labour draw more dole

Wife wants glasses, teeth and pills
All are free we got no bills
White man say he pay all year
To keep National Assistance here
Bless all white men big and small
For paying tax to keep us all
We think England damn good place
Too damn good for white man's race
If he not like coloured man –
Plenty room in Pakistan

Anon

The reverse of this popular coin shows the realities of Bedford in June 1969. At that time, there were 596 men and 84 women unemployed in the town; there were 465 vacancies for men and for women 374. The manager of the Bedford employment exchange estimates that immigrants of all kinds make up about 35 of the 596 men and about 6 of the 84 women. In brief, while immigrants make up some 20 per cent of the whole population of Bedford, they represent only about 6 per cent of people unemployed. The verses quoted above, therefore, though not without appeal, are without foundation.

These facts reinforce the point that immigrants have come to Bedford to do the work that British natives will not do. The main reasons for their presence are the needs of the local brick industry, and the main employer of labour is the London Brick Co. Ltd, with its Stewartby, Coronation, Elstow, Marston and Ridgmont works. The two last-named were acquired towards the end of 1968, following a take-over of the Marston Valley Brick Co. Ltd. Stewartby employs 2,172 men on the clock (i.e. manual workers on weekly wages), Elstow 150, Coronation 220, and Marston and Ridgmont together 1,635.

Analysis of records at Stewartby,[1] which is in fact the largest brickyard in the world, shows the extent to which the brick industry has come to rely on immigrant labour since 1947.

Prisoners-of-war provided the first main source of foreign labour. Thereafter, Poles were taken on in increasing numbers, and by the time the POWs were repatriated in early 1948 the number of Poles employed had reached its maximum. That same year, recession in the brick industry created redundancies and by July 1948 the number on the clock had dropped to 1,772.

[1] See Table 1.

STEWARTBY LABOUR RECORDS (SELECTED DATES)

W/E	Total No. on clock	POW	Poles	EVW	S. Irish	Italians	W.I.	Pakistanis	Indians
30.11.47	2,090	473	311	112	56				
4. 1.48	2,179	284	332	176	58				
28. 3.48	1,798	—	189	148	—				
2. 1.49	1,911	—	210	274	—				
26. 6.49	2,236	—	200	531	—				
1. 1.50	2,308	—	161	577	—				
25. 6.50	2,349	—	142	590	16				
7. 1.51	2,394	—	133	626	6				
30. 6.51	2,257	—	118	542	—	23			
6. 1.52	2,264	—	112	411	—	144			
4. 1.53	2,522	—	110	388	—	242			
3. 1.54	2,531	—	111	378	—	247			
2. 1.55	2,377	—	99	350	—	242			
6. 3.55	2,410	—	93	346	—	276	6		
8. 1.56	2,486	—	93	327	—	276	12		
6. 1.57	2,516	—	94	317	—	365	7		
6. 1.58	2,546	—	91	297	—	359	129		
14. 9.58	2,518	—	82	284	—	341	88	35	33
4. 1.59	2,551	—	84	278	—	360	85	43	34
10. 1.60	2,629	—	83	276	—	368	76	95	67
8. 1.61	2,541	—	84	270	—	367	73	75	75
7. 1.62	2,595	—	81	264	—	351	81	69	120
6. 1.63	2,537	—	78	254	—	338	74	83	137
5. 1.64	2,502	—	77	244	—	319	65	100	180
8. 1.65	2,538	—	74	230	—	265	76	170	178
7. 1.66	2,445	—	72	221	—	353	62	130	164
8. 1.67	2,380	—	70	196	—	429	50	106	154
5. 1.68	2,255	—	63	189	—	365	46	106	162
3. 1.69	2,172	—	247		—	334	42	95	174

European Voluntary Workers were recruited in growing numbers from this time and reached their maximum in early 1951. Labour was still inadequate to meet the demands of production, however, and after unavailing attempts to recruit British labour agreement was reached in 1951 with British and Italian ministries of labour for the bulk importation of Italian workers. Italians began work in the brickyards in June 1951.

The build-up of Italian labour continued until the end of the fifties, when the borough of Bedford, faced with a growing crisis in local housing, imposed restrictions on the importation of Italian labour. The effects of this control can be seen in the levelling-off of the number of Italian workers in 1960, although numbers did not drop significantly until mid-1964. Thereafter, importation of Italian workers on a personal basis (e.g. on the recommendation of Italians already working in Bedford) was allowed where local labour was not available, and Italian numbers rose slowly again during the mid-sixties.

West Indians were first recruited in 1955. Their numbers rose rapidly to reach a peak in early 1958 and thereafter very slowly declined (from 129 in January 1958 to 42 in January 1969) following the introduction of Asian labour. Figures in recent years suggest a preference for Asian workers over West Indian workers.

Asians first appeared in the autumn of 1958. Until the mid-sixties, Indians and Pakistanis were recruited in roughly equal numbers, and the preponderance of Indians after that time suggests a preference for Indians over Pakistani labour. In 1967, recession in the brick industry led to a temporary measure of redundancy and numbers fell from 2,380 in January to 2,156 in March. Many of those who were put off at the time were taken on again later in the year.

In 1969, the labour needs of the London Brick Co. still exceeded supply. Once more, they are forced to recruit foreign workers, for although the current national unemployment figure is about half-a-million and the current local figure 600 recent attempts to recruit British labour have proved unavailing. A recruitment campaign in the spring of this year was followed by a series of interviews with unemployed men at the local Labour Exchange. Most refused point-blank to work in the brickfields, and of those who accepted not one reported for work. In the face of this evidence, permission was given for the company to recruit 30 more workers from Italy.

The situation at the other local brick company, Redlands

Fletton, shows a similar pattern. Of 400 staff (including office staff), 190 are English, 79 Italian, 32 other Europeans, 90 Asians (including about 12 Indians), and 15 West Indians. Since the borough imposed its restrictions on Italian labour, the company has been forced to recruit on a 'catch as catch can' basis. Like the London Brick Co., their need for manual labour remains as great as ever.

The local brick industry thus employs just over 4,500 men in manual work on weekly wages. The percentage of immigrants at Stewartby is currently 41 per cent, but in the local brick industry as a whole it is almost certainly higher, since certain works such as Marston are less highly mechanised than Stewartby. Overall, then, it seems that of these 4,500, nearly half are immigrants.

In the other industrial firms of Bedford, as in the brickfields, the presence of immigrants is directly related to the number of semi-skilled and unskilled jobs available. Out of just over a thousand at Britannia Iron & Steel Works Ltd, for example, there are 119 unskilled and 496 semi-skilled jobs for men. Many of these jobs, especially in the foundry, involve hard, dirty work. Britannia currently employs 132 West Indians, 64 Asians, 32 Italians, and 30 post-war Europeans. The firm was responsible for recruiting the first West Indians to the town in 1955 and thereafter something of a tradition of West Indian labour was established.

At Brookhirst Igranic Ltd, makers of electrical components, the number of skilled jobs is higher, that of immigrants correspondingly lower. In a total work force of some 2,000 people, there are relatively small numbers of immigrants working at various levels, from Poles and EVWs in the machine shop and in technical trades to West Indians in labouring and craft jobs. The growing reputation of Sikh workers in recent years has led to some moving up into the skilled trades, and at the time of writing a Sikh is the highest paid worker in the machine shop.

W. H. Allen & Sons & Co. Ltd also employ about 2,000 people, 1,300 of them on the shop floor. Their main products are turbines and switch gear, with many one-off orders of high quality requiring skilled labour. These skilled jobs have long been a preserve of local families, in some cases for generations. The need for immigrant labour is therefore small and resistance to the intrusion of 'outside' sources of labour is considerable. The only significant group of immigrants working at Allen's is that of some twenty West Indians who act as internal truck drivers and fork lift drivers.

The pattern of immigrant labour in these three large firms is representative of the area as a whole. Most immigrants find employment in the dirtier, less skilled jobs in industry, relatively few in the public services. (The United Counties Bus Co., for instance, currently employs three Jamaican bus-drivers, and four Jamaican and two Pakistani bus-conductors. Language and education barriers make it difficult to find men of the required level of skill and responsibility.) A number of immigrants living locally are employed outside the area, notably Indians and West Indians in the car firms of Luton. They find it difficult to obtain suitable accommodation in Luton and many share car expenses to their place of work. The current charge for car transport to Luton and back over a five-day week is £1.

A small number of immigrants are self-employed. Of some twenty-five to thirty businesses run by Poles and EVWs, most are based on skilled crafts. Italian businesses now number about two dozen, mainly service trades such as hairdressers, cafés, food stores, etc. There are also four or five Asian food stores and four Chinese restaurants. Further expansions into business life, particularly by Italians, Indians, and Chinese, are to be expected.

Employers' views on the work qualities of immigrant men are remarkably consistent. Post-war Europeans rate highly as good, conscientious workers, many of them in skilled trades. A number are engaged in research and higher technical work, and one EVW has achieved executive status in the brick industry. Italians also enjoy a high work reputation. Most are not fussy about the nature of the work as long as wages are good. Nothing deters them, not even cleaning the flues in the brickyards. Lack of technical skills and education, particularly lack of English, inevitably confine the advancement of Italians, as well as making it difficult for them to adapt to mechanised processes. The few northern Italians are reckoned a good deal superior to southern Italian in this respect.

West Indians are less highly regarded by employers. Though the more educated and skilled have good work reputations, employers complain of a lack of conscientiousness and of high fall-out rate among the unskilled and semi-skilled. One company estimates that they may need to recruit six West Indians for every one who satisfactorily takes his place on piece-work after training. They are also frequently reckoned to be 'arrogant' and 'difficult', liable to ascribe criticism to colour prejudice, and to become involved in squabbles and quarrels. Such quarrels often derive from inter-island jealousies and some have resulted in grievous bodily harm (one firm had two cases of stabbing involving West Indians). Where there are tensions between groups, it is mostly between Italians and West Indians, although cases of open conflict between groups are relatively few.

By contrast, the great virtue of Asian labour in employers' eyes is that of docility, although this often goes hand-in-hand with poor physical condition, especially among Pakistanis. With their high incidence of respiratory disease, poor diet, and a background of deprivation, the reputation of Pakistani labour is inevitably low, though some employers have noticed signs of improvement recently as a result of better living conditions and feeding habits in this country. Certain employers seem unable to make a distinction between Pakistanis and Indians, but those who can have a growing regard for Indian labour. Though less docile than the Pakistanis, they are in general more active, and Sikhs, in particular, are fast gaining approval for their disciplined and hard-working qualities. One manager reckons that an Indian can do the work of two Pakistanis, and in the brick industry today there are far more Indians than Pakistanis on piece-work.

Tension between Asians and other groups arises mainly through difference in cultural habits, toilet hygiene being the greatest cause of tension. British and European workers often complain bitterly of fouled toilets, and in some works separate toilets have now been established for Asian workers. British and European workers also object to the smell of Asians' body oils, particularly among Pakistanis. There have been cases of men refusing to work with Pakistanis on hot days, and one such incident in the brickfields was settled by a wise foreman who put the Pakistanis down-wind.

Of immigrant women there is a fair sprinkling in these industrial concerns. Britannia currently employ 62 (25 West Indians, 20 Italians, 8 other Europeans, 8 Indians, and 1 Malay), and Brookhirst Igranic has some 60 Italian women on the assembly line. Many more work at cleaning and domestic jobs, and the town hall and other council offices, the local hospital and local schools, all rely heavily upon them. Most of these women are Italian, whose capacity for hard work and natural feeling for cleanliness make them highly valued by employers. Italian women are also beginning to find work in retail trades, although, so far, there is virtually no sign of Asian or West Indian girls serving in these trades.

The two most important single employers of female labour are

Tobler-Meltis Ltd and Texas Instruments Ltd. Tobler-Meltis, the chocolate and confectionery manufacturers, employ between seven and eight hundred women on the production floor. Much of the work is of an unskilled, repetitive nature with virtually no language requirements: 212 Italian women are employed, about 100 Asians (mostly Indians) and about 25 West Indians. The best-paid jobs are those on the packing lines or 'webs', and these demand unflagging concentration and dexterity. One line has an Englishwoman at each end, all those between them being Italian with the exception of two Yugoslavs. The women's fingers move like lacemakers' at Bruges. The nature of the work and the friendly atmosphere have helped to create a tradition of Italian labour, and an Italian personnel officer is employed to handle recruitment and welfare.

Few West Indian or Asian women work on team piece-work of this kind. Backgrounds of poor health and feeding habits are often painfully apparent in their movements, and by far the most animated and dexterous are the younger women who have lived longest in this country. Yet, even though their manual skills are limited, Asian girls, in particular, are willing and co-operative in their work attitudes. In will to work, English girls present more problems than any other national group.

Competition for local female labour is now intense; and its supply has been unable to keep pace with the very rapid expansion of Texas Instruments Ltd in recent years. Established in Bedford in 1957, the company forms part of the semi-conductor component division of the parent corporation in Dallas, Texas. The Bedford plant, with its identity tabs, its gloss of Christian name egalitarianism, its excellent working conditions and the apparent paternalism of its industrial attitudes, has, in fact, very much the 'feel' of an American corporation, despite company insistence: 'We are British to the backbone.'

Texas Instruments employ some 2,500 people in Bedford, of whom about 1,500 are women. Most of the women perform comparatively unskilled tasks requiring good eyesight and manual dexterity. Despite recent programmes of work simplification and the lowering of recruitment standards, T.I.'s difficulty in recruiting labour now leads them to curtail further local expansion and to lay down plants in other parts of the country.

While visiting the T.I. plant, I was informed that the company keeps no records of the nationalities of its workers on the grounds that this is discriminatory. The sentiment is admirable, the logic doubtful. Even if the company does not think it useful to keep records of the numbers and performance of the various groups of immigrant workers, I would have thought it important both for the town, and the country, to know in detail the extent to which industry depends on immigrant labour, and to know something of the work performance of the various groups. T.I. officials also seemed loath either to discuss or admit problems on immigrant labour, and before being walked round the plant I was told, 'The company would prefer for you not to communicate with the operatives' – a phrase to treasure.

Texas Instruments are not alone in their reluctance to give information or to discuss issues. Among most firms, to a greater or lesser degree, fears of competitors, fears of trade unions, and fears of the Race Relations Act join with traditionally distrustful and conservative habits of mind to create an atmosphere where mere recognition of problems, let alone analysis, becomes a matter of difficulty.

Despite this, the general pattern of immigrant employment in the Bedford area is quite clear. Immigrants have come to take on the lower levels of work. In effect, they accept a situation of job segregation. Given the local context of full employment, economic conflict has thereby been kept to a minimum. Conflict has only occurred where there has been a challenge to established economic preserves and privileges. In the mid-sixties, for example, Allen's recruited an Indian turner; within a few hours, there were mass demands from plant workers that the company get rid of him. They saw his presence as a threat to their traditional preserves and as the beginning of a movement that could undercut, first their wages, then their jobs. Since he was a fully qualified man, management and unions found themselves in a cleft stick. The man was suspended pending discussions of the issue; and, while talks went on, the Indian, rather than be the cause of resentment and unrest, found employment elsewhere.

To label this episode 'colour prejudice' would be to miss much of the point. The real root of the workers' objections was economic fear of 'foreign' labour of any kind. In the early days of immigrant labour in Bedford, discrimination against foreign workers was often quite explicit. At Britannia in 1955, for instance, shop stewards agreed to the company engaging Italians for the foundry and upgrading them if no British labour was available. In return, the company undertook: (1) not to reduce working time in any department below forty-four hours before declaring Italians in that department redundant; (2) not to reduce Saturday morning overtime in any department where Italians were working; and (3) not to engage Italians free from working restrictions for more than a year at a stretch. Later, at a time of economic recession, some Italian workers were laid off Saturday morning overtime, while British workers were kept on. The local Italian authorities immediately referred the matter to the Ministry of Labour, but luckily improvement in the economic situation allowed matters to be righted before issue was joined.

Since that time, the rights of foreign workers have gradually become more fully recognised and more closely defined. In the brick industry prior to June 1963, it was established practice that, in the event of redundancy, foreign workers were the first to go, and that British workers should be given preference of consideration for promotion. From 1963, foreigners who were trade union members were given equal rights with British workers. Thus, when redundancies came about in 1967, it was agreed that 'foreign workers who are not trade union members will be the first workers redundant', and that thereafter the principle of last in, first out, should apply. Such agreements have not been operative since the passing of the Race Relations Act.

As the rights of foreign workers have become more fully recognised, so they have come to participate more fully in trade union affairs. In the climate of the mid-fifties, it was hardly surprising that many Italians saw little point in union membership and many still resent the payment of union dues. Italians want something back for their money. A number of West Indians also question the value of membership, though Asians, in general, pay their dues without demur. Many employers recommend or require immigrant employees to join a union; and membership may well become compulsory for all foreign workers before long.

The value that most immigrants put upon acceptance in the host society, the fear of bureaucracy and officialdom bred among them in their own countries, and their lack of English, all join to inhibit immigrants from active participation in union affairs. Participation has increased in recent years, however, and may be reasonably measured by the number of shop stewards in the brick industry. London Brick Co. has a total of 75 shop stewards, 5 of them women. Of the remaining 70, 11 are immigrants (4 Poles and

EVWs, 4 Italians, 2 West Indians, and 1 Pakistani). Redlands Fletton have 2 immigrant shop stewards – one post-war European and one Indian – out of a total of 6.

Though discrimination against immigrants in employment is now strictly controlled, there is evidence of discrimination against immigrants seeking employment. Men applying for advertised jobs have sometimes been told that the jobs have been taken, though later they have found that the posts were filled *after* they had been turned away. More than one Sikh, when told a job was taken, has returned home, shaved, and successfully re-applied for the same job. Again, colour prejudice is too simple an explanation. Shaving, after all, does not change a man's colour, but it may make him more acceptable by ordinary British standards.

For unskilled tasks there is, of course, no competition. Virtually any pairs of hands are welcome. Skilled tasks are another matter. Here, local management attitudes to immigrant labour closely resemble those of those local householders to the European immigrants who sought accommodation here after the war. Here, too, is enacted the classical, if moderate, pattern of British xenophobia: an initial period of wariness, suspicion and reluctance to accept the newcomer followed by a transition or trial period where a few immigrants of particular groups are admitted on probation. At this time prejudices are either confounded or confirmed, and from this experience all future policies derive.

Among recent immigrant groups, Sikhs have been particularly successful in proving themselves, and many of them now find the former climate of antipathy turning to one of acceptance. Recently I heard a story of a Sikh who some years back was deeply distressed when forced to shave in order to gain employment. His work qualities so impressed his employers that not only did they make no objection when he began to grow his hair again, but they took on ten or a dozen more 'turban men'. The story may be apocryphal, but one point is clear: that, whatever the nature of employers' initial reservations about immigrant workers, final considerations and valuations are economic.

The attitudes of British workers to immigrants have also changed a good deal in recent years. A West Indian's summing-up of the present situation is that 'the British are prepared to accept you as a worker, but they resent you as the boss'.[1] Where a senior position involves a purely technical function, it is relatively easy for an

[1] But not necessarily as employer.

immigrant to gain acceptance. Immigrants in supervisory or minor managerial roles meet far greater resentment and resistance.

The other main factors governing local attitudes are those of personal experience of immigrants' work qualities, and the pressures of the local employment situation. Antipathy towards immigrants is thus not a fixed quantity. It develops or diminishes in relation to prevailing economic conditions and pressures. In this context, the conclusion of a recent survey that 10 per cent of the British people are prejudiced has little reality. In Bedford, at least, the only real 'fact' is that a favourable economic situation, together with effective social organisation, is likely to allow a gradual, if grudged, acceptance of immigrants to continue, while a cold economic wind could well fan antipathy into open hostility. The concept of 'prejudice', moreover, is not of great relevance. There are few local pre-judgments these days for the simple reason that most people have some experience of immigrants; and local antipathies are usually based on some kind of personal observation, however inadequate.

Complaints of discrimination from immigrants come mainly from those of the second generation. While their fathers were prepared to accept inferior jobs and inferior living conditions, the younger people look for opportunities equal to those of their British contemporaries. Few will be ready to accept jobs as manual labourers in brickfield or foundry, not least *because* their fathers had such jobs: and the fathers themselves want their sons to do better than they have done. Among most immigrant groups the drive for education and training is intense, and the sons' aspirations are towards skilled craft and technical jobs, and towards apprenticeships.

Of no groups is this more true than of the Indians; while ambition sometimes leads them to over-estimate their abilities, there is also evidence that a number of young Indians are confined to jobs incommensurate with their skills and qualifications: a welder working as a labourer; a young man with 3 'A' Levels in a poorly paid clerical post, etc. Recently, I heard a local official state in public that 'young Asians and West Indians with qualifications have an equal chance of taking up employment with British youth'. Complacency is a great maker of blinkers.

In matters of employment, as in all matters affecting immigrants, Bedford is all too prone to self-congratulation. The peace of the local immigrant scene is in no way an achieved peace. Bedford is peaceable mainly because it has not yet been tested. The test is now beginning as the children of immigrants come on to the labour market in growing numbers. By 1980, Bedford should know better whether she has cause to rejoice or not.

A useful test for the future is the extent to which apprenticeships are made available to qualified immigrant youth. In the past, in old-established firms such as Allen's, many apprentices have come from families where fathers, and often grandfathers, have created a work tradition. Now that immigrant children make up about a quarter of the children in Bedford schools, competition between the sons of local families and the sons of immigrants will inevitably become more fierce, and the bases on which apprenticeships are given will be ever more closely scrutinised on both sides. Certain firms such as Brookhirst Igranic have already demonstrated willingness to consider the qualities and qualifications of applicants for apprenticeships without reference to nationality; and Indians and Italians have been notably successful in gaining access to their apprentice schemes. How far local firms are willing or are able to follow this kind of lead will be crucial factors in the making of the local industrial scene during the seventies.

It is the future of the brick industry, of course, which dominates the local scene. Already it has been the main motive force for bringing 14,000 immigrants to Bedford and its need for unskilled labour remains unassuaged. Unless there are drastic changes in methods and conditions of work, it seems unlikely that the industry will attract British workers. Continued reliance on foreign labour may, therefore, be inevitable. But where will it come from? Southern Italy is unlikely to continue long as a source of labour. Industrial development is rapidly creating there new forms of employment and higher wages; and the whole tradition of Italian emigration may now be near its end. If southern Italians do look outward in the future, it is most likely to be towards the other countries of the European Economic Community. For sources of manual labour the brick industry will therefore have to look further afield, possibly to Turkey. If so, the town must expect influxes of a new group or groups of non-English speaking people with backgrounds of poverty and illiteracy, with a consequent new wave of demands on local social services.

Even then, the needs of the brick industry will not be satisfied. Many of the British workers are those of long standing. They are ageing and as they retire it will be difficult, to say the least, to replace them with other British labour. In previous generations, the local ways of life decreed that sons replaced fathers. This is no longer so. It is also certain that few second generation immigrants will come to join their fathers or replace them when they retire. (Many Italians have already worked more than fifteen years in the brickfields.) As with the British miners of post-war days, fathers want their sons to do better for themselves than they did. As for the sons, they tend to look at the brickfields as a modern Colonial looks at the old sugar plantations, identifying them with the degradations of the past. If the sons come to the brickfields, it will only be for apprenticeships or for skilled work associated with machines rather than with manual work.

Is there, then, an alternative to a further build-up of immigrant numbers in the area? Trade union leaders argue that the brick-works could still do a great deal more to attract British labour. Health, safety, welfare, and general working conditions could all be improved. Certainly, in the bleak of winter, with men in old army greatcoats stamping against the raw cold under the smoke outside shabby buildings, the brickfields look for all the world like postwar DP camps.

The unions further suggest better financial inducements to British workers entering the industry, in particular during settling-in periods on basic rates of pay while they are training to go on piece-work. Failing new influxes of British labour, the only long-term alternative to further importations of foreign labour is the further replacement of manual work by machines. Though the nature of many tasks in the brick industry could make this difficult as well as costly, an increased measure of mechanisation may well prove inevitable.

Union leaders are understandably reluctant to agree to new influxes of foreign workers. In Bedford, the social consequences are far from reassuring. And since foreign workers are no longer subject to three- or four-year contracts, there is a fear of foreign workers coming to join the brick industry and then quickly drifting off to aggravate the national unemployment situation. High rates of labour turnover in the brick industry reinforce these fears.

Beyond this are fears about the vulnerability of the brick industry to national economic pressures. Even in the current year, an unwonted measure of stockpiling accompanies demands for more labour. With only a limited movement to economic recession, co-existence would be replaced by competition between British and foreign workers in Bedford, and relationships might thereby – for the first time – be cruelly tested.

Such a context dictates rigorous planning, starting with a skilled assessment of the future development of the brick industry in relation to national needs: of the extent to which further mechanisation is practical, and of the extent to which the industry will need manual labour. If these labour needs remain considerable, how far can they be supplied by British labour? If they cannot be, consider which other countries can supply labour, and the nature and the quality of the people likely to come as workers. If they come, on what terms would they come? Should it be as short-term workers or as true immigrants? If as immigrants, consider the social consequences, in particular the demands they will make upon local social services. Who is to be accounted responsible for these consequences? Should the brick industry be required to make some contribution, in cash or in kind, towards the education, housing and health services required? Or, if it were found that the brick industry had no alternative but to recruit workers abroad, should this be made a national responsibility?

Such planning demands, firstly, detailed and accurate information about the numbers and the work performance of each of the immigrant groups. The keeping of such records by individual firms should thus be made a national requirement. Planning further demands that all immigrants be given common status as foreign workers. The present two-tiered system of commonwealth citizens and aliens, apart from having no human justification, only serves to confuse planning and to create resentment.

Up till now, there has been little evidence of planning immigrant policies in relation to local and national needs. Locally, employers have coped on a make-do basis, recruiting labour for their immediate needs as and where they could. Relationships between these labour needs and the social consequences for the local community seem to have been virtually ignored by employers, and even by some local officials. Yet this relationship should surely be the central consideration in making rational immigration policies. How long, I wonder, can we afford to go on discussing immigrant matters in terms of subsidiary issues such as that of colour instead of getting down to the main issues of economic and social planning?

11

Education

THE recruitment of immigrants by local industry has imposed severe burdens on the social services in Bedford. In education, the build-up of immigrants within the borough schools over the last fifteen years is given in Table 2. The main trends are:

(1) The levelling-off of the number of European pupils in recent years. At the beginning of 1969, there were 1,393 in borough schools – 1,180 Italians, 84 Poles and 129 other Europeans.

(2) The rapid growth in the numbers of West Indian and Indian pupils. Totals in January 1969 were 688 West Indians and 471 Indians (including 50 Kenya Indians), the greatest concentration of both nationalities being between the ages of five and seven. The present pattern of growth will thus continue for some years.

(3) The small number of Pakistani pupils – only 55 in early 1969. This reflects the lack of a settled pattern of family life. It is notable that borough schools have no Pakistani girls over the age of eleven, whereas the majority of the boys are in the eleven to fifteen age range. This suggests that Pakistani children are brought over mainly as potential wage-earners.

The distribution of immigrant children in borough schools at 23 January 1969 is given in Table 3.[1] It is apparent:

(a) that immigrants have come to live in the older and poorer areas of housing in the town, and that their children attend mainly the schools which are older and poorer in facilities; and

(b) that the distribution of immigrant children in borough schools is remarkably uneven, varying between 0 per cent and 80 per cent.

A map of Bedford (p. 163) shows the nature of the distribution of immigrant children, with the placing of the various infants', junior, primary and secondary schools. Roman Catholic schools are not included, since they are not neighbourhood schools and

[1] See also Appendixes I and II.

NUMBERS OF IMMIGRANT CHILDREN IN THE BOROUGH OF BEDFORD SCHOOLS 1955–69[1]

	Italy	Poland	Yugoslavia	Latvia & Baltic States	Hungary	Ukraine	Germany	Other European Countries	Malta & Cyprus	Africa (inc. Kenya Asians)	India	Pakistan	Other Asians	West Indies	N. America	Australasia	Others	Total	No. of Children on Roll	Percentage Immigrants in Schools
1955	82	17	12	0	0	0	5	0	0	0	0	0	0	0	0	0	0	116	4,309	2·7
1956	190	38	15	0	1	0	2	2	0	0	1	0	0	1	0	0	0	250	6,000	4·1
1957	289	39	8	2	3	4	3	0	3	0	3	0	0	2	21	0	0	380	7,131	5·3
1958	376	56	15	5	2	8	11	5	2	0	7	3	1	11	7	0	0	509	7,277	7
1959	525	69	10	6	11	2	4	4	1	3	11	1	0	3	31	0	0	686	7,480	9·2
1960	628	63	16	4	9	4	5	2	10	3	18	1	0	13	29	0	2	807	7,601	10·7
1961	789	84	26	13	10	11	9	84	6	3	22	4	0	28	58	0	1	1,145	7,987	14·2
1962	934	105	24	17	13	16	12	86	6	7	41	8	0	29	33	0	2	1,333	8,252	16·0
1963	952	104	37	17	19	15	7	45	11	4	71	20	4	61	31	0	2	1,415	8,510	16·6
1964	957	86	53	12	22	14	13	65	18	4	108	11	4	98	25	0	4	1,499	8,983	16·6
1965	969	85	69	18	23	23	13	70	11	5	140	25	6	144	45	0	12	1,658	9,451	17·4
1966	1,548	87	63	19	16	25	11	56	6	5	235	20	6	253	64	0	10	1,939	10,073	19
1967	1,136	66	124						10	3	295	29	8	369	57	0	0	2,097	10,337	20
1968	1,136	72	105						12	7	384	57	12	515	38	1	1	2,365	11,015	21·5
1969	1,180	84	129						16	58[2]	421	55	14	688	53[3]	7	4	2,709	11,477	23·4

(For 1967–69 the figures under Yugoslavia combine Yugoslavia, Latvia & Baltic States, Hungary and Ukraine.)

[1] See Appendix I on the statistics given in this chapter.

[2] 50 out of 58 Africans are Kenya Asians, almost all of Indian descent.

[3] The figure of 53 American children includes 49 children of temporary residents.

TABLE 3
IMMIGRANT CHILDREN IN BEDFORD SCHOOLS
(JANUARY 1969)

	Australia Canada N. Zealand	Cyprus Malta Gibraltar	Pakistan	India	Kenya Asians	Other African Commonwealth	Other Asian Commonwealth	West Indies	Italy	Poland	Other European Countries	USA	Rest of World	Total	School Roll	% (to nearest whole no.)
PRIMARY SCHOOLS																
Ampthill Rd. Junior	0	0	0	61	11	0	5	23	77	0	16	0	0	193	280	69
Ampthill Rd. Infts.	0	0	1	69	2	0	0	30	61	4	4	0	0	171	222	77
Brickhill Junior	0	0	1	0	0	0	0	2	0	0	1	0	0	4	343	1
Brickhill Infts.	0	0	0	0	0	0	0	1	0	0	0	0	0	1	265	0
Clapham Rd. Junior	0	1	2	25	0	0	0	83	100	1	7	0	2	221	349	63
Clapham Rd. Infts.	0	0	0	11	1	1	0	90	68	1	3	1	1	177	267	66
Goldington Green Primary	1	0	0	0	0	0	0	1	0	0	0	0	0	1	605	0
Goldington Rd. Junior	1	3	4	3	0	0	0	45	59	5	10	0	0	130	421	31
Goldington Rd. Infts.	1	1	4	4	0	0	1	47	39	2	5	0	0	104	270	39
Hazeldene Junior	0	0	0	0	0	0	0	0	0	0	2	0	0	2	319	1
Hazeldene Infts.	0	0	0	0	0	0	0	0	5	0	1	0	0	6	274	2
Kingsbrook Junior	0	0	0	14	0	0	0	1	5	1	1	0	0	21	484	4
Manton	0	0	0	5	0	0	0	1	2	0	0	0	0	9	279	3
Parkdene Infts.	0	0	0	1	2	0	0	1	14	5	0	0	0	21	266	8
Pearcey Rd. Junior	0	0	0	7	2	0	0	4	13	0	0	0	0	26	270	10
Pearcey Rd. Infts.	0	0	0	4	0	1	0	7	23	1	7	0	0	43	176	24
Priory Infts.	0	0	0	7	0	0	0	41	59	1	0	0	0	108	150	72
Putnoe Junior	0	0	0	0	0	0	0	0	0	0	0	0	0	0	361	0
Putnoe Infts.	0	1	0	0	0	0	0	0	1	0	0	0	1	2	290	1
Queens Park Junior	0	1	9	50	0	0	0	73	148	3	5	0	1	290	456	64
Queens Park Infts.	0	0	4	18	0	0	0	47	64	6	0	0	0	139	240	58
St Joseph s Junior	1	0	0	0	0	0	2	6	15	10	9	0	0	40	402	10
St Joseph s Infts.	1	2	0	0	0	1	1	4	12	8	8	0	0	37	244	15
SECONDARY SCHOOLS																
Goldington Sec.	1	3	7	4	4	2	2	36	57	4	4	0	0	124	716	17
Newnham Sec.	0	0	0	2	0	0	0	9	10	2	5	0	0	28	702	4
Silver Jubilee Boys	0	0	6	58	2	0	0	10	36	6	6	0	0	124	470	26
Pilgrim (Selective)	0	0	0	0	1	0	0	0	3	0	3	0	0	7	860	1
St Gregory R.C.	1	4	0	2	1	2	0	7	125	14	11	3	0	170	465	37
Silver Jubilee Girls	0	0	0	37	15	1	0	16	48	7	14	0	0	138	437	32
Westfield	1	1	17	39	11	0	3	102	136	3	7	0	0	320	594	54
TOTALS	7	16	55	421	50	8	14	688	1,180	84	129	4	4	2,660	11,477	23

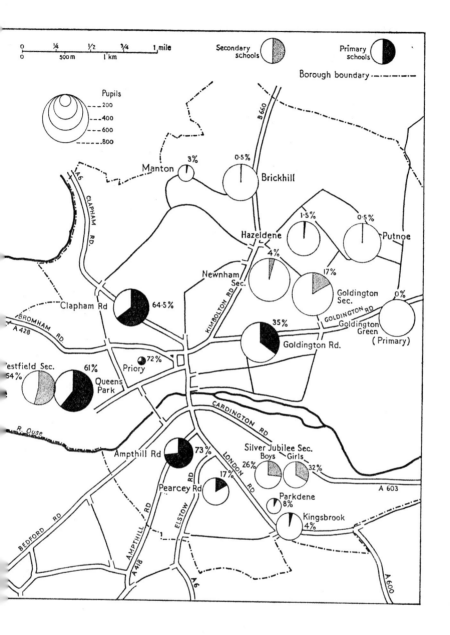

The Distribution of Immigrant Children in the Borough
of Bedford Schools (January 1969)

therefore give no accurate guide to the general distribution pattern. Also omitted is the one selective borough secondary school, where, in January 1969, immigrant children numbered only 7 out of 860 pupils: 3 Poles, 3 Italians and 1 Indian.

Of the other secondary schools in the area, four are administered by the Harpur Trust, two being public schools and two grant-aided. Immigrants number no more than a score among their 3,455 pupils. Only at one partly selective school, the Convent, is there a significant number of immigrant children: 60 in a total of 310 (11 Italians, 44 other Europeans, including some 20 Poles, 1 West Indian, 1 Guyanan, 1 Kenya Indian and 1 other Asian.) In brief, immigrant children have very little place in the selective schools of Bedford.

Immigrants have tended to concentrate in the west end of the town. The rambling Victorian houses built for Colonials seeking cheap education have become their lodging-houses and the older, working-class houses the first homes that immigrants could afford to buy for themselves.

The Queens Park area, in particular, is truly polyglot. Here, all variations of colour of skin, and hues and styles of dress, com-mingle in the streets. It is also an area of much coming and going, and the problems of neighbourhood schools derive not only from a concentration of immigrants but also from a shifting population. At Queen's Park Junior School, for instance, just over one-third of the children are English, just under one-third Italian, one-sixth West Indian, and most of the rest Indians. The school provides education over four years, with about 110 children in each year. During the 1968–9 session, some 110 children – one-quarter of the school – left and were replaced. This is mainly due to English people moving out of the district and immigrants moving in.

To the north-west of the town is the greatest concentration of West Indians. They make up nearly 30 per cent of all pupils in the Clapham Road schools, just slightly more than the Italians. Since most of the West Indians are younger children, the percentage of them in these schools will continue to grow.

The Indians are fast concentrating to the south of the town, particularly in the Ampthill Road area. The schools here show immigrant problems in their most exacerbated forms. At 1 May 1969, the situation at Ampthill Road Infants' School was that of the 241 children on the school roll, there were 86 Indian, 67 Italian, 29 West Indian (28 from Jamaica, 1 from Trinidad), 4 Polish, 4

Yugoslav, 1 Pakistani, and 50 designated 'English'. Of the 50 English, 6 were children of mixed marriages, 3 Irish, and half of them from poor, deprived homes, many with backgrounds of broken family relationships. The tasks of teaching the English children alone would be intensely demanding, and to these must be added the enormous problems of teaching in a school with almost 80 per cent immigrant children. Over the three months until 1 May, the school roll increased by 19, 17 of whom were Indian. Indians now make up nearly 36 per cent of all pupils and the build-up of their numbers will obviously continue rapidly. The situation here is not helped by borough council policy of buying up old houses in the district for a development area and letting them to the needy – often immigrants – on a short-term basis.

The central problem in the Ampthill Road school is that of teaching English as a common medium of communication. Difficulties here are not so much a function of the percentage of immigrant children as a whole within the school, but rather of the percentage of individual groups. Where the percentage of English children is smaller than that of any other national group, then English becomes *a* language rather than *the* language of communication, and teaching problems escalate. In the case of the Ampthill Road Infants' School, there are two national groups larger than the English group, and reasonable standards of English are being circulated only by the teachers and a small handful of pupils. Both from a human and from an academic point of view, the situation is hardly tolerable: and if basic circumstances remain unchanged, it will certainly get worse. Unless some measure of redistribution is attempted, moreover, the multiplicity of problems in the Infants' school – which its junior school shares – will, by the early seventies, have been handed on to the secondary schools of the area.

In this unenviable context, in an old school deficient in reasonable facilities, the good and devoted head teacher, Mrs Coley, soldiers on as best she can. Her achievement seems to me remarkable. She has not only coped for many years with kindness and competence, but has also inspired a small band of teachers to share her uphill struggle for most of that time.

It is an incredibly difficult though not an unrepresentative situation. In the immigrant schools of Bedford as a whole, the all too typically British picture is of good people making do over many years with little effective direction from official sources. It is probable that the teachers have suffered, in fact, from their own capacities to improvise. 'We should have struck,' an experienced headmaster said recently. In the event, of course, they carried on, head teachers making stop-gap solutions of a kind which seemed to them most appropriate for their own schools.

Despite all efforts, it is inevitable that academic standards decline. A number of English parents have clearly come to feel that their own children will have better educational opportunities in areas that have fewer immigrants. One cannot say exactly how strong or how widespread this feeling is as a motive for people to leave immigrant areas, but it is certainly there.

'The boy didn't seem to be doing much at school. That helped us decide to move. Just before we went, I thought, well, I would go and thank his teacher. She said, "Yes, he is a very good boy. I give him crayons and he sits quiet all day, while I get on teaching the immigrant children." When he went to the new school, of course, he was far behind the others. I had to teach him myself every night for a long time. Now, at last, he is holding his own. For his sake alone, we are thankful we moved. No doubt of it.' This father has moved to the north-east of the town. It is notable that there, in the Brickhill and Putnoe junior and infant schools, immigrants number only 7 out of 1,459 pupils or less than ½ per cent.

Most immigrant children, West Indians excepted, enter schools with little or no knowledge of English, perhaps, at best, one-hundredth of the vocabulary of a normal English child. (West Indians have their own problems of inaccurate forms of English.) Few of the immigrant children, moreover, have anything like an English child's 'feel' for his own way of life, his background knowledge of his society, his everyday experience of numeracy, nor even of playthings and play habits. Many are children of parents alien in culture, barely literate in their own language, humanly and economically under-privileged. They may possibly come to school inadequately dressed and ignorant of the most elementary forms of behaviour expected of them. Many of the Asians, in particular, have to be taught basic hygiene and toilet habits.

To assess with accuracy the abilities of these immigrant children when they first enter school is, in itself, an exacting task. Children newly arrived in this country present a particular problem. Apart from the great barrier of language they have to surmount, many may suffer a period of cultural shock: the shock of a new country, new habits, customs and values, new tastes, smells and sounds. To absorb this bewilderment of new ideas and new impressions, to adjust to new standards, for many proves demanding, for some overwhelming. During this period, a child may well give an impression of mental backwardness, and whether this is real or not may for some time be virtually impossible to discern.

Such time of pause varies from child to child. Difficulties of dealing with children at this time also make great demands on the teachers. One child, who came straight from Italy to junior school at the beginning of a school year in September, said not a word for weeks. As time went by, his teacher grew more worried. The headmaster counselled patience and persistence. In mid-November, the teacher called excitedly to the headmaster. He came to where the boy was sitting, bent down, and very softly the boy said his first words in English, 'One. Two. Three. Four.'

The headmaster, Stanley Fisher, was recently awarded an M.B.E. for his services to the education of immigrant children. It was at his school in the early sixties that separate 'English Progress' classes for newly entered immigrant children were instituted, aiming to give them the competence in English they would need to take a full part in school life and work. Other headmasters followed this example, and made their own solutions to immigrant language problems as best they could or as circumstances decreed.

The lack of common pattern in these developments reflects the lack of clear direction in local policy-making; and here the situation has not been helped by very British confusion between county and borough authority. Although officially independent in administering borough schools, the borough is financially dependent on the county administration. The results of this anomalous relationship have often been duplications of services and confusions of policy.

One headmaster appointed locally in 1963 was amazed to be asked no questions about the teaching of immigrants at his appointment interview. Later, he took a course on the teaching of English as a foreign language on his own initiative and at his own expense; he also joined with a group of senior teachers in Bedford to form the Association for the Teaching of English to Pupils from Overseas (ATEPO). Teacher members tell me that for long they were given neither official encouragement nor an allocation of funds for their work.

Official concern for immigrant problems did begin to grow

during the sixties, however, and in September 1967 the Schools Council project for the teaching of English to immigrant children was put into operation in borough schools. Various forms of organisation are used to tackle language problems, from 'D' stream classes within the normal school structure to special 'withdrawal' classes for immigrant children.

Indians and West Indians make up the bulk of the children in these separate language classes. Most teachers find that Indian children, despite their initial barriers of language, are particularly quick and eager to learn. Recently I saw the work of a Kenya Indian girl of thirteen. In September 1968, she had only elementary English, just managing to write simple sentences. By December, she had made an imaginative little essay on the wonder of first impressions of Africa. By March 1969, she had produced a delightful and competently written story of her grandmother's visit to England. The child's advancement was, by any standards, astonishing, not least in comparison with that of her West Indian classmates. She is clearly as bright as a button, a child to go farther faster than her fellows. All this is excellent, of course, though one pauses to wonder whether the characteristic Indian drive for education may not, in later years, create resentments among other immigrant groups.

With the exception of English children from deprived backgrounds, West Indians are generally considered by teachers to present most problems. The reasons are complex. Initially, it seems, their Creole forms of spoken English act against the learning of standard English. In effect, they have English and they do not have it. Their difficulties are thus the more difficult for teachers to define and for them to accept.

The anomalies of their position reflect those of their educational background as a whole. Many have had some measure of 'British' education in their home islands, where school conditions and facilities, and teaching standards and methods, have been very different from those which obtain in Bedford schools. Many West Indian schools consist simply of a large, bare, single room where several hundred children crowd in groups for instruction, much of it by rote by ill-trained and underpaid teachers with poor academic standards. The head teacher's table is in the midst, his strap at the ready for 'licks'. It is not a system to encourage interest, initiative or activity of mind. Its methods are highly at variance with the heuristic approach of most English schools today. So, the West

Indian child often finds himself at a loss in his new situation, bewildered by a new ambience, so overcome by freedoms that he may abuse rather than use them.

Teachers suggest, moreover, that many West Indian children do not have such great will to learn as Italian and Indian children. This may in great measure reflect the respect for education and educationalists among Italian and Indian parents. Teachers naturally appreciate this respect, although the decreasing regard in which they are held in their own society tinges their appreciation with a certain sense of irony. The value placed on education can be two-edged, of course. One headmaster told me of a scene constantly enacted in his office: the Indian father (his wife hovering respectfully in the background) uttering the now familiar words: 'He does not learn. You must beat him.'

Many immigrant parents are impatient and distrustful of current activity and play methods. To them, education is book and discipline; and they are intent to preserve the forms of authority that England now lets slip. On the one hand, then, is real authority, with deep concern for a child's advancement; on the other, the kind of misapplied energies that led one proud Indian parent to say, on his child's entry to school, 'You will have no trouble with him. I have taught him to be silent', or an Italian parent to hang his child up by his wrists in a coalhouse and to thrash him there for his mistakes in learning.

Enthusiasm for the best in English education at times assumes a wholly distasteful form – the objection of Italian parents to an Indian teacher, for example, 'Put child with English teacher. . . . Not lady with coloured skin. . . . Must have English teacher.' It is evident that prejudice of colour is also involved here. An Italian mother recently irrupted into a classroom at work, yanked her child from his desk, pointed at an Indian child sitting next to him, and declared, 'Not sit here.' She did not stay long. Growing evidence of feuds between Italian and West Indian children in some playgrounds also points to the antipathies of some Italian parents being passed on to their children. Expressions of colour antagonism can at times be bizarre – witness the New York West Indian boy who was heard to call a Barbadian girl a 'bloody Zulu bastard'.

Some teachers feel that the currents of prejudice and hostility are growing stronger. In an address to teachers in January 1969, for instance, Mrs Coley directly associated them with Enoch Powell's speech on immigration in April 1968: 'I could give you chapter and verse, date and time, of immigrant parents showing hostility to teachers and English children since that vital date last April. . . . Remarks have been made such as "you would like to send us back on a banana boat" – I have omitted the colourful epithets – "you take in white children, not us blacks. . . ." You know, and I know, that this is not true, but human nature being what it is, they must hit back. . . .'[1]

'Integration is in the classroom, but not in the playground,' said one secondary school head teacher, meaning to point a general trend rather than a whole truth. On the whole, mixing is freest among the younger children, those most spontaneous by nature and least influenced by the views of parents and local society. As a child moves towards adult consciousness, he tends to seek, or to be driven towards, the security of his own group. This grouping is not a 'colour' grouping, but a national grouping. When I visited a secondary school recently on a wet day, at a time when several hundred children were gathered informally in the school hall, this kind of grouping was very plain to see: West Indians, Italians, Indians, all distinct.

Despite this tendency, the children born to immigrants in this country have little sense of connection with a way of life other than that of England. Talking recently to children in an infants' school where there are many West Indians and Italians, I asked where their mothers and fathers had come from.

'My dad came from the West Indies.'

'He never did,' said his neighbour. 'He come from Birmingham.'

'Before that he did. . . . Which island? . . . Oh, I don't know.'

Only a few had heard of Jamaica, and to all of them it was no more than a name. Bedford, that's what they knew: that's where they came from.

Most Italian children knew their parents came from Italy and many had been there on holiday. Only one or two knew the name of their parents' home town or village. They only remembered what they had felt or seen. 'The sun shining, all hot, and when it rains, all the earth gets muddy.' 'And I got a horse in Italy. Don't know his name but he's smashing.' All these children are Bedfordian, no doubt of it, in their relationships and in their expectations. Ten years from now, most of them will be on the labour market, with expectations vastly different from those of their parents.

Teachers' tasks in immigrant schools are legion, beginning on the first day of a new school with toilet drill for new entrants. Even

[1] From a report in the *Bedfordshire Times*, 31 January 1969.

such a mundane task as giving advice on clothing against the English winter is not always plain sailing. A head teacher who gave a little Indian child a warm vest was shocked to discover later that the child had been badly beaten at home on suspicion of thieving it.

Unpunctuality is a constant bugbear; and this derives mainly from parents' work needs. Father may be coming off night shift as mother goes on early turn. The child is then aroused immediately for school or left to sleep on. In consequence, some are late for school, while others gather in playgrounds long before school begins. One teacher, passing his school at 8.15 a.m. on a winter morning, found about 80 out of a total of 400 children already in the playground. What happens during holiday periods, when the children are no longer subject to supervision, care and feeding in the schools, must be a matter for grave concern.

Particular problems derive from the lack of Asian records and documentation. The task of establishing a child's identity and age is often in itself complex, and some headmasters complain of Asian parents seeking to change this information where new needs arise – for the child to take a county assessment test, for example, or to leave school.

Some teachers resent these additional burdens, others rejoice in the wider social significance that immigrant problems give to their jobs. One headmaster, at least, believes that in immigrant areas the teacher can recover his ancient force in society. He keeps in close touch with the area health visitors to trace his children's problems in their homes. His office is open to parents as well as children needing help and advice. He welcomes the chance to break down the compartment walls which normally surround education and to develop relationships with the life of the neighbourhood as a whole. In his kind of area, indeed, the case for a real integration of policy in the social services, for continual interchange between those working in different spheres and for their involvement in policy-making, seems brutally plain.

Whatever is done in this respect, however, the basic educational problems of immigrant schools remain. Language, home background, and culture confine many immigrant children to the lower levels of educational achievement. The academic standards of many immigrant schools are comparatively low, and a number of immigrant children still leave them without the basic competence in English to permit future advancement. Particularly difficult is the situation of immigrant children who have had only a few years' schooling – a smattering of education – prior to seeking a job.

This is a context which gives added importance to the local technical college, Mander College, in Bedford's structure of education. It is already doing a good deal to help immigrant youth to improve their educational standards and to advance their ambitions for better jobs, though its potential in this sphere is still in some measure frustrated by the deficiencies of some of these young people in basic educational standards.

Such deficiencies mainly affect the most recent arrivals in Bedford, particularly the Asians and West Indians. They numbered only 223 out of a total of 6,443 enrolments (3½ per cent) at Mander College for the 1968–9 session.[1] Of these, more than half were Indian men. Almost all are studying at craftsman level, very few at technician level. In the department of production engineering, for example, out of 215 studying for technician examinations, there are 11 European students but no Asians or West Indians; and out of 307 students at craftsman level, there are 24 Italians, 6 other Europeans, 18 Asians, 15 West Indians and 2 other Commonwealth students.[2]

Lack of competence in English is clearly a major factor in preventing immigrant youth from realising their potential. Just as it stops some from embarking on courses, so it checks others in mid-course. A limited number seek to help themselves by enrolling in language classes. In the 1968–9 session, 9 Indian boys and 1 West Indian girl registered for the G.C.E. 'O' Level English course at Mander College, and 28 Indian boys, 1 Indian girl, and 1 West Indian boy signed on for a general course of English for overseas students.[3] The college itself, moreover, has lately come to require that more time be devoted to English studies.

It is probable that more radical solutions are required. It is clear that many immigrant youths will not be able to cope with vocational courses until they have greater proficiency in general and basic technical English. One suggestion is that an intensive course in English should form the first part of certain vocational courses. Another proposal of a more comprehensive kind is that of a full-time course at school-leaving age aimed to give students proficiency

[1] I am obliged to Mr Harry Sutcliffe for these figures, collected for his report on immigrant youth.
[2] Figures supplied by Mr R. E. Roe, head of the Department of Production Engineering.
[3] Figures also supplied by Mr Harry Sutcliffe.

both in the English language and in the supplementary language of mathematics, and oriented towards their work needs in adult life. Such a scheme would demand experienced teachers capable of understanding both the needs of the students and those of local industry, backed by technical training facilities and the resources of a language laboratory. It would be logical to ask local industries, especially those whose labour needs have, in effect, made Bedford an immigrant town, to aid such schemes.

Beyond this are more general problems of adult education among first generation immigrants, particularly those of helping immigrants to surmount barriers of language and culture, and to fit into the normal fabric of everyday life in this country. To attempt this within the usual pattern of English adult education – through English classes at further education centres, for example – would be a waste of time. The only approaches likely to be successful are those used for functional literacy projects in developing countries, designed to serve the needs of particular groups in particular ways. These might be applied to certain key areas of need in Bedford – for example, to help Indian women to cope with the everyday demands of family living here. Again, this kind of project is only likely to be carried through successfully by working through the leaders and institutions of the group concerned – for example, by using Sikhs to teach their own people in the *gurdwara*.

In sum, it is clear that very great problems face educational administrators. There are material problems such as providing better facilities, smaller classes, more teachers and more generous financial recognition for the specialist work involved in immigrant schools. There are planning problems, particularly those to obviate further concentrations of immigrant children. Most teachers agree that, however desirable a policy of 'dispersal' is in principle, the time is long past when it could be effectively implemented in the Bedford area. The problems of who would be moved to which school and from where, and on what grounds, would cause intense resentments among parents and children, great administrative difficulties, and frustrate the whole concept of neighbourhood schools. Nevertheless, there is clearly a case for a more equitable distribution of immigrant children in borough schools, and probably for modifications to the present system of school catchment areas. It is particularly important to ensure that the situation in the Ampthill Road schools does not deteriorate, and that similar situations are prevented from developing.

Perhaps the greatest problem is to check the tendency to educational segregation in the area. If the children of immigrants are confined to lower educational achievement in the schools, if they are unable to develop opportunities for further education in the technical college and come to feel themselves trapped inexorably in lower paid jobs, then the calm of Bedford could well be disturbed within a decade.

The past has been bleak, but recent senior appointments in educational administration are now giving greater hope that this knotted complex of problems may be tackled with intelligence and energy.

12

Housing

JUST as most immigrants came to Bedford to do the jobs the British did not want to do, so they came to occupy the houses the British did not want to live in. Most immigrants are still to be found in the older, poorer houses of the town.

To find accommodation of any kind has been a hard struggle for each and every group. Of late, difficulties experienced by West Indians and Asians have been quoted as evidence of colour prejudice. However true that may be, the essential fact is that there is no national group which has not suffered in this way. Each in turn – Poles, Latvians, Ukrainians, Yugoslavs, Italians, West Indians, Pakistanis and Indians – have come to share the common history of tramping innumerable streets; of enduring local suspicion and antipathy; and of being turned away from many doors before finding a place to live.

The first places the immigrants could find were near the railway station, to the west of the town centre. In this area some 70 per cent of the buildings date from before 1875. Many were big old houses too inconvenient and too costly for English families to maintain. These became the first lodging-houses. There the immigrants crammed together, partly from a need for the security of their own kind but mainly because these houses were all they could get. After months, even years, of searching, they were glad to get anything, and almost on any terms. The inevitable results were, on the one hand, overcrowding and poor living conditions; on the other, a rash of stories of immigrant slum conditions. These were righteously circulated among local residents as sure evidence of the dirty, degrading ways of foreigners and of the innate superiority of British ways. Certain British landlords, meanwhile, fattened visibly.

Slowly there emerged a cyclic pattern of immigrant housing. At first, the arduous search. Then a foothold in an old house; and, as trust was established, more of the same group admitted to the lodging. There they lived, often hugger-mugger, scrimping and saving until one or more of them got money enough to buy up a house for themselves where they could live and which would be a lodging-place for their own people. As others of the group got money, they left to find rooms on their own, or married and bought a house where they could afford it – for the most part in the poorer areas of town. Then, as the group dispersed, the new immigrant landlords, together with the local landlords, let their rooms to the next wave of immigrants. These, in turn, re-enacted the original pattern.

The southern Italians brought a new dimension to the problem. Few wanted to linger long in brick company hostels on the diet provided by English and Polish cooks. They came to town in increasing numbers. Since poverty had driven them here, they endured poor and overcrowded conditions with equanimity, even cheerfulness. By the end of 1955, many of the men had been joined by their families and 1,414 Italian adults and 285 children under twelve were living in multiple occupation. The west central area of town was virtually a colony of Italians. Here they huddled together in the security of their own ways in the face of a strange, cold people. In the pleasant homes of these people, stories of dirty foreigners were transformed into stories of dirty, noisy foreigners; and the number of stories grew in proportion to immigrant numbers.

The old houses strained at the seams with unaccustomed numbers. Exploitation had a field day. The need for control was immediate. The local authority took three main courses of action. Firstly, mortgages were granted to immigrants to buy their own houses. Secondly, agreements were made with the Italian authorities and local industry that Italians could not send for their families until they had rented accommodation, the accommodation had been vetted by the public health department, and their financial circumstances confirmed by their employers. Thirdly, landlords were required by a private Act of Parliament on behalf of Bedford Corporation (1956) to provide rent books and to make them available for inspection by the council. Evasions of the law were frequent. Some landlords gave token breakfasts to their tenants to avoid its requirements, while others continued to rely on Italian ignorance of language and their rights.

For the public health inspectors, there were constant difficulties to determine just how many people were living in a particular house. Beds occupied by night-shift workers during the day could well be occupied by day-shift workers at night. Some inspections were therefore carried out on Sunday nights – the only night when the brickyards did not work a night-shift – to find out what the real situation was. Slowly, numbers were determined, standards enforced.

The numbers living in multiple occupation continue to grow, however. By the end of 1958, 3,131 Italians were in multiple occupation out of a borough total of 5,636. In 1959, the borough prohibited the brick industry from further bulk importation of Italian labour. It was a decision justified by the immediate situation, although later regretted by many local people.

This measure did not stop the flow of immigrants. The brick industry simply looked elsewhere for its labour, and found it among the West Indians, Indians and Pakistanis who had begun to appear in Bedford after the mid-fifties. During 1959, the numbers of Indians and Pakistanis living in multiple occupation nearly doubled, and their numbers have continued to grow during the sixties.

The overall situation of nationalities in multiple occupation since 1955 is given in Table 4. The main trends are:

(1) The number of Poles has gradually decreased since 1955. Most Polish families have their own houses.

(2) Latvians and Ukrainians have followed the pattern of the Poles. Their numbers came to a peak in 1956, and thereafter slowly decreased.

(3) The peak of Yugoslav numbers was not reached until 1959 – Yugoslavia, unlike the Soviet Union, allowed some freedom of movement to England, and a number of Yugoslavs came to join their families here during the fifties.

(4) Italian numbers continued in excess of 3,000 from 1958 to 1962. They still represent 36 per cent of all people in multiple occupation. As Italians saved money for their own houses, so their 'near-ghetto' began to disperse. Many bought property in the smaller, older houses of the Queen's Park area. In the late sixties, as that area becomes increasingly polyglot, as savings grow, and desire for return to Italy wanes, there is a further slow dispersal of Italians to more well-to-do areas of the town.

(5) West Indian numbers came to a peak in 1964, and since then have been slowly decreasing as people buy their own homes.

T.

NATIONALITIES OF OCCUPANTS

NATIONALITY	1955		1956		1957		1958		1959		19
	Ad.	Ch.	Ad.	Ch.	Ad.	Ch.	Ad.	Ch.	Ad.	Ch.	Ad.
Albanian	1	—	1	—	—	—	—	—	—	—	—
American	20	4	11	3	12	3	14	5	20	3	30
Arab (Aden)	—	—	—	—	—	—	—	—	—	—	5
Austrian	—	—	—	—	—	—	—	—	—	—	2
West Indian	—	—	199	8	220	21	388	43	364	53	381
Chinese	—	—	—	—	—	—	—	—	—	—	—
Czech	8	3	4	—	4	—	5	—	2	—	4
Dutch	2	1	3	1	—	—	—	—	—	—	—
English	278	54	237	30	198	31	196	36	274	63	313
Estonian	1	—	2	—	2	—	2	—	1	—	1
German	8	2	11	—	7	—	7	—	5	—	5
Greek	10	3	6	2	6	2	4	4	4	2	1
Hungarian	4	—	4	—	6	—	18	1	33	8	32
Indian	25	—	24	—	34	—	82	7	140	17	135
Irish	92	15	96	17	101	22	127	27	200	32	199
Italian	1414	285	1895	510	2065	642	2244	787	2122	980	2116
Yugoslav	74	13	93	24	94	31	98	39	103	39	100
Latvian	51	4	70	7	64	5	62	9	61	12	48
Lithuanian	1	—	3	—	2	—	2	—	3	—	2
Maltese	4	—	—	—	—	—	—	—	3	—	3
Nigerian	—	—	—	—	—	—	—	—	2	—	3
Pakistani	—	—	—	—	38	—	132	3	242	2	248
Polish	219	55	211	54	191	50	189	50	158	43	147
Romanian	4	1	5	1	4	1	4	1	3	1	6
Russian	1	—	—	—	—	—	—	—	1	—	—
Spanish	—	—	—	—	—	—	—	—	4	—	5
Ukrainian	33	9	41	3	38	5	37	13	36	8	36
TOTAL	2250	449	2916	660	3087	813	3611	1025	3781	1263	3826
	2699		3576		3900		5636		5044		527
No. of Houses in Multiple Occupation	226		341		375		458		521		578

Ad. – A

JLTIPLE OCCUPATION SINCE 1955

1961		1962		1963		1964		1965		1966		1967		1968	
.	Ch.	Ad.	Ch.	Ad.	Ch.	Ad.	Ch.	Ad.	Ch.	Ad.	Ch.	Ad.	Ch.	Ad.	Ch.
—	—	—	—	—	—	—	—	—	—	—	—	—	—	—	—
o	9	36	7	44	8	29	5	30	5	12	7	17	4	23	7
3	—	3	—	—	—	—	—	5	—	3	—	4	3	4	3
2	I	2	I	I	—	I	—	—	—	I	—	—	—	—	—
I	129	717	151	807	216	808	248	703	247	682	272	639	272	654	263
7	—	7	—	18	—	9	—	28	4	30	3	42	4	33	4
6	—	2	I	4	—	2	—	2	—	2	—	2	—	—	—
—	—	—	—	—	—	—	—	—	—	—	—	—	—	—	—
9	72	322	67	567	113	492	92	548	128	491	109	563	124	546	115
—	—	—	—	I	—	—	—	—	—	2	—	—	—	—	—
3	—	4	I	5	—	2	—	4	—	I	—	I	—	I	—
I	—	12	7	12	9	10	6	2	I	4	2	—	—	6	6
a	9	29	11	47	21	42	17	20	7	5	3	15	5	19	—
5	4	341	68	458	104	534	124	599	180	588	228	595	291	828	442
9	43	227	40	241	37	169	24	169	48	140	39	204	40	153	25
7	1094	2015	897	1812	812	1740	755	1951	850	1806	693	1520	654	1533	650
6	52	98	53	70	29	72	37	84	42	41	13	47	15	43	6
I	9	39	7	53	7	29	4	51	13	14	—	20	—	20	—
2	—	3	—	3	—	2	—	2	—	I	—	2	—	—	—
4	—	2	—	—	—	2	—	3	—	2	—	2	—	—	—
3	—	3	—	—	—	2	—	2	—	2	—	—	—	—	—
o	29	394	11	456	8	506	25	541	24	548	36	524	23	553	20
4	48	136	39	133	36	132	37	128	31	118	24	117	16	110	11
2	2	—	—	—	—	—	—	—	—	—	—	—	—	—	—
I	—	—	—	—	—	—	—	—	—	I	—	I	—	I	—
4	—	3	—	I	—	I	—	I	—	I	—	—	—	—	—
I	6	32	7	31	5	33	7	29	9	26	7	24	4	22	—
4	1507	4427	1366	4744	1405	4617	1381	4902	1589	4521	1436	4339	1455	4549	1552
5491		5793		6149		5998		6491		5957		5794		6101	
598		643		637		962		747		713		703		715	

Children

The movement has been slow and numbers living in multiple occupation fairly constant (between 900 and 1,000) in recent years. West Indians represented 15 per cent of all people in multiple occupation at the end of 1968.

(6) Indians are making a greater commitment to Bedford than other commonwealth immigrants. Their numbers continue to rise and many of the recent arrivals are dependants. At the end of 1965, there were 180 children with the 599 adults in multiple occupation. Two years later, there were 291 children with almost the same number of adults. The dramatic rise in numbers from 886 at the end of 1967 to 1,270 at the end of 1968 is partially explained by the influx of Kenya Indians during that year. At the end of 1968, they represented 21 per cent of all people in multiple occupation. Indian families are also fast establishing roots in Bedford by buying or renting small properties, particularly in the Ampthill Road area, to the south of the town.

(7) Pakistani numbers have been more or less constant, between 500 and 600, over the last five years. To some extent they are a floating population and the Pakistanis are the only national group who have not yet established deep roots in Bedford. Only of late is some semblance of a family pattern of life becoming established among West Pakistanis. It is notable that the percentage of children in the Pakistani group at the end of 1968 was only 3·5 against 35 among Indians, 30 among Italians, 28·5 among West Indians, and 21 among English.

(8) Of the other nationalities in multiple occupation, the English make up 11 per cent. Irish numbers came to a peak in 1963 and there are still a sizeable number of them in lodgings, mostly itinerant labourers. There are also a number of Americans in temporary residence while working with local firms or studying. Since the mid-sixties, Chinese numbers have increased and the decrease of those in multiple occupation from 46 at the end of 1967 to 37 at the end of 1968 is not evidence of a movement away from Bedford. The four Chinese restaurants now established in town, together with the opening of take-away food shops, imply a commitment to Bedford by a small, though growing, number of Chinese. In mid-1969, the Chinese community totals some seventy people.

The Pakistanis form the hard core of housing problems in Bedford today. Conditioned to poverty and deprivation, submissive by temperament, often with the apathy that derives from poor health, they accept exploitation and poor conditions, and have comparatively little thought to improve their lot. Many insist only on low rents – £1 a week is the magic figure at the present time – and are prepared to put up with almost anything rather than to pay more. Landlords who, under pressure from the public health authorities, provide better facilities and then try to raise rents to cover their expenses, often find themselves losing tenants. It is a situation that makes both for constant changes of ownership and for continuance of poor living standards. The lack of many women in the houses also means neglect and disorder, together with a rash of health and social problems, while absentee landlords make it difficult to determine ownership and to bring about improvements.

Over the years, in this often unpromising context, the borough public health department has done fine work in determining standards and improving conditions. It is work that calls for patience and perseverance as well as skill, for constant visits, advice, persuasion, and direction. Only when all else fails do inspectors resort to law. The following record of a round of visits may help to convey the nature of their problems and the value of their work.

Semi-detached house, neglected in appearance, window curtained over. Inspector knocks on back door, immediately enters. Four men in bleak, bare scullery; old stove burned black. Do all four live here? Replies hesitant. One smartly dressed man says he does not live there. Owner's representative says owner is in East Pakistan. All people living here are from East Pakistan. We mount bare stairs. To the left, a small cubicle with a single bed, a towel hanging on a piece of string. This is the status – i.e. single – room of the owner's representative.

Most rooms are locked. 'Can you open the door?' 'Lock,' is the usual answer, or 'gone away'. Coughing within. The inspector knocks. Silence. Knocks again. Pause. Sound of the door being unlocked. It is not opened. We enter. A woman, a girl and a child sitting on an old double bed against the wall. 'How many people live here?' 'Three people.' Inspector smiles. 'Well, you couldn't say less, could you?'

Another room with two double beds and a very young baby in a cot. The child-like mother has just arrived from Pakistan. She speaks no word of English. In each of the other rooms, two or three double beds. A man asleep in most of them. Two men in one bed under coarse blankets. Some groan and turn. One looks up, eyes red, apprehensive. The sense of inertia is overwhelming. They are on night-shift, we are told.

In every room a poor minimum of furniture, few possessions. On cheap, rickety tables, collections of half-empty packets of food, washing and shaving materials, a confusion of old pots and pans. But little dirt. Evidence of walls recently decorated. The lino on the hall floor looks as if it has been recently polished. All evidence of recent visits by the inspector.

The smartly dressed man reveals that he is the owner's cousin. The inspector tells him of further improvements needed. 'How many families live here?' Pause. 'Two.' 'How many people in all?' Pause. 'Fourteen.' 'There's more than that, isn't there?' 'I am giving notice to some men.' Does he mean that? Who could say? Is this a pious expression of intent to satisfy the inspector or will the intent become reality? The inspector has doubts: 'Sometimes you can get an idea of the real situation by the number of clay boots at the back door. We'll have to keep an eye on this house – may even have to do a Sunday night inspection.' That means three inspectors: 'to count heads, to stop everyone moving round and out of the house, and to check on conditions.'

Opposite is a house occupied by West Pakistanis. There the door is opened by a boy in thin shirt and pyjama trousers. It is winter. The kitchen is bare, with a burnt stove and a black tava, a round iron griddle for making chappaties.

A man lies shivering under army blankets on an old sofa. 'He sick.' The man groans. His eyeballs roll. The boy is fifteen. 'Why aren't you at school?' Shrug. 'Is this your father?' 'Yes, father.' 'Not at school because your father is sick?' 'Yes, father sick.' The words are mechanical. Is this the truth or does he say this because he thinks this is the required answer or is he simply clutching at straws? Who can say?

The house is in better repair than the last and much cleaner. Clean toilet, an old bath scrubbed clean, with old plastic pots in it. Clean lino. The boy accompanies us obediently. 'Why aren't you at school?' Shrug. 'What do you do when you leave school?' 'Work.' 'Where do you want to work?' Shrug. 'In a factory?' 'Yes, factory.' 'In the brickyards?' 'Yes, brickyards.' Total acceptance. Total inertia. Numbers in the house accord to regulations. Outside the front door are eleven pints of milk.

Then to a West Indian lodging-house of four families. The

owners, a Jamaican couple, are both at work. One Jamaican tenant at home. Upstairs a young white girl, seemingly sub-normal, and a Jamaican woman. The men work in Luton and live in Bedford, because here rented accommodation is cheaper and easier to find. The men share the cost of car transport to Luton. The house is poorly but adequately furnished. Clean, but with an air of shabbiness and some neglect. The inspector outlines the minor improvements that are needed. 'Sure, sure, man, I'll tell them about that. I'll tell them you came.' Relationships with West Indians are improving. In the past, some interpreted the work of inspectors as acts of prejudice against coloured people. Nowadays, inspectors' visits are increasingly accepted as a normal part of life.

Lastly, to an Italian lodging-house. Neat, well-painted exterior, with a rack of plants outside the front door. Within, everything in order, spotless, trim, with the usual profusion of family photographs on the wall and a cocktail-cabinet of decorated glass in the parlour. The kitchen scrubbed clean. 'I'd be glad if all the British kept their houses like this.'

In foodshops and businesses, the story is similar. Few Italian premises need attention or advice. This butcher's shop is a model of hygiene: that ice-cream factory impeccable. Here the owner consulted the public health department before he purchased the premises, and the new buildings were planned and designed in collaboration. Pakistani shops have greater need of inspectors' services, although new paint, new tiling, new refrigeration, and signs of sweeping and scrubbing in these shops are all evidence of inspectors' influence.

The case study of a single house demonstrates how exacting the work of public health inspectors can be. Substantial in the nineteenth century, now seedy and decayed, it has become a constant headache to the public health department over the last decade. In 1958 it came into Pakistani ownership with a permitted number of sixteen tenants on the basis of 70 sq. ft. per man and 50 sq. ft. per child under the age of twelve. Since that time, the record is as follows:

1958   *July:* change of ownership. *November:* warning notice of overcrowding.

1959   *September:* change to joint ownership. *November:* owners asked to provide rent book.

1961   *May:* change of ownership, followed by a complaint on

behalf of the then thirty-one lodgers: 'The house is shock-
ingly overcrowded. In some rooms, seven persons sleep
together sharing the bed with each other. We pay a very
high rent, i.e. 18s per head per week. They keep the house
so nasty, we cannot breathe in the house.'

1962   *January:* prosecution for overcrowding. Owners pleaded
guilty and fined. Unsuccessful attempt to sell house to
corporation, followed by change of ownership.

1963   *February:* warning notice to the three owners to improve
management standards, although difficulties were found in
establishing who and where the owners were. *March:*
order applying management standards. *April:* two notices,
one requiring owners to provide a fire escape, the other for
improving facilities.

1964   A brief period of Italian ownership – required improvements were not completed. *October:* house reverted to
Pakistani ownership. Notice then given of the need for
radical and immediate improvements. *November:* joint
ownership established.

1965   *July:* warning of overcrowding and of the need for a fire
escape. *October:* report of overcrowding (twenty-one
occupants). *November:* prosecution and fine.

1966   *May:* notice of defective sewer. No action taken, so the
council did the work and charged the owner. *August:*
prosecution and fine for overcrowding. *September:* notice of
the need for cleaning, repairs and of added facilities.
December: fire escape at last installed.

1967   *November:* reverted to single ownership.

1968   *March:* notice of overcrowding. *June:* prosecution and
fine. Management regulations imposed. *July:* notice to
improve hot-water supplies.

1969   *March:* notice of repairs and improvements required.

This formidable record has made enormous demands on the time,
skill and patience of the local public health inspector. He estimates
that, over the last eighteen months, he has made at least one visit a
month to the house, one night visit (when he was refused access),
and one visit with an interpreter – the owner, after some time of
dealing in English, having suddenly refused to speak the language.
(He also told the interpreter, in Urdu, that he could not speak
Urdu.)

All in all, the fines imposed on the owners over a decade may be thought poor compensation for the cost of work incurred by the public health and legal authorities in dealing with this one house, and they probably represent not much more than 10 per cent of the profit that accrued from overcrowding. On the other hand, conditions in the house have gradually improved, although some repairs are outstanding, and better kitchen and hot-water facilities are still needed. In general, there is a greater air of tidiness and cleanliness about the place than previously, and this process has been helped along as single men begin to be replaced by families. That conditions are as good as they are is largely due to the skill and patience of the public health inspectors.

The work of defining and improving standards of public health and living conditions in Bedford owes a great deal to Ernest Avison, chief public health inspector since the end of 1956. His success is rooted in a rare understanding of immigrants' needs and aspirations, and his kindness and help to the various groups have extended far beyond the confines of his job. The founding of local Pakistani and West Indian clubs, in particular, derived largely from his encouragement, advice and support. In the peaceful making of Bedford as an immigrant town he is a key figure.

Although local problems of immigrant housing standards have often been acute, they have been handled for the most part with good sense and with a merciful lack of that mass media publicity which so often breeds more controversy than it reflects. On the allocation of local council property to immigrants, however, opinion is far more divided and criticism more frequent.

At the present time, the council control about 20 per cent of town property, some 6,000 tenancies in all, ranging from one-room flats to houses of all descriptions. Council policy in making allocations is to balance urgency of need against priority of application. The housing manager informs me that a check on the allocation of council properties over the first ten months of 1968 established that 40 per cent of all allocations were to immigrant families or to families where either the husband or the wife were immigrants, and that these families were drawn from ten nationalities.

Criticisms of local housing policies concern both the criteria for allocating houses and the placing of immigrant families. Some of the criticism is highly informed, some mere tattle. A good many local inhabitants think that an excessive number of tenancies are allocated to immigrants while others complain that immigrants are often pushed to the back of the queue. The best way to dispel criticism of this kind would be for the council to define more fully to the general public their criteria for allocating houses, their methods of establishing priorities, and the aims and purposes of their policies in general.

A major criticism is that many immigrant families are being allocated tenancies in older houses in the poorer areas of town, and that council policies are thus serving to create a ghetto situation. It is certainly clear that in recent years there has been a growing concentration of immigrant families in areas of old housing scheduled for redevelopment, notably in the Ampthill Road area:[1] and the build-up of the number of Indian families in this area gives particular concern to the teachers, health workers and others who have to cope with the myriad problems that this concentration imposes. There is no doubt that these problems are fast intensifying. At the end of January 1969, for example, 69 per cent of all pupils at Ampthill Road Junior School were the children of immigrants. On 1 October of the same year, the percentage was 77, the great majority of the newcomers being Indian. Teachers coping with this kind of situation feel that they have already suffered enough from the failure of past educational policy without having their problems exacerbated by current failure in local housing policy.

There has also been criticism that houses allocated in this area are sub-standard, and that some lack normal bath and washbasin amenities. This evokes a good deal of bitterness from landlords of private property, who maintain that some council properties do not conform to the standards laid down by the council's own public health department. 'Why the hell should we have to conform to these standards if the council themselves don't?' is the familiar argument.

The local council maintains that these tenancies are short-term expedients to tide people over until new housing areas are established. Critics fear that current curbs on new building will mean that immigrant families will have to live in makeshift areas for far longer than was expected, and that by the early seventies, a vast problem area of poorer immigrants, many ignorant not only of the English language but of elementary health procedures, will have been created in the area to the south of the town centre. Since many of these immigrant families come from backgrounds of poverty and

[1] See map on p. 163

illiteracy dominated by a strong traditional culture, their needs for the security of their own kind will inevitably impel them to stay together, thus reinforcing tendencies towards concentration and its attendant social problems.

Whatever the rights and wrongs of local housing policies, it seems clear that they are insufficiently co-ordinated with policies in the other social services. The moral is simple: that the social services can only be fully effective when conceived and organised in unity. It is apparent that in Bedford, as in many other towns, the departmental structure of the social services acts against rational planning, i.e. recognition of overall objectives and co-ordination of action to achieve these objectives. It also seems that there is insufficient consultation between policy-makers and the teachers, health visitors, social workers, policemen and others who are bearing the main brunt of local social problems. The continuing build-up of immigrant families to the south of the town and the consequent intensifying of social problems point the urgent need for fresh, co-ordinated and informed policies.

13
Health[1]

IMMIGRANT groups bring with them their own ways of life and their own social and welfare problems. These modify the patterns of local life and the nature of local problems, not so much in proportion to immigrant numbers as to the extent to which immigrant patterns of life differ from our own. The social welfare problems of the immigrants from 'underprivileged' or 'developing' countries, in particular, will surely modify the nature of local problems and of local policies.

In some measure, a modern immigrant society such as Bedford *is* an underprivileged society. It is more useful to recognise this than to hide it. One can then go on to look at Bedford in the way one looks at any underprivileged society.

Consider briefly the condition of a small Caribbean island. The principal causes of death are gastro-enteritis and malnutrition. (Infant mortality is of the order of 100/1,000 and one-third of all deaths are of children under the age of one year.) Bad living, feeding and sanitary conditions, together with constant suffering from various kinds of intestinal worms, have created a people poor in physical and mental initiative. Their deficiencies are reflected in every aspect of life, from family welfare to economic production.

Two principles become clear: that the island's fundamental problems are health problems; and that at root these health problems are essentially problems of fundamental education. The main enemy is not so much disease as ignorance, and the inertia that accrues from centuries of ignorance. In the main, problems will be solved by helping people to understand why and how they should keep themselves and their houses clean, dispose of waste, rear and feed their babies, feed themselves, guard against common infections, and so on. This situation demonstrates, in sum, that the

[1] I am deeply indebted to Dr John Harte for allowing me to make extensive use of his paper on 'Clinical Problems in Immigrants' in this chapter.

usual 'compartmenting' of the social services is artificial and disabling; and that these services cannot be fully effective unless conceived and organised in unity. It may well be that our own immigrant society demands similar emphases and approaches to its social problems, in particular where large numbers of immigrants are from underprivileged backgrounds.

From a health point of view, it is useful to consider the immigrants of Bedford in two main groups: those from relatively privileged, European backgrounds, and those from other, relatively underprivileged areas.

Among the war refugees – the Poles, Latvians, Ukrainians, and Yugoslavs – a main factor is the legacy of war and post-war strain and suffering. This becomes increasingly apparent with the years. Torn from their own land and their own families, often enduring intense physical and mental hardship, long periods of poor feeding, and the degradation of jobs for which they were quite unfitted by nature and intelligence, these refugee groups show a high incidence of mental illness and coronary disease. Years of loneliness in lodging-houses, without meaningful work or community, have also often led to alcoholism, breakdown and suicide. Psychological illness is commonplace and several men take permanent refuge in physical illness under the burdens of loneliness and deprivation.

Of all immigrant groups, the Italians most resemble the British in health standards. Few have the background of suffering of the European refugees and most live to a settled pattern of family life. Yet the transfer to an alien, industrial environment and long, hard experience of shift work in local industry have served to create some incidence of strain, stress, and duodenal ulcers.

As for the health problems of local immigrants from underprivileged countries, the most useful source of reference is the very able paper on 'Clinical Problems in Immigrants' presented by Dr John Harte to the Royal College of Physicians in June 1967.

I have a Group Practice of three doctors and one lady assistant with a practice list of about 7,000, of which just over one-tenth are coloured immigrants, mainly Pakistanis and Indians. The first immigrants joined the practice ten years ago and the numbers started to increase in 1961. The women and children came in 1963 and there are now 757 Asians predominantly in the young healthy age group aged twenty to thirty and few are over the age of fifty. This is quite different from the average age distribution of an English population, where the case load is heaviest in those under ten years and over sixty-five. In the last quarter of 1966 the immigrant population attended my surgery about twice as frequently as the other patients and took about twice as long for a consultation because of the language difficulty.

Dr Harte made a study of his practice and of attendances at local hospital clinics. It showed 'a much higher than anticipated attendance rate by immigrants at the obstetric, orthopaedic, venereal disease and eye clinics, with also an increase in the medical, skin and gynaecological departments, and a low attendance at ear, nose and throat, surgery and psychiatric clinics. The re-attendance rates for the hospital clinics follow much the same pattern as in my own practice, and certain departments such as the chest clinic have a very high re-attendance rate.'

Dr Harte went on to discuss the clinical problems in detail. He found 'a high attendance rate by immigrants at the venereal disease clinic, especially for gonorrhoea among West Indians and Asian men, but low among immigrant women, the source of infection by the immigrants being predominantly from English women, usually prostitutes on visits to Bedford.'[1]

It is useful here to compare the figures that Dr Harte provides covering the last quarter of 1966 with those obtaining two years later. (See Tables 5 and 6.)

The comparison suggests an increasing adjustment of the various immigrant groups to British norms. On the one hand, the percentage of West Indians and Pakistanis fell sharply over the period of two years. West Indians represented one-third of all conditions in 1966, one-sixth of all conditions two years later. The percentage of Pakistanis fell from about 20 in 1966 to just over 5 in 1968. On the other hand, the number of Italians, negligible in 1966, rose sharply within two years to account for one-eighth of all conditions in 1968. A small number of Indians also appeared in 1968 for the first time. The most significant figure of all, perhaps, is that of the very considerable increase of venereal conditions among British women. In 1968, they made up one-third of all conditions seen at Bedford Hospital.

The orthopaedic problems are mainly hand injuries among a predominantly manual working population. There is also a high incidence of muscle strain and backache, both among the women and the men, but for different reasons. The women come from

[1] See also pp. 201–3

TABLE 5

Number of Conditions Seen at VD Clinic, Bedford General Hospital during October, November and December 1966

Nationalities	No.	M	F	M	F	M	F	M	F
		Totals		Syphilis		Gonorrhoea		Other Conditions	
UK	62	41	21	1	–	9	12	31	9
West Indians	49	41	8	–	1	25	3	16	4
Pakistanis	28	27	1	1	–	9	1	17	–
Others	5	4	1	–	–	1	–	3	1
TOTAL	144	113	31	2	1	44	16	67	14

TABLE 6

Number of Conditions Seen at VD Clinic, Bedford General Hospital during October, November and December 1968

Nationalities	No.	M	F	M	F	M	F	M	F
		Totals		Syphilis		Gonorrhoea		Other Conditions	
UK	97	43	54	1	2	9	14	33	38
West Indians	27	22	5	1	–	11	1	10	4
Pakistanis	9	9	–	1	–	3	–	5	–
Indians	3	2	1	–	–	–	–	2	1
Italians	20	15	5	–	–	–	–	15	5
Others	9	7	2	–	–	2	–	5	2
TOTAL	165	98	67	3	2	25	15	70	50

villages where they have been used to working in the fields in a warm climate. In this country they tend to sit around at home and their complaints may reflect loss of muscle tone and also underlying psychological factors. In the men the strains relate to poor physique subjected to hard physical effort. I feel that much more could be done in the industrial/medical field in looking at the work problems of the immigrants. It is important also not to dismiss backache as psychogenic without a careful examination because of the high incidence of bone disease in the immigrants.

Among Asian immigrants, diseases of the eye are common, together with skin diseases and infestations derived from poor hygiene – this despite the fact that 'on the whole, the immigrants are particular about their personal cleanliness'.

As for respiratory diseases: 'Several Papers have been written about the well-recognised increased risk from tuberculosis in immigrant groups of rural origin. For the Irish this is times 3, for the Indian times 7, and for the Pakistanis times 30 (Dolton W.D.).' Bedford experience confirms a high incidence of respiratory diseases among Pakistanis, and second cases among Asian families are also prevalent 'probably due to the custom of Asians to crowd into the room of the sick patient. I get the impression that there are more upper respiratory infections since the children have come to this country and they probably represent the reservoirs of infection.'

Among Asian women, apart from respiratory diseases, there is a high incidence of anaemia and diabetes, and the frequency of their attendances at gynaecological clinics 'probably indicated considerable underlying psychological problems in adaptation and marriage in a strange country'.

[It is notable that] there is a higher incidence of anaemia and infections in children born in the United Kingdom than of those born abroad. The anaemias become noticeable in the third year of life and this points to the need to understand the early feeding habits of the children. It is generally known that Asian children are smaller and weigh less than English children of the same age and their growth rate is slower. It is important to recognise this distinction and not to compare the Asian children with the normal growth rates of English children. . . .

Psychological symptoms are present frequently in the immigrant population and they are the most difficult to diagnose and treat. There is probably less breakdown than would be expected because customs and communal living provide some, albeit limited, emotional support. . . . There are many cultural as well as language differences which make it difficult for the Doctor to give psychotherapy to help emotionally disturbed patients, and the only course open is to accept the frequent visits and give kindness and patience as the main supportive care. . . .

It is in the doctor/patient relationship that the major difficulties arise. The first consultation with an immigrant is usually long and frustrating, trying to establish a relationship frequently through an interpreter often a child. It is in this situation that the help of specially trained social workers knowing the customs and language of the immigrant would be of great value. Otherwise it is very difficult to elicit a history and to explain treatment to an immigrant patient. Several drug firms have prepared printed cards with advice on diets and contraceptives and these are printed in Urdu and Hindi, but not all villagers can read.

Dr Harte concludes that, of the problems he discussed:

The most important are the recognition of anaemia especially in the children and women, in the higher incidence of primitive forms of respiratory infections, in the chronic infestations and the continuing problem of the unmasked psychological difficulties. There is a need to develop special techniques of history-taking where the customary methods are inadequate because of the language problem and the lack of understanding of social and cultural patterns. This highlights the importance of team work, especially of the doctor working with social workers. There is a need for research to study some of the patterns of illness mentioned and for more health education, especially among the women in the first year of their arrival in the United Kingdom; and in studying the clinical problems affecting the immigrants not only will we know more about these strangers who have come to make their home among us, but we shall know more about ourselves and the diseases from which man suffers.

This perceptive Paper is clearly based on close observation, sympathy, and understanding. The rewards of a practice such as Dr Harte's are certainly medical rather than financial, for, apart from the time demanded by individual consultations, the high percentage of Asians in the practice has often brought complaints from British patients. Their objections, it is worth noting, have been to the persistent smell of Asians in the waiting-room. These smells derive from aromatic oils rubbed on the body and from garlic and other herbs used in Asian diets. Since Dr Harte installed extractor fans in his waiting-room, complaints have ceased. His analysis of such situations leads him to conclude that a main root of British objections to Asians is not race or colour, but smell.

Dr Harte's paper confirms the proposition that many Asian health problems are essentially those of education and communication, and that there is urgent need for medically trained advisers and interpreters working at fundamental level among their own people in immigrant communities.

The activities of Bedford's one Indian clinic nurse, Mrs Chima, admirably reinforce this point. She works both with health visitors and at town clinics. Her functions are of particular value in the Ampthill Road area of town, with its concentration of Asians from backgrounds of poverty and illiteracy. Together with the two health visitors of the area, she makes an admirable team. Their task is not only to advise but to gain the confidence of immigrants often fearful of English life and organisation, and ignorant equally of good health habits and social service facilities.

In Urdu, Punjabi and Hindi, Mrs Chima gives advice on simple and basic needs: what to wear to keep warm in an English winter; how and why to keep the house clean; to combat anaemia and worms; to feed the family, especially the children; to prepare food for the baby; to sterilise milk and feeding utensils; to bath baby; to visit the clinics for inoculation or examination; to keep to a regular timetable of health precautions, etc.

Advice on rearing babies has a central place in her work. Of the 1,279 babies born in Bedford in 1968, 10 per cent were Asian. (This compares with percentages of 10 Italian, 5 West Indian, and 5 mid-European.) The birth rate of Indians is higher than that of any other immigrant group; and even at the present time, 200 out of 800 health visitors' cards for children under five in the Ampthill Road area are for Indians.

The work of health visitors in such an area makes heavy demands upon time as well as upon sympathy and understanding. Since many Asians are illiterate even in their own language, notices of medical attendance for inoculations, examinations, etc. have to be delivered personally rather than through the post. The volume of work alone is therefore immense; and accompanying Mrs Chima and the health visitors on their rounds makes it clear that Asian women love to gossip, especially about their personal relationships.

Problems can rarely be dealt with quickly and health visiting inevitably takes longer here than in English households.

This is far from being a waste of time. Such visits do much more than help to keep people healthy. It is only by this kind of human interchange that Asian immigrants can be gradually drawn into the ambit of the medical service as a whole. Asian women now attend baby clinics in increasing numbers, often in the brilliant plumage of a social occasion. Many also take advantage of birth control clinics, where current reservations about the pill lead them to prefer inter-uterine devices. (West Indians tend to be more casual in these precautions and indeed in their health habits as a whole.)

At these clinics Mrs Chima's presence often proves essential. Although pamphlets on health matters are sometimes available in Urdu, Hindi, and Punjabi, the illiteracy of Asian women means that the pamphlets have only limited use. The prime need is for direct personal interpretation. 'On the day she doesn't come, we often can't get through to them at all.' This opinion of a doctor at the Queen's Park clinic was repeated almost word for word to me by a doctor at the clinic in the Ampthill Road area.

It seems clear that in an immigrant society, the 'bridge' function, the role of the skilled interpreter – whether relating doctor to patient, health visitor to family, teacher to parent, police to public – is of central importance. In the sphere of health, there is evident and urgent need for more people of Mrs Chima's kind, particularly to work as health visitors among the Asian communities, those most cut off from British ways of life and organisation by barriers of language and culture. Such work has much wider purpose than that of a purely medical function. In Mrs Chima's own words, it is 'to teach people to live life in England'.

Medical considerations engage most fully with general social considerations during immigrants' early years of residence in this country. When allocating hospital beds for confinements, for example, health authorities find that social considerations such as poor housing conditions and language difficulties figure most prominently in the cases of newly arrived immigrants, and that, as immigrant groups become established locally, such considerations gradually decline in importance. Thus, in the late fifties, 90 per cent of Italian immigrants applying for a hospital bed on social grounds were admitted; by 1968, the percentage was considerably lower, roughly on a par with that of West Indians. The great pressure at the present time is from Asian applicants, nearly 90 per cent of whom were admitted on social grounds in 1968. Comparative figures for that year are as follows:

Applications for Confinements in Bedford Hospital[1] on Social Grounds, 1968[2]

	Indians & Pakistanis	West Indians & Africans	Italians & Mid-Europeans	Others	British	Total
Total						
Applicants	82	25	60	5	134	306
Recommended	72	13	28	5	60	178
Refused	10	12	32	0	74	128

This situation reinforces the point that a primary purpose of local social services is to draw immigrant groups into the normal fabric of life as quickly as possible. To do so requires well-co-ordinated policies on lines already suggested, supported by programmes of research such as that already initiated by Dr Harte, and by collective advice from working parties of practitioners in every sphere of local activity – doctors, health workers, public health inspectors, housing officials, social workers, policemen, teachers, and so on. There is also a clear case for special projects to tackle key problems, such as those of Asian families. What could be more useful in Bedford, for example, than a programme of literacy and fundamental education for Sikh women in their own *gurdwara*, with teachers of their own kind using such literacy techniques as those worked out by UNESCO in developing countries, designed to teach them how to cope with the demands of everday life in the country?

To draw immigrants into the fabric of British life does not mean to encourage them simply to imitate our ways and values. In

[1] I am indebted to Dr J. G. M. Mortimer, medical officer of health for Bedford, for this information.

[2] It is pertinent here to note the extent to which the local hospital depends on the services of people of other countries. Of forty senior medical staff, one is Indian and one Mid-European. Of twenty-eight junior medical staff, seventeen are from overseas, the great majority of them being Indian. A considerable proportion of the nursing staff are also from overseas, while local immigrants – particularly Indian and West Indian women – form a large part of the catering and domestic staff.

certain spheres of life – in the case of old people, for instance –
immigrant groups show considerably higher general standards of
concern and responsibility than does the local British community.
Among no immigrant group could be found the kind of attitude
recently met by a health official when she called at the home of a
local English lady. The lady asked for her mother to be taken
away to a home. She explained that she had just had a new carpet
fitted, and that as her mother tended to be incontinent it was clear
she would have to go away in case she wetted the new carpet. Is it
really desirable that the immigrants from 'developing' or less
'advanced' countries should make themselves in our image? Are
we really sure that we know what we mean by 'development' and
'advancement'?

14

Immigrants and the Police

MOST first generation immigrants ask no more than acceptance in Britain. They want no trouble; they take pains to avoid it. It follows that immigrants are responsible for fewer crimes in proportion to their numbers than are the natives. Crime statistics, however, are rarely accurate guides to the nature and quality of police work; and the fact that immigrants' crime statistics are comparatively low does not mean that the police are seldom involved with them.

The problems that the immigrant groups present to the police in Bedford derive directly from their ways of life and their personal experiences. Among the Slav and Baltic peoples who came here after the Second World War, there is little incidence of crime, though a small number of them, mainly men living lonely in rented rooms, are still booked for habitual drunkenness. One man has more than fifty convictions to his name. In the early days, arrests were sometimes accompanied by shouts of 'Gestapo' against the police, but such hostility has long since waned. Today it is rare to find anything but respect and admiration for the police among the European refugees: 'One thing that impressed me when first I came to this country, that was English policemen. You could not find friendlier people. Ninety-five per cent of English policemen are gentlemen.' This representative opinion of a Slovene is echoed by another from a Pole: 'I have seen many countries. I have never seen such kind, good, polite policemen as in this country.'

Many of these refugees now live settled family lives in Bedford, and, since the pattern of that family life often has a stronger basis of authority than is common among English families, the incidence of crime among their youth also tends to be less than among English youth: 'Generally, you don't get among the Europeans what you find in some British families: parents who couldn't care less about their kids . . . nor such loutishness among the youth. . . .'

Policemen's comments are often as blunt as they are realistic.

The small group of Hungarians proved an exception to the general pattern of law-abiding European immigrants. Indeed, their crime rate in Bedford in relation to their numbers has been greater than that of any other immigrant group. Those who came here after the Budapest uprising in 1956 comprised a number of brave and hard-working people interspersed with petty criminals, social misfits, and those anxious to avoid military service. These latter people proved anti-social in behaviour, hostile to authority, and reluctant to take useful employment. One small group of women, for example, was responsible for persistent shop-lifting in Bedford, while a group of young men soon built up a vicious record of violence, drunkenness, traffic offences and larceny. 'A parasitic band of layabouts' was the description of them in one official report. Their record made it an appropriate summing-up.

At the other end of the scale are the Italian immigrants. In the first generation, they still live to a rigid traditional pattern. Most are industrious and abstemious, with a great respect for the family, for the Church, and for traditional sources of authority of every kind. It is a community which, on the whole, has regulated itself. It has also kept its sins to itself. Among this first generation, crimes are few; those against property are rare, and those such as drunkenness are virtually unknown. Such crimes as there have been have derived mainly from strong personal emotions: domestic disagreements leading to violence, together with a few cases of sexual assault and rape.

The Italian community in Bedford has therefore come to enjoy a great local reputation for its law-abiding qualities. Only recently has this reputation been dented, and the dents can be directly associated with the growth of a second generation intent on renouncing traditional ways of life. Since so many local people so constantly insist that immigrants should adopt our ways, that 'these people should learn to be like us', it is not without irony that only since young Italians began to be like us, by imitating the ways of British youth, has the crime rate of the local Italian community – like its VD rate – been at all significant. And as second generation Italians become increasingly anglicised, there is no doubt that more Italian girls will break violently with their home ways of life and that more Italian young men will follow the delinquency patterns of British youth. The desire of young Italians to belong to British society may well make them particularly vulnerable to group pressures and influences, and several Italian youths are already involved in the local drug scene.

I have heard local people seek to establish connections between the development of the drug scene in Bedford over the last decade and the build-up of immigrant numbers in the town over the same period. Though some immigrants of certain groups figure in the margins of the scene, they have virtually no connection with its main stream of development, which is rather to be associated with such factors as the increased accessibility of drugs in recent years and the growing climate of doubt and disaffection as to the whole meaning and purpose of life in modern urban, industrial society.

Apart from a very few young Italians, it is doubtful if any immigrants figure among local hard drug addicts. Reliable evidence suggests there are some forty such addicts[1] in Bedford at the time of writing, for instance, and that both suppliers and customers are nearly all British. Where immigrants are involved in the taking and passing of drugs, it is almost invariably in continuation of traditional habits. There is certainly some private smoking of opium among Asians in Bedford, for example, and recent finds by local police suggest that Bedford may well be used as a staging post in the transfer of opium from London airport to Pakistanis in Bradford.

Of greater importance is the circulation of cannabis among some local West Indians. Though there is no evidence of them extending their tastes to the more sophisticated drugs of 'advanced' Western societies, the police are concerned about cannabis distribution at West Indian parties, where 'social reasons' may encourage others to try the weed. A particular matter of concern is that the increasing numbers of British youths and girls at such parties may not be able to control use of the drug as West Indians do, and that some may eventually progress on to heroin and the more dangerous hard drugs.

Most local policemen count West Indians their greatest problem among immigrant groups. This is not so much a matter of their aptitude for crime as of their attitudes towards authority. Police complain that their inquiries are often met with insolence and defiance, and nothing antagonises them more than attempts to

---

[1] The local drug scene is changing and developing so fast that estimates of numbers on soft drugs are virtually worthless. At the end of 1969, it seemed certain, however, that at least one per cent of the local population were on soft drugs, and that young people were rapidly turning from pills to cannabis and acid. One local drug pusher numbers local cannabis smokers in thousands.

discredit their inquiries and actions with labels of 'colour prejudice': 'You only pick on me because I'm black.' The more the police meet this response, the more they resent it: 'What we get prejudiced about are the buggers that use that argument.' They feel it as a slur on their integrity and as creating a climate in which it becomes more difficult to act objectively. The pity is that some policemen are thereby led to cast all West Indians in the image of the offensive minority, with the consequence that relationships are further impaired.

Overall crime statistics for West Indians are low. There is little planned crime, such as breaking and entering. Similarly rare are crimes deriving from sexual repressions. Indecent exposure, for example, has never been recorded among West Indians in Bedford, nor is it likely to be. And where violence occurs, it is usually spontaneous in nature, deriving from sudden quarrels, perhaps over or with a woman, often with drink taken. In general, West Indians are involved less in deliberate breakings of the law than in evasions of it such as failure to take out motor insurance.

The complaint most commonly lodged against West Indians is that of the noisy party – another sore point with the police, because they can do so little about it. Such parties are most frequent at week-ends and in summertime, and the parties organised for profit, in particular, draw considerable numbers of West Indians from different parts of the country. Local residents complain. The police make a call. The lull is temporary. An inevitable and vicious circle of noise, complaint and remonstration follows. The outcome is inconclusive and all concerned – the party organisers, the neighbours, and the police – are left simmering with resentment. Of such stuff is racial antagonism made. Nobody regrets these disturbances more than the majority of West Indians in Bedford, for it is they who suffer most from the backlash of local reactions.

Of all areas of local crime, West Indians are most seriously involved in that of prostitution, although it needs to be said immediately that many of the organisers and most of the girls are British. Prostitution in Bedford is a good deal more widespread, and a good deal more serious as a social problem, than most local authorities are prepared to admit. Crime statistics are almost meaningless here, for the simple reason that Bedford has no regular system of brothels in the usual sense. Contacts are commonly made in pubs and clubs, and services are commonly rendered by girls moving around, or being delivered, to lodging-houses and other private addresses. There is also a growing business in parked cars. Many of these girls are not town residents, but come in, or are brought in, from other areas, mainly at week-ends. In brief, it is a moving trade and, as such, successfully confounds most police attempts to obtain convictions.

A good deal of local prostitution has been of the lowest grade, often involving girls poor in intelligence and with pathetic histories of broken homes and broken relationships. Such girls frequently give themselves over entirely to the first man who shows them affection or even mere recognition as women; and a number finally accept the will of the men – West Indians included – that they should prostitute themselves. Such girls may be found doing the rounds of certain lodging-houses on pay nights, their current prices ranging from 5/- to £5.

It is not a trade to evoke erotic interest. Silken dalliance has no place in the dingy, airless rooms of Pakistani lodging-houses, for example, on beds of old army blankets. A girl who has earned up to £40 a night at £1 a time in a lodging-house was asked how she could stomach it: 'Ah, they get so excited, they come as quick as they get in you.' She returned home thereafter for 'proper sex' with her West Indian protector.

This pattern of prostitution is being modified as more attractive girls take to relationships and to whoring of this kind, and as the line between amateurs and professionals becomes ever more blurred in our society. Prostitutes and others involved on the scene confirm the opinion that 'most girls won't go with Pakistanis. The places they live in are filthy. If they do, like when they really need money, it's no kissing. Just plain sex. . . . It is Pakistanis and West Indians do business with the girls. Very few Indians do business with them. Indians treat a girl very honourable and nice. If one should want to go to bed with a girl, it must be in secret, so that no other Indians will know.' Local venereal disease statistics also lend some weight to the generalisation;[1] and here the most significant figure of all, perhaps, is that of all venereal conditions seen at Bedford Hospital in the last quarter of 1968 one-third were in British women.

As prostitution extends locally, and becomes more affluent, West Indian girls are becoming involved for the first time, catering almost entirely for British clients. Yet, despite the growth of the

[1] See chapter on Health, p. 191.

trade, the system of 'visiting' makes it as difficult as ever to control by normal police methods. Where charges are preferred, they often derive from other, minor charges, such as a breach of the peace or a motoring offence. In a case that came before local magistrates recently, for example, the police were called to a violent disturbance in a private house to find furniture damaged and a West Indian man and an English woman exchanging blows. The woman, a mother of three, told how she had met the man in a local pub and gone to live with him: 'He asked me to hustle for him,' the statement alleged. 'I refused at first, then later I agreed. He would have three or four men waiting for me when I got home. The men paid £3 each, which they gave to X. These were usually Chinese.' Mrs Z. alleged that he also brought Pakistanis and others who sometimes paid £4 or £5. 'He got them from local pubs,' she said. Mrs Z. went on: 'X made me go to bed with the landlord because he was short of the rent.' She also alleged that X was 'running other girls'.[1]

Current punishments for charges of immoral earnings do little to discourage enterprise. A fine of £25, a day's 'work', is hardly likely to deter any pimp from his way of life; and, as often as not, the woman involved takes up with him again after he leaves the court. At times, the pattern of fidelity is bizarre. A girl found in wretched conditions among Pakistanis in a lodging-house was asked why she did not leave them: 'That wouldn't be right,' she said. 'They paid £50 for me.' So the squalid trade continues, difficult to check or control, dangerous not least in its high risk of venereal disease. In 1968, an outbreak of 23 cases of syphilis among Pakistanis in Bedford was traced back to one local prostitute. The case for a properly supervised official brothel system could hardly be more clear.

The Pakistanis, as the only group in Bedford without a well-established pattern of family life, are prominent as prostitutes' customers. And since by language and culture they are separated more completely from English life than any other immigrant group these women are at once their only sexual outlet and one of their few points of social contact.

Most of the Pakistanis are, in every sense, underprivileged. Docile, submissive, bewildered by the transition to an alien, industrial society, they have little initiative for crime and are anxious only to avoid trouble. Ironically, it is this which leads them most often into illegality, mainly through the giving of false

[1] From a report in the *Bedfordshire Times*

information. The commonplaces are false documents, passports and tax returns. How far the illegality is wilful, how far it is due to ignorance, how far to the advice and direction of a few fellow-countrymen eager to exploit that ignorance, is impossible to determine. Certainly the worst dangers are from the exploiters. They 'help' the ignorant and illiterate to fill in tax forms, counsel false returns, and take most of the benefits for themselves as fees. They lure those fearful of authority into labyrinths of false statements, not only charging them exorbitantly, but making them increasingly dependent on their services. For such people the pickings are great, the harm incalculable, not only in material terms to their countrymen, but to the relationships of their group with the police and with the British public at large.

The problems of communicating with Asian groups, and of creating understanding of British standards, are as complex as they are important. A central problem for the police in this sphere is that of finding suitable interpreters: people both willing and able to undertake inquiries, question suspects and record evidence. It has never been an easy task. Many suitable immigrants are fearful of helping in this way lest they become identified with the police in the eyes of their own people and so jeopardise their personal positions. This social worker fears that by so doing she may impair her capacity to help her people; this businessman that he will lose trade; that leader that he will lose influence, and so on. The police, on their side, are aware that not all interpreters have been trustworthy; that this man was rewarded with unofficial fees for his services to one side in a dispute, and that man interpreted evidence in ways designed to protect his community rather than to reveal the truth. Inevitably, in such a context, distrust proliferates.

This situation is not helped by the predilection of some Asians for making anonymous allegations to the police against their own kind: 'Dear Sir, It has come to my notice that a certain gentleman has entered England on a forged passport, etc, etc.' A number of these allegations show the touch of a literary hand.

> 'Dear Sir, I thought it best to tell you something about those Indian people who are throwing dust in the eyes of this Government. And first I am writing about one named BLANK. . . . He has changed his passport by hook or by crook. . . . As a citizen of this country, I have done my duty and hope you will try to give a keen attention towards this case. Thanking you in anticipation. Yours very truly. Signed.'

Bedford police suffer also from the ingrained distrust and fear of authority in general, and of police in particular, which many Asians bring with them from their own countries. A curtain of ignorance descends in the face of most inquiries. How far is it real, how far assumed? The police can rarely, if ever, know for certain. At every turn they meet frustrations: 'We do not know him. . . . He does not live here. . . . He has gone away. . . .' Such are the standard responses. Or else faces of blank incomprehension. At times there could be serious consequences. Item: a Pakistani immigrant lands at London airport. She undergoes a standard test for TB. The results are inconclusive. She gives a Bedford address and is asked to report to the local medical authority. She does not do so, and the local medical officer contacts the police. She may be a case of open TB. The police find the house she named occupied by Indians. 'How could a Pakistani live here?' The police inform leaders of the local Pakistani and Indian communities. They can only hope they will be lucky enough to discover the woman's whereabouts.

There are also constant problems of illegal entry, mainly concerning those Asians who arrived in this country as visitors, and thereafter simply disappeared from view. Checks and inquiries all too often meet a blank wall; and sometimes the innocent suffer. A Pakistani takes a holiday in Europe; an irregularity in his passport causes the immigration authorities to stop him on his return to England. Indignant, he gives an address in Bedford. Immigration contacts the local police, who visit the house. 'We do not know him. He does not live here.' It is probable that he does live in Bedford, but the police are unable to confirm it. The man is therefore returned to the country from which he travelled to England. He may still be there.

With the Asians, then, police problems concern not so much the incidence of crime as the complexities of coming to terms with people alien to them in culture, customs and language, many of whom have little or no understanding either of the norms of British law or of their responsibilities as citizens. It is evident, moreover, that Indian and Pakistani communities at times settle affairs that should properly be settled in courts of law – that judgments are enacted, punishments exacted within those communities. That the police know of this, and can do so little about it, only serves to foment further suspicion and distrust.

Investigations of Asian crimes thus often prove intensely

demanding, wearisome and confusing. Item: an Indian is wounded – a deep single cut from hairline to the end of his nose. How did the wound come about – from a punishment or from a casual brawl? A whole year of investigation follows: a year of evidence often changing and conflicting; of allegations and counter-allegations; of witnesses retracting evidence or simply disappearing. Finally, those responsible are brought to trial and sentenced to varying terms of imprisonment. The police are by no means certain that this is the end of the affair.

In general, the Sikhs of Bedford, like the Italians, are law-abiding and self-regulating as a community. The record of crime is slight, and mainly confined to a few crimes of violence, although the violence can assume disturbing forms, and may have disturbing under-currents. Item: the police are called to find a Sikh girl of fourteen bleeding badly after sexual assault. She is profoundly frightened and tells a story of being gagged, blindfolded and raped by masked men who threatened her with death. Reality is finally found to be more prosaic. The real offender is a family acquaintance. Although the crime is punished in a British court of law, a deep sense of shame remains both with the family concerned and with the Sikh community as a whole, for virginity is sacred. Fears persist that some within the community may take the law into their own hands.

In sum, though the crime rate of the various immigrant groups in Bedford is comparatively low, their presence imposes on the local police a whole new range of complex problems for which their formal training gives them little or no preparation. The central problems seem to me those of communicating with the various groups, of surmounting the barriers of culture and language, of creating a climate of mutual understanding and of establishing effective working relationships. To achieve these objects requires of the police understanding as well as experience.

Of late, some areas of police training have been extended to include studies in contemporary society, including immigrant problems. This book, in fact, has its origin in a residential seminar for police sergeants in 1968, the first of a series initiated by the chief constable of Bedfordshire, open to police sergeants throughout Britain, aiming to explore the changing patterns of police work in a rapidly changing industrial society.

Police officers seem to find it of real utility to discuss immigrant themes: how the ways of life, habits and values of the various groups have been created; in what ways they differ in family and community organisation and values, in aspirations and purposes; their characteristic patterns of crime and how these are likely to develop; what problems they pose for the police, and what effective action the police might take to meet and solve them, etc. For my part, I have found interchange with the police on such matters extremely rewarding, not least because most bring to their studies profound personal experience rather than the wearisome slogans of liberal or illiberal ignorance.

Yet this experience may create its own dangers. It naturally inclines police officers to see each group in the image of its malefactors. In this distorting mirror, Asians become liars, West Indians pimps, and so on. They can deal with hosts of British malefactors without it distorting their judgments on the local community as a whole, simply because they know what the standards of British society are. Few police officers know much about the standards of the immigrant groups, so that their approach to them is often coloured by distorted assumptions and unnecessary suspicions. In short, they tend to look at the immigrants very much as the immigrants look at them.

The one way to overcome such mutual distrust and common distortions of viewpoint is to extend contact and interchange between police and immigrant groups. A few days ago, for example, a group of police sergeants on a residential course visited the Ampthill Junior School in Bedford, which currently (October 1969) has 77 per cent immigrants.[1] They saw and talked with immigrant children in a normal situation: Italians, Indians, West Indians, British and many others, all with Bedford accents, learning and playing together. The understanding gained from their visit was worth far more than anything discussion alone could give.

Far more extensive and systematic interchange with immigrant groups, especially through community leaders, could do much to create understanding, dispel fears, and increase that awareness of British norms and standards among immigrants without which police action can never be fully effective. This is particularly necessary among Asian groups, those most sharply differentiated from British life by language and culture, though in practice such a policy is likely to be far less successful with the loose-knit Paki-

[1] This represents a rise of 8 per cent in nine months (see also Appendix 1).

stani group than with the close-structured Indian community.

Some traditionally minded policemen remain sceptical as to the use and value of discussion of immigrant affairs. 'A villain is a villain, no matter his background or his colour of skin.' It is an admirable argument, though here it is hardly relevant. What is relevant is that police cannot work efficiently except in a climate of mutual trust, confidence and understanding. It is not much use saying that a villain is a villain if you are unable to say who is a villain and who is not because you have made no effort to come to terms with the people you are talking to. The real villain in this situation is voluntary ignorance.

Despite the persistence of such attitudes, the local police force as a whole seem to me far more open to free and frank discussion of immigrant issues and problems than most other local authorities or local employers. The police, at least, are refreshingly free of local tendencies to whitewash, adopt defensive postures or play games of blind man's bluff. The pity is that most 'documentary' presentations of the police to the public through the mass media seem concerned only to beat the fashionable anti-authority drum and to perpetuate the hidebound reactionary image. My own impressions of the local police force are quite different: of conscientious and responsible people intent on preserving their traditions of public service yet ready to look at fresh approaches with open and agreeably practical minds. A good many more immigrants in Bedford share my respect than either the image-makers or even the police themselves are inclined to think.

15

Clubs, Culture and the Community

IMMIGRANT groups, in greater or in less degree, want to preserve their identity. They serve this end with their own clubs, societies and schools; they make their own communities with only limited reference to local British society; and they have virtually no contact with other immigrant groups.

This does not mean that they are unresponsive to the values of British society. Since they want to live in peace and set high value upon acceptance, they seek, often anxiously, accommodations with British norms and with British methods of organisation. They want to fit into the structure of British society, though not into its modes of consciousness. In brief, they want to belong in terms of organisation, not in terms of being.

To belong in a full human sense would mean, in effect, to forfeit themselves. For this reason the concept of integration, implying the merging of parts into a single whole, is rarely found on immigrants' lips. Most leave the notion, with a certain smile, to British liberals and to community relations professionals.

Even in the second generation, immigrant youth put primary emphasis on making their own societies. In Bedford, every major group of second generation immigrants has its own youth club. The Young Indians Association has 180 members, the Italian youth club 120, the West Indian and Polish youth clubs each over 60. Their participation in local 'open' youth clubs is, with few exceptions, slight.

While making a survey in 1969 of Commonwealth immigrant youth in Bedford, Harry Sutcliffe assembled information which makes the point clear.

Thus, in 67 youth clubs, West Indians make up 2·9 per cent of the total membership, Indians 0·6 per cent, and Pakistanis 0·1 per cent. Together, they represent 3·6 per cent of all youth club

TABLE 7

COMMONWEALTH IMMIGRANT MEMBERSHIP OF YOUTH CLUBS IN BEDFORD (1969)

	Indians		Pakistanis		West Indians		All membership			Commonwealth Immigrant Members as % of total
	boys	girls	boys	girls	boys	girls	boys	girls	total	
6 Provided Clubs with paid membership	11				8	1	809	361	1,170	1.7%
16 Clubs connected with religious organisations	4				20	7	391	268	659	4.7%
4 units, Red Cross and St John's	3	2		2	3	16	28	101	129	20%
14 groups, Scouts, Boys Brigade					4		450	—	450	0.9%
20 groups, Guides, Rangers, Girls' Brigade		1				25	—	495	495	5.2%
7 units of pre-service organisations				2	14	4	606	31	637	2.8%
TOTALS in 67 Clubs:	18	3	2	2	49	53	2,284	1,256	3,540	3.6%

members, one-third of the percentage they represent in local schools.

That West Indian representation is far higher than that of Asians may be explained principally by their lack of a strong indigenous culture and by their habituation both to British culture and to the structure of British organisation. The clubs to which the West Indians belong in Bedford are almost exactly those they could have been expected to join in the West Indies: the religious and uniformed organisations, especially the Red Cross, St John's, and the guides. In the West Indies, the boys might well have belonged to scouts and 4H clubs rather than to pre-service organisations, but principle and appeal remain the same. Inevitably, they prefer the clubs in which relationships are given a formal, hierarchical structure, in which one knows precisely where and in what role one belongs, and where one is recognised as a 'role' – patrol leader, corporal, or whatever – rather than as a 'free' – or isolated – individual.

It is notable that participation in locally provided general activity clubs is minimal. Where it does occur, participation is confined almost entirely to a single sex club – the Bedford Boys' Club – and activities are confined almost entirely to a set pattern of physical recreation and exercise. In sum, there is virtually no general social and cultural intermingling by immigrants in the 'open' youth clubs of Bedford.

The situation is brought about by a complex of factors, varying in emphasis from group to group. Those young people whose cultural backgrounds are least firmly defined and who most seek acceptance in British society – West Indians, in particular – fear most to expose themselves to rejection. There is little evidence of much effort or imagination in 'open' youth clubs to help overcome their fears and to gather them in; few qualities of that 'quick-eyed Love', which,

> observing me grow slack
> From my first entrance in,
> Drew nearer to me, sweetly questioning,
> If I lacked any thing.[1]

All too often, the attitude of young British people to unfamiliar immigrants seeking entrance to their clubs resembles that of local householders to unfamiliar immigrants seeking lodgings or that of local employers to unfamiliar immigrants seeking jobs. In sum, the

[1] George Herbert, 'Love bade me welcome', *The Temple*, 1633.

classical pattern of British xenophobia re-enacts itself, from an initial attitude not so much of antipathy as of wary and fearful neutrality, allied to insular shyness and sheer ignorance of how to cope with people. The onus, as always, is upon the 'bloody foreigner' to prove himself worthy of acceptance. If he passes the appropriate tests – which usually involve enacting British ways and demonstrating British values – then his acceptance is total. He becomes 'one of us'. He enjoys the full protection of the tribe. More often than not, the tasks prove too demanding, and the young immigrant turns away discouraged and sometimes bitter, to seek the security of his own kind. To the British, it is just another instance of foreigners not wanting to fit in. They feel, in all sincerity, that no sin of commission can be laid at their door.

If anything, the climate of the times tends to damp down rather than to kindle the light of understanding. Discussion of immigrant issues by delegates at a recent local youth conference led a youth officer to confess, 'They shook me with their bigotry. It was like listening to a race of Alf Garnetts.'

The reference is telling. Over recent years, the TV programme *Till Death Us Do Part* has, to some measure, given a vocabulary to hardening anti-immigrant opinion in this country. As Powell the politician did much to create the climate of opinion, Speight, the script-writer, however unwittingly, did much to create the words. Alf Garnett's strictures on 'bloody coons', however satirically intended, became national currency. They still persist as fashionable usage. To young people in particular, their crude assertiveness sounded attractively smart and 'with it'. They even gave the illusion of honest thinking, refreshingly free of hedgings and hypocrisies. 'Coon' became an 'in' word, and in Bedford has been indiscriminately applied not only to 'coloureds' but to foreigners of all kinds.

How far, then, is the antipathy expressed by young people against immigrants a matter of fashionable attitudes and words, how far is it reality? Ask the same question of the same person in a different situation – first as an individual and then as a member of a group – and you may well get different answers. He who has grown up among immigrant children, like many people in Bedford, may naturally incline to tolerance and understanding. As a member of a group, however, he may have to subordinate his feelings to group opinions. 'If you took two twins and put them in different circumstances, they could well end up in different groups that exclude each other.' These words of a local youth officer point the force of group pressures on the individual in our times. As they grow more rigorous, while contemporary fashion grows more imperious, it seems inevitable that they will increasingly act against the spread of tolerance and understanding.

The climate of antipathy or aversion to immigrants is thus composed of many elements, most of them not amenable to quantitative analysis. This climate varies according to circumstance and environment. Even a temporary recession in the local brick industry, for example, could transfer the store of antipathy into active currents of hostility. Economic fear already begins to strengthen antipathy in local youth groups. As more immigrant youths come on to the labour market and competition for apprenticeships grows more intense, so fears may develop and opinions harden.

Immigrant groups, on their side, make objections to local youth clubs. The stronger the culture of the group, the stronger the objections. Indian parents, in particular, fear that attendance at youth clubs may expose their sons to a corrupting moral climate, as well as frittering away time that could be better spent in work and study. As for the girls, traditional values and traditional systems of social restraint before marriage virtually rule out any kind of participation. West Indian parents are, by contrast, less bound by traditional family organisation and values, but they also resemble the generality of immigrant parents in their fears and reservations about contemporary patterns of behaviour amongst British youth.

In varying measure, young immigrants share something of their parents' attitudes, even those young Italians who are consciously turning away from their parents' ways of life. Young Indians, especially, share the value that their parents put upon study and advancement, and are often shocked by contemporary abuses of social freedom among British youth. Seeking meaningful relationships in British society, they are often dismayed to find human relationships degraded into terms of mere sexual usage. The more sophisticated note with distaste the force of conditioning influences in the society, not least the ways in which the media of mass communication through popular reading matter, television programmes and commercials endorse and enforce the concept of women as objects of status and consumption. As for the range of activities in general purpose youth clubs, they find little to attract them. 'Physical jerks all week and snogging at the week-end dance . . . it's just boring.'

Many young immigrants, especially Asians, simply do not share the hearty philistine traditions of British youth. They aspire to a wider, more satisfying range of social and cultural activities; and in their own clubs they can, at least, attempt to make patterns of activity to their own cut and liking, in the security of their own kind.

In this climate, the recommendations of Lord Hunt's Committee on 'Immigrants and the Youth Service' are, for the most part, likely to remain pious hopes. This report is based on the premise that colour is the fundamental divisive force among youth groups of different nationalities, and that the essential task is to seek means to overcome that force in order that the various groups can mingle freely together. This line of reasoning is eminently well-intentioned and riddled with questionable assumptions. If colour is the fundamental divisive force, why is it that divisions between the coloured groups themselves, especially between Indians and West Indians, are deeper than those between either Indians and British or West Indians and British? Why is 'non-coloured' immigrant participation in British youth clubs as slight as 'coloured' participation? And why does each and every immigrant group, irrespective of its skin colour, seek rather to develop its own club rather than to participate in British clubs?

The one answer to this question, the one explanation that makes sense of these facts, is that the fundamental force which impels each group is that of its culture. Though colour of skin is one dividing force, it is not the heart of the matter. To make it so both falsifies reality and leads us to misinterpret immigrant needs and aspirations. Though most immigrant youth seek interchange and equality of opportunity with British youth, their fundamental purpose is to preserve themselves, their own being, their own cultural identity. What meaning would their lives have were they to forfeit this? Recently, I heard a young Indian say: 'To an Indian, the notion of integration is irrelevant. . . . We want to be ourselves, first-class Indians, not second-class Britons.' The force of this feeling among immigrants depends, of course, on the strength of their cultural background. It is predictably stronger among Indians than among West Indians, for example, although the figures for the national youth clubs show that it remains true for all.

If we make premises of culture rather than those of colour, we are led to lines of reasoning and courses of action at once more humanly right and more practical than those of Lord Hunt's Committee. Recognise, first, the force of national cultures and that they exist in equal right. Admit, therefore, the principle of cultural diversity rather than that of integration. The development of national clubs can then be seen as natural and inevitable. At this point, doubts arise. Will this separate development not create cultural isolation and perpetuate divisions? The activities of the Italian youth club in Bedford already demonstrate otherwise. Although nationally based, about a third of its members are not Italian; and the plain fact is that no British general purpose youth club in the area achieves anything like the same measure of interchange between young people of different cultural backgrounds.

Let us, then, adopt policies which put emphasis upon interchange within national groups and between national groups rather than upon integration within British groups. Such patterns will be more rational and more successful, and interchange will assume full human meaning, because it will be between equals meeting on terms of mutual respect. The range of activities will also prove more satisfying than those obtaining in British general purpose clubs. In particular, there will be the chance of genuine cultural interchange through performances of national songs and dances, recitals of national music, exhibitions of national arts and crafts, and kindred activities.

National groups in Bedford have already proved that they have the will, the talent, and the pride to create activities of this kind.[1] The task now is to make local policies aimed to encourage group activities and to provide local facilities for interchange between the groups. The ideal would be to provide a civic cultural centre for use by national groups for activities between groups and for musical, dramatic, and cultural activities of all kinds. Such a centre could well prove a key factor in the making of Bedford as an immigrant town, as well as giving dignity to its civic life and – just conceivably – providing a source of local revenue.

The question then arises: how and by whom can policies affecting immigrants best be made? Is this more effectively done by voluntary organisations or through official bodies at local and national level? It is pertinent here to look at the nature and quality of the work of the voluntary organisation representing immigrants' interests in Bedford – the Bedford International Friendship Association.

BIFA was founded in 1967. In the previous year, the local rotary club had made a report on immigrants in Bedford as a result of which a steering committee was set up. This was joined

[1] Notably in the Bedford International Festival of 6 April 1968.

by representatives of the Bedford Council of Churches, contacts were made with the National Committee for Commonwealth Immigrants (NCCI), and in May 1967 a meeting of interested parties and leaders of immigrant groups was convened, and BIFA inaugurated.

It made an impressive start. In September 1967, proposals for setting up local playgroups secured a grant of £3,270 over three years from the Gulbenkian Trust. The local council gave a grant of £300 for the financial year 1968–9, and a full-time liaison officer was appointed on 1 October 1968, her salary guaranteed by NCCI, her office provided by the Bedford Council for Social Service.

Since that time, BIFA has handled both personal and general problems affecting local immigrants. They have ranged from housing difficulties to disputes between Pakistanis and the local tax office. In the latter case, BIFA brought tax officials and Pakistani leaders together to discuss and resolve problems arising from false tax declarations and accusations of discrimination. BIFA's main achievement over the past two years, however, remains the creation of the playgroups; and this was largely the work of Mrs Anna Tapsell. Five groups now operate – three in the borough, two in Kempston – providing for nearly 120 children, half of them English, half of them born of immigrant parents. Most of the groups meet for two half-days a week under the supervision of a paid organiser assisted by voluntary helpers. The majority of the immigrant children attending the playgroups are Indian, and most of the others are West Indian. Italian children number only three, all in the Queen's Park group; and at this centre also, language classes are being given to several Indian mothers by voluntary teachers. Given the lack of official provision of playgroups in the area, there is little doubt as to the overall value of the scheme.

Despite its achievements, the BIFA voluntary organisation faces difficult problems of relationships. Firstly, it has the task of reconciling within its own ranks disparate national interests and disparate points of view ranging from mild clerical-liberal to racialist. Fundamental to this task is the question: Who does BIFA really represent? Is it *all* immigrant interests or only those of certain groups? 'BIFA is concerned with improving relationships and understanding between all sections of the community,' says its constitution. Increasingly close relationships with NCCI (now the Community Relations Commission) and heavy emphases upon the 'colour' issue by BIFA officials, however, are serving to sow ever more doubts among the Italians and other European groups that BIFA really is intent to serve 'all sections of the community'.

BIFA's annual general meeting in May 1969 did little to allay these doubts. No European immigrants were voted on to the executive committee, and the dominant theme of most speakers, from Miss Nadine Peppard of the CRC to the local Community Relations Officer, was that 'colour makes the difference' and that 'colour' is the central issue in immigrant affairs. Not only is the argument of doubtful validity, but many immigrants feel that, in the long run, such views will do more harm than good to BIFA's capacity for helping local immigrants as a whole. More and more Europeans gain the impression that BIFA's original aims are not being carried through as intended, that 'BIFA is not for us', but is being given over to the interests of commonwealth or 'coloured' immigrants.

It might be argued that this change of emphasis is right, that commonwealth immigrants have little in common with European immigrants anyway, and that BIFA's essential task *is* to serve 'coloured people'. But does the term 'coloured people' itself represent any real community of interests? I see little evidence to support the claim. Not only is awareness of colour far less pervasive among Indians than among West Indians, but one would be hard pressed to find two groups in Bedford who have less in common. Even the fact that BIFA's community relations officer is an Indian itself creates reservations – in some cases, resentment – among West Indians: 'If the West Indians have a problem, they want to tell it to their own people.'

In the event then, BIFA may find the task of unifying disparate interests too great; and individual immigrant groups may come to think it both more desirable and more effective to act on their own account. Most of them, after all, had already shown they could help themselves to very good effect long before BIFA appeared on the local scene.

A further problem is that of BIFA's relationships with the local council. Though the mayor of Bedford is ex-officio president of BIFA, the council has no official representatives on BIFA's executive committee, and its attitude to BIFA has, in the main, been wary, and never more than lukewarm. Also involved here are the general questions and dilemmas which almost inevitably plague relationships between voluntary and official bodies. If the voluntary organisation shows itself too critical of council policies, it invites rejection, and its capacity to influence the council may be permanently impaired. If it follows a line of acceptance of council policies, it may ensure itself a measure of co-operation at the cost of a loss of confidence among its own members. In Bedford, certainly, an effective working relationship between BIFA and local council has yet to be made.

One set of questions remain. Can an unofficial organisation of this kind – either at national or local level – ever be really effective? By its very nature, can it ever do more than scratch the surface of immigrant problems? If one accepts that the problems of an immigrant society, whether on a national or local scale, necessitate a greater measure of economic and social planning, a more effective co-ordination of social services, an extension of liaison services between immigrants and public servants, and so on, then the question arises: can there be any real hope of achieving these objects through an unofficial organisation?

The unofficial organisation may finally prove more of a drag than an aid to effective action. Its mere existence creates a natural tendency for other agencies to leave to it all matters affecting immigrants; and two dangers lurk here. By focusing excessive attention on the subsidiary issues of colour relationships, the unofficial organisation may tend to obscure the main issues of economic and social planning: and because of its own anomalous position vis-à-vis official organisation, it has no effective power to translate ideas into action.

In sum, I would have thought it evident that unofficial organisations are unlikely to prove very efficient instruments; and that the needs of a society with immigrant problems – Britain as a whole, or Bedford as a microcosm – can only be satisfactorily met by effective thought and action *within* official governmental or local council organisation.

For official thought and action to be fully effective, it must first be fully informed – by employers, social service practitioners and others deeply involved in immigrant affairs, and by the leaders of the various immigrant groups themselves. Official immigrant councils or committees comprehending all such interests, working as integral parts of national and local organisation, would at least give some hope both of bringing thinking and action on immigrant problems into effective relationship, and of putting them into the essential context of national and local planning as a whole.

16

Conclusions

A man can abandon everything – home, country, land – but he
cannot abandon himself, that by which he lives and by virtue of
which he is what he is. . . .

> (Milovan Djilas: *Montenegro*.)

The majority of men commonly dislike foreigners, and are easily
inflamed against them; and it is not possible for the majority to
know much about foreign peoples.

> (T. S. Eliot: *Notes Towards a Definition of Culture*.)

Other nations of different habits are not enemies: they are godsends.

> (A. N. Whitehead: *Science and the Modern World*.)

BEDFORD is a middling, average sort of town. Like other towns in
Britain at this time, it is in process of losing distinct identity and
community, and the people of many different countries and
cultures who have come to Bedford since the war now live together in a condition of reasonably peaceful coexistence.

This peaceful coexistence is rather a matter of luck than of
judgment, the luck being the state of more or less full employment
that Bedford has enjoyed since the war. After 1945, the brick
industry needed unskilled men to do the work that British workers
would not do: immigrants have come to Bedford to satisfy those
needs: and in 1969, the needs are neither fully satisfied nor are
likely to be, short of a recession in the industry or a radical programme of mechanisation. This situation has meant that there has
been virtually no economic competition between natives and
foreigners; and it is this factor, above all else, which has allowed
Bedford to develop in relative peace as an immigrant town.

The various immigrant groups have little in common except
their problems of settling here. All in turn, irrespective of their
backgrounds or skin colours, have faced similar difficulties in

making a life for themselves in Bedford. In looking for accommodation, or for jobs, or for entry into clubs, or simply in doing the daily shopping, all in turn have met the fear, suspicion or antipathy which the majority of natives show to all people and all customs foreign to themselves. Though they have also met a great deal of kindness and help from individuals in Bedford, the general rule has been that what is least congruous to the natives is also least pleasing; and the degree of antipathy met initially by each group may be measured by the extent to which they were alien in their ways, appearance, attitudes and values. Thereafter, local attitudes have been modified according to the willingness of each group to accommodate itself to English ways and to conform to English standards. In effect, the natives have instinctively put each immigrant group to a series of tests to determine how worthy they are of acceptance.

Inevitably, there have been tensions between these native attitudes and the aims and aspirations of the immigrants. If immigrant groups have anything in common, it is firstly, their attitude of reservation or antipathy towards the ways and values of contemporary British society, and, more fundamentally, their wish to preserve their own identity, to *be* themselves. For all of them except the West Indians, whose cultural background is quasi-British, the notion of 'integration' with British life and culture is irrelevant and degrading. They do not wish to be combined into a new whole. They do not want to be anything except themselves. Indeed, they *cannot* be anything except themselves. 'A man can abandon everything – home, country, land – but he cannot abandon himself, that by which he lives and by virtue of which he is what he is.'

In this context, the only principles that make sense are those of cultural diversity and interchange, whereby each group can preserve intact its own being yet be helped to play as full a part as possible within the fabric of British life and organisation.

Given a suitable economic climate, the latter aim can best be realised through effective social organisation. In Bedford, a large immigrant population has meant great pressures upon local social services. Some, such as the public health service, have coped intelligently and therefore well. Others, such as the education service, have coped comparatively poorly. The failures, of course, have not been among the people in direct contact with the immigrants, the teachers, but among the policy-makers, who have so far failed to make a reasonable context for teachers to work in.[1] Beyond that has been an overall failure to conceive and direct the social services in unity and to create a situation whereby health, housing and education policies all aid and reinforce each other. The essential task of drawing the various immigrant groups into the ambit of English life as quickly as possible is thereby obstructed and delayed, and the work of individual practitioners – teachers, medical and social workers, doctors, policemen, and the like – is thereby thwarted and frustrated.

Good policies are invariably well-informed policies, and the most successful local policy-makers have been those closest in touch with immigrant needs. More systematised interchange between policy-makers, practitioners in every sphere of local life (including local industry), and leaders of the immigrant groups themselves – on a consultative council, for example – could do much to create wider understanding of immigrant needs, more accurate identification of their problems, and more effective solutions to those problems. (Such matters are too important to be left to a voluntary body like BIFA, limited both in its powers of action and in its capacity to represent the interest of immigrant groups as a whole.)

In Bedford at the present time, the key immigrant problem may well be that of drawing the great mass of Asian peoples into the fabric of local life as soon as possible. Particular needs are for Asian health visitors and other medical-social workers to advise the women in their own languages how to cope with the demands of everyday living in this country; and for fundamental literacy programmes on similar lines given by Asians for their own people in their own institutions (e.g. by Sikhs for Sikhs in their *gurdwara*).

To create a climate where understanding of immigrant affairs may breed an interchange of ideas, and information be stimulated, is also of first importance in Bedford. Most practitioners welcome interchange. All too many officials still seem to fear it. 'We prefer to write things down rather than to write them up.' Some go as far as to say that 'there are no special immigrant problems', while others seem to think that their primary duty is to hide all information from the public's eyes.[2] It goes without saying that those most

[1] See map on p. 163.
[2] While writing this book, not the least of my pleasures has been to give talks about immigrants and their problems in Bedford on behalf of authorities who have refused me even basic information.

ready to give and discuss information are invariably the most competent.

Underlying these considerations of cultural relationships and social organisation are those of the economic environment. It was the needs of the brick industry, above all else, which made Bedford an immigrant town. How it develops as an immigrant town depends very largely on how that industry develops. A fair economic wind will give Bedford every opportunity to create the kind of social organisation that makes for harmonious relationships. A contrary wind could set its peoples cruelly at odds with each other. In that climate, prejudice – or rather, hostility – would breed, for it is not a fixed quantity but the product of economic and social circumstance as well as of cultural tradition. It follows that the main issues of the contemporary debate on immigration are those of economic and social planning, and that the most logical way to determine immigration policy is to balance the long-term needs of the economy for foreign workers against the social consequences of their entry.

No easy task, for a whole complex of dilemmas and opposing interests spring immediately to mind. At the present time, the brick industry wants to import yet more foreign workers. Are national interests best served by letting it have its way? Or, by so doing, are we also allowing it to postpone a vital act of recreating itself with new, mechanised production processes? And will a further consequence be to put excessive strains upon already overloaded social services? And how far would this prejudice our chances of making effective social organisation, and thus of creating harmonious relationships? These are cruel dilemmas: but one thing is sure. If they are not faced and met, they will become more cruel, i.e. the economic and social stakes which they represent will become ever greater.

'Colour' is, by comparison, a subsidiary issue in Bedford. There is no clear evidence to connect 'colour' with the rebuffs and rejection experienced by the various immigrant groups. The European refugees suffered in this respect as much as any, and no people have borne all with greater dignity and fortitude.

Of antipathy on grounds of colour, there is limited evidence; of 'colour prejudice' very little. Not only is the time for pre-judgments in Bedford long past, but most local criticisms of Asians and West Indians are directed not against 'coloured people' in general, but against specific nationalities for specific reasons: 'I don't like Pakis because they smell and because they keep their houses badly.' 'I don't like Indians because they don't try to fit in with our ways and because of the smells of their cooking.' 'I don't like West Indians because they are noisy and because they have chips on their shoulders.' Where the term 'coloureds' is used, as often as not it is identified with West Indians only.

Such comments are widespread in the town, and all too often they are labelled 'colour prejudice'. To call them so is to obscure their real nature, which is that of cultural antipathy. ('Dislike' is too active a word.) If Bedford is a reliable guide, such antipathy is pervasive in our society. Local employers' reluctance to take on Sikhs, for example, was far more a matter of their turbans and their beards than of their colour of skin. Brickworkers' objections to Pakistanis on buses to and from the brickyards, or while working in the kilns, were essentially those of smell, as were the objections of Dr Harte's English patients to his Asian patients.[1] The latter case illustrates classically how easily confusions between 'colour' and 'culture' can arise. It took Dr Harte's intelligence and his extractor fans to establish the fact that he was dealing with cultural antipathy and not with colour prejudice.

It is a matter for regret that contemporary obsession with 'colour', reinforced by a welter of vested interests, has made it the centre of much debate on immigration. In Bedford, colour of skin has been important as one of the marks of difference between peoples, though it is no more than one mark among many. It has major importance only for the group whose cultural history has made it important to them – the West Indians. In brief, the importance derives from their distinct *cultural* plight. Born of a divisive, transplant society, they have been nurtured in traditions which they assumed were wholly British; and have found themselves at best only partially acceptable as British. This discovery has meant for many tensions and lacerations of consciousness cruel in intensity; denied identity as British, they have had no other identity to fall back upon but that of their skin colour. In this sense only – and for these West Indians only – is there a 'colour problem'; and, given their cultural insecurity, it is inevitable that many will seek as well as find offence, and that they will translate it into 'colour' terms. The wonder is that so many West Indians in Bedford are living at peace with the world about them. How far the children of the West Indian immigrants inherit their parents'

[1] See pp. 193–4.

unique cultural dilemma depends largely upon the measure and quality of understanding that is given them.

This dilemma is 'unique', of course, only in terms of British experience, for there are certain parallels between the condition of the West Indian in Britain and that of the American Negro. The latter was also born to a transplant society, and, denied full identity as a US citizen, has been falling back to concepts of 'black people-hood'. From the transplant slave societies of the Americas, then, has come an interpretation of history in 'colour' terms. The pity is that so many concerned with immigrant affairs should have failed to see that this interpretation applies only to the societies from which it sprang, and that for contemporary immigrant problems in this country issues and interpretations based on 'colour difference' have only very limited relevance – in fact, to the West Indians alone.

The great false step in the contemporary debate has been to associate West Indians and Asians together under the identity of 'coloured people'. No immigrant groups have less in common, and Asians share none of the West Indians' innate awareness of colour. Apart from what has been dinned into them since they came to Britain, colour of skin has meaning neither for the Punjabi Sikhs nor for the multi-racial community of Islam; it is notable that in Bedford most local hostility has been directed against the Paki-stanis, in general the *lightest* of the misnamed 'coloured' group. The reasons for this hostility are primarily, of course, those of *culture*: the Pakistanis are the most alien in their ways and have done least to accommodate themselves to British standards.

As time goes by, the essential differences between the various immigrant groups, between Asians and West Indians, and between Asians themselves, will become more overt. Indians – or more correctly, Punjabi Sikhs – will forge ahead in establishing a strong, purposeful community in Bedford. Given a favourable economic climate, they will wring acceptance from Bedford in much the same ways as the southern Italians have done. Indeed, there are real resemblances between Indians and Italians, notably their capacities for hard work, the capacity of their communities for self-regulation, the influence of religious faith on their lives, and their close, disciplined patterns of family life.

In the second generation, however, the pattern of Sikh culture will prove more enduring than that of southern Italy. Because interpretations of immigrant problems in cultural terms have been so few, there has been little or no public recognition that a key problem area is that of the crisis within the Italian family. While the immigrants cling fast to southern Italy, most of their children want only to break the bonds of traditional culture and merge into 'Englishness'. The violence of reaction against the parents is already creating profound unhappiness and divisions of conscious-ness, and could well go on to create a formidable record of suffer-ing and even of delinquency.

Among second generation Sikhs, by contrast, traditional bonds will hold. They will seek further accommodations with English life and a great measure of outward and visible resemblance. They will also insist on recognition and treatment equal to that of their English contemporaries (in Sikh traditions, militancy mingles curiously with acceptance). Yet the outwardly emancipated Sikh will still marry according to caste, still observe the seclusion of women before marriage, and still cling to the fundamental tenets of his faith. Compromises with Bedford, in brief, will be a matter of outward forms rather than of inward realities. Real change will be a very gradual matter and will bring little joy to the apostles of integration within their lifetimes.

The Kenya Asians – Sikhs, Hindus, and a handful of Muslims – in many ways form a distinctive group of their own. 'In energy, application and ability, there is no one to touch them,' said a local secondary school headmaster recently. 'I'd take on a school of 600 of them at any time. The only thing that can stop them getting to the top is discrimination.' Here, certainly, is one of the key areas for testing the future. My own guess – again, given a stable econ-omic climate – is that they may find it easier to realise their aspirations at graduate and technologist level than other young Indians will do at technician and craftsman level. Local experience suggests that there is greater resistance to immigrants in these lower-middle levels of employment – particularly in directive functions such as those of foreman and supervisor – than there is either at unskilled or very skilled levels.

The advance of Pakistanis and West Indians will be much more an individual matter depending on each young person's ability and initiative, and on the strength of family backing and encourage-ment. Among Pakistanis, this is likely to be stronger in Punjabis and Mirpuris than in Sylhetis; and, among West Indians, stronger in Barbadians than in Jamaicans, since general standards of education are higher in Barbados than in Jamaica and respect for education more widely pervasive.

H

Lacking the context of a strong and purposeful community, however, the advance of second generation West Indians as a whole will be a good deal slower than that of the Indians, and this could eventually give rise to tensions and resentments between the two groups. (Why is it that integrationists are so deeply concerned to establish closer relationships between the British on the one hand and immigrant groups on the other, and so little concerned with the almost complete absence of positive relationships between the various immigrant groups themselves?) Such tensions between the descendants of the Indians and the descendants of the Negroes have arisen in classically predictable ways wherever they have found themselves together. I see no reason why Bedford should prove an exception to the rule. Perhaps, then, at least, the myth that the central issue in the immigration debate is that of the relationship between 'whites' on the one hand and 'coloureds' – implying West Indians and Asians together – on the other, will finally be blown up out of the arena of immigrant affairs in the way it deserves to be.

What of the future of the other, too often forgotten, immigrants, the political refugees of Central and Eastern Europe, and our comrades in arms, the Poles? In Bedford, all of them, in the earlier years, endured much and demanded nothing, though the EVWs were more restricted in civil rights than any other group has ever been. They made no protest. They were kept quiet by their pride in *being* Poles, Latvians, Ukrainians, Serbs or Slovenes. (The peoples of Yugoslavia show that nationality, like colour, bows the knee to differences in culture.) Bedford has done these people all too little honour, the Poles for what they were as soldiers, and all of them together for what they have been as citizens.

The future of each of these groups depends a great deal on how far physical connections between each country and Bedford have been maintained. For the Poles, there are still such connections, and Polish consciousness lives on in some, at least, of the second generation. Among the Serbs and Slovenes, political idealism and political hatreds are both too intense to allow their consciousness as separate peoples to live beyond a second generation. For the Latvians, there are few strands connecting them with the homeland, and for most of the young people, Latvia remains a dream country. As for the Ukrainians, their country has lived underground for centuries, and the light of their resolution is still undimmed. In that faith they are as united as any people in Bedford, and however few there may be to carry it on in the second generation, they will do so.

It is possible that something more than all this will come from the presence of immigrant groups together in Bedford – that which the young Ukrainian, himself a passionate nationalist, glimpsed: 'You know, I wish it was possible to have lots of parents of all different countries. British, Ukrainian, Italian, West Indian, the lot. Then you would know every way of life. You could choose the best of each.'

Bedford is a fortunate town. While 'it is not possible for the majority to know much about foreign peoples', in Bedford it *is* possible to know a good deal about foreign peoples. It is possible to know about them the best way, by living experience, to compare many ways and many conditions of life, and to make a choice of life. In brief, it is possible to find that 'other nations of different habits are not enemies: they are godsends.'

This possibility of life now stands in the shadows of the brick-works chimneys. Will the economic wind blow fair? If it does, and if local social organisation is intelligently conceived and directed, then the immigrants of Bedford may be able to live in the peace which that original, Joe Clough, the doyen of Bedford's immigrants, has found in the town.

Education in Bedford, January 1970

FOR reasons discussed in Appendix II, a detailed comparison of the number of immigrant pupils in Bedford schools in January 1969 with the number in January 1970 would be of little value. It is possible, however, to show the trends in the key areas of the town, since most of the head teachers in those areas have followed consistent policies in making their yearly returns.

In the Ampthill Road area numbers of immigrant pupils have built up as anticipated, the most notable increase being in the Ampthill Road Junior School where the percentage of immigrant pupils has risen by 9 per cent (from 69 per cent to 78 per cent) over the past year. The two main reasons for this development are the increase in the local Indian population and the passing of the 'bulge' of immigrant pupils from the Infants' to the Junior School. Unless decisive action is taken by Borough authorities, this 'bulge' can be expected to pass to the secondary schools of the area in September 1973.[1]

In the Clapham Road area, with its heavy concentration of West Indian and Italian immigrants, there has been a slight increase in immigrant numbers in the Junior and Infants' schools from 63 per cent and 66 per cent respectively in January 1969 to 66 per cent and 67 per cent in January 1970. The main increase here has been a 20 per cent rise in the number of West Indians in the Junior School (from 83 to 104).

There has also been some increase in the polyglot Queen's Park area, with more Italians moving into the Junior School, together with a few more Pakistani children. In the Infants' School, the increase has been mainly of Indian children. It is not possible to estimate accurately the increase at Westfield, the district secondary school, since returns for 1970 were made on a different basis from those of January 1969. It is clear, however, that there has been a

[1] And onto the labour market by 1977-8.

significant increase here in the numbers both of Indian and West Indian children.

There is virtually no evidence of dispersal of immigrant children from these areas of greatest concentration to those of least concentration. In the four Brickhill and Putnoe schools to the north-east of the town, for example, immigrant pupils in January 1969 numbered 7 out of a total of 1,262, and in January 1970 8 out of a total of 1,356. (2 Kenya Asians, 1 Indian, 1 Pakistani, 1 West Indian, 1 Italian, and 2 other Europeans.)

There has also been no more than a marginal increase in the number of immigrant pupils in the one Borough Selective or Grammar School. Whereas immigrant pupils numbered 7 out of a school roll of 860 in January 1969, they numbered 11 out of a school roll of 924 in January 1970, West Indians (3) figuring on the roll for the first time.

The over-all situation thus shows that the trends discussed in the chapter on Education have developed on predictable lines, with the mal-distribution of immigrant pupils in Borough schools continuing unchecked. In this discouraging context, head teachers and their staffs continue to cope manfully. A notable achievement has been that of the Headmaster of the Ampthill Road Junior School, Mr Harry Brunjes, who, despite an almost overwhelming concentration of immigrant children, has created a school of excellent spirit and good academic standards. (Of 10 passes obtained by his pupils in the 11 + test during the year, 4 were by immigrants.) About a hundred of some three hundred children on the school roll are now Indian, and they alone number about one and a half times the number of British: Italians also substantially outnumber British pupils in the school.

Unfortunately, there is virtually no sign of the Borough education authorities taking decisive action to create a more rational context for teachers to work in. There is also little sign of any degree of co-ordination between education and housing authorities to prevent an even further build-up of immigrants in the vital Ampthill Road area.

Immigrants – Facts and Statistics[1]

WHILE writing a book on the life of an immigrant town, my doubts about official statistics have grown ever stronger. The 'facts' about immigrants, as I discovered them, often differed radically from the 'facts' of official statistics: and this disparity was noted with some concern by the reader to whom my publishers sent the manuscript for comment. He pointed out, for instance, that whereas the sample census of 1966 gave the number of Pakistanis in Bedford as 390, I had given an estimate for 1969 of at least 1,000 Pakistanis in Bedford. These totals were difficult to reconcile. Who was right? What were the facts? The publishers, very reasonably, wanted to know. At a time when immigrant issues generate so much emotional heat and where so many interests seem intent either to inflame or gloss over such issues rather than to analyse and explore them, the tasks of establishing the 'facts', they felt, were clearly of first importance.

I could reassure them about certain past statistics. In the year that official statistics had given 390 Pakistanis in Bedford, for example, the Borough Public Health Department had registered 584 Pakistanis living in multiple occupation *alone*. From experience of that department, I knew their figures were fairly reliable, and by relating them to what I knew of the pattern of Pakistani family life in Bedford, estimated the probable number of Pakistanis in town in that year to have been between 800 and 900. In brief, I could demonstrate that official statistics were sometimes not merely inaccurate but even grossly misleading.

In view of the current climate of anxiety and contention about immigrant issues, I wish I could assure my publishers that official statistics are likely to grow more accurate. Present evidence, however, is not reassuring. Whereas latest official figures (the Registrar-General's) give 4.6 per cent Commonwealth immigrants in Bed-

[1] First published as an article in *The Times*, 24 March 1970, under the title 'Why Immigrant Statistics Are Unreliable'.

ford, for instance, my own researches suggest that this figure is approximately 60 per cent inaccurate and that the true percentage is nearer 7 per cent (2,000 West Indians, rather more than 2,000 Indians, and rather more than 1,000 Pakistanis in a town population of 70,000).

As for the future, I can say with certainty that, in the sphere of education at least, a good deal of statistical evidence about immigrants now in preparation is also going to be erroneous and misleading.

This situation is being classically demonstrated in the collection of statistics about the number of immigrant pupils in our schools. Accuracy here is foundering on the way in which an 'immigrant pupil' is defined in the Department of Education and Science Form 7(i) Schools (1970). The 'Notes for Guidance' on the Form state:

(1) (a) For the purpose of this return immigrant pupils are defined as
    (i) children born outside the British Isles who have come to this country with, or to join, parents or guardians whose countries of origin were abroad; and
    (ii) children born in the United Kingdom to parents whose countries of origin were abroad and who came to the United Kingdom on or after 1st January 1960.
(b) The return should *not* include
    (i) children from Northern Ireland or Eire; or
    (ii) children of mixed immigrant and non-immigrant parentage.

The rub, of course, lies in the way that the meaning of 'immigrant pupil' is limited to the children of immigrants who came to the United Kingdom during the past 10 years. In Bedford, at least, a number of head teachers to whom I have spoken feel strongly that this limitation is utterly artificial, and that to abide by the DES definition in making their returns would only serve to falsify the numbers of immigrant pupils in our schools, would act against any accurate assessment of their educational problems, and could well mislead the public. Their experiences are that the children of immigrants suffer more or less equally the characteristic deprivations of an immigrant home background, no matter when the parents arrived in this country. They find no essential difference between the children of southern Italian immigrants who came here in the early fifties and the children of those who came a decade or more later. At whatever time southern Italians came to Bedford, they brought and preserved their own language and their own ways of life, and they will preserve them, only partially modified by the experience of Britain, until they die. The same couldbe said of the Asians who settled here in the fifties and sixties.

Knowledge of this context leads many head teachers instinctively to reject official attempts to limit the meaning of 'immigrant pupil'; and in filling in Form 7(i) most of them simply ignore the governmental ruling. They return the numbers of *all* immigrant pupils irrespective of when the parents arrived in this country since the Second World War. Considerations of expediency reinforce their commonsense. They know that the task of collecting officially 'correct' statistics from immigrant children who are rarely more than semi-literate and from immigrant parents who are often totally illiterate, would be intensely difficult and immensely time-wasting.

Local practice and national policy are thus poles apart. Knowing this, I could say with some confidence that local returns for January 1969 were, in 'real' – or non-governmental – terms, reasonably accurate. Official figures gave just over 23 per cent immigrant pupils in Bedford schools at this time. This meant that, in reality, rather more than one in four of all pupils were the children of immigrants.

Further than this accuracy cannot go: nor can any reliable comparisons be made of the situation from year to year, since in each year local practices change. Looking at the January 1970 returns in the Borough Education Offices recently, I was amazed to find that a school which in January 1969 returned 37 per cent immigrant pupils was now returning only 12 per cent. A phone call established the fact that the head teacher was ill and that a conscientious staff had contrived to fill in the form 'honestly'. Another school which had returned 54 per cent in 1969 was now returning rather less, although I knew that there had been a notable increase in the number of immigrant pupils during the year and that the real figure was probably nearer 60 per cent. Another phone call made it clear that a newly appointed head teacher, by dint of enormous effort, had obeyed the official ruling.

Now, I know as a fact that the number of immigrant children who are really 'there', in front of the teachers of Bedford, has shown a marked increase during the past year. An increase will be shown on the local returns, but it will certainly not be a true measure of the real increase; and, short of a completely new survey, there is no possible way of determining accurately either the true figure or the true rate of increase. The best I can do is to make a rough estimate, and at least I know that this will be nearer reality than the official statistics.

Project this local situation to a country-wide scale. Is it not as plain as a pikestaff that, throughout the land, the books must be cooking themselves, and that errors and confusion must be compounding each other?

A further phone call to the Department of Education and Science. My question evokes a gurgle of mingled laughter and horror at the other end of the line.

'Yes, we know it's absurd, but this definition of an immigrant as one who came within the last 10 years has been in effect since 1966 and there's nothing we can do about it.'

The DES official tells me that the definition derived from a recommendation by a governmental inter-departmental committee; and that the Home Office has insisted that the DES stick to it.

'It means, of course, that all statistics about immigrants and immigrant pupils based on this definition will be as confused as they will be misleading.'

'Oh, yes,' says the official voice. 'Well, maybe, one of these days we will be able to get back to a rational basis.' The voice does not sound very certain about it.

On, then, to the Immigration Department of the Home Office. I tell them about the definition of an immigrant on the DES form. What is their own definition of an immigrant? Nobody seems quite sure. Helpful noises are made and a promise to ring me back. Within a quarter-of-an-hour, the Immigration Department rings back.

'We do not use the term "immigrant" here. We divide people into those who come from abroad for settlement and those who come on a temporary basis.'

So here I am, more or less in mid-air; and filled with wonderment. All I know for certain is that national returns of the number of immigrant pupils in British schools have been, are, and, at least in the near future, will be, confused, inaccurate, and misleading. I know, too, that all speakings and writings that have been, are being, or will be, based on such statistics are virtually worthless.

Beyond that, one can only wonder: why, by whom, and for what reason has the 10-year limit been placed on the meaning of 'immigrant'? Was it misplaced liberalism, mere stupidity or deliberate intent to mislead the public that framed this definition? And how widely is it used? Is there a governmental definition of an immigrant that is used consistently by all departments of government? Or does each department have its own definition? Do some indeed so scorn definitions that they are not really sure where they stand?

One question lies at the root of all. What is an immigrant? I think I know the answer in 'real' – i.e. human – terms. But what is it in governmental terms? Before the problems of immigrant peoples living in this country are blackened or whitewashed any further, and yet more claims and counter-claims, arguments and counter-arguments, are propounded on a basis of worthless statistics, is it not worth while to spare a moment to define our fundamental terms?

Without that definition, it is inevitable not only that our anxieties about immigrant issues will be further confused, but that a climate of utter distrust will be created for all official statistics in this sphere. Such scepticism, of course, may not be amiss. Statistics are so very far from being 'facts'.

Index

Allen & Sons & Co. Ltd, W. H., 149, 153, 157
American Negro, 224
Americans, 11, 180
Ampthill Road area, 164, 186, 194–5, 231
Ampthill Road schools, 162, 164–5, 173, 186, 207, 231–2
Anders, Gen., 39
Anglican Church, 99, 108
Anguilla, 98, 101
Antigua, 103
Antilles, 99
Asian Society, 128–9
Asians, 12–13, 15, 116–42, 221–6; and education, 166, 171–2; and employment, 148–9, 152, 154; and health, 189–96; and police, 200, 204–7. *See also* Asian Society; Chinese; India; Kenya Asians; Pakistan
Association for the Teaching of English to Peoples from Overseas (ATEPO), 167
Auschwitz, 33
Avison, Ernest, 138, 185

Baltic States, 35, 44, 58, 66, 167, 198
Barbados, 102, 104–6, 110–11, 169, 225
Bedford Corporation, 19, 176, 217, 218; education policies, 160–74, 186–7, 188, 196, 220–1; housing policies, 165, 185–7; Public Health Department, 176–85, 233
Bedford Hospital, 190–1, 195–6
Bedford International Friendship Association (BIFA), 66–7, 107, 215–17, 221
Bedfordshire Times (and *Bedford Times*), 21, 27 n, 170 n, 203 n
Bible Way Pentecostal Church, 111-13
Birkenau, 33

birth control, 110, 195
births, immigrant, 11, 194
Black Power, 99, 224
Blacke Booke (1563), 19
Bradshaw, Robert, 101, 115
Brereton, Dr, 22
brick industry, 11, 23, 26, 27, 28, 30, 31, 37, 49, 50, 51, 52, 53, 55, 61, 66, 73, 80, 83, 89, 132, 140, 146–51, 153–5, 157–9, 177, 213, 219, 222, 223, 227; London Brick Co., 27, 146–9, 154; Marston Valley brick-yards, 146, 149
Brickhill School, 162, 166, 232
Britannia Iron and Steel Works Ltd, 21, 101, 102, 149, 151, 153–4
British Council for Aid to Refugees, 30
Brookhurst Igranic Ltd (and Igranic Electric), 21, 149, 151, 157
Brunjes, Harry, 232
Buchenwald, 33
Bunyan, John, 20

Carriacou, 98, 103, 104
Chetnik organisations, 70–2, 78
Chima, Mrs, 194–5
Chinese, 11, 180
Clapham Road schools, 164–231
Clough, Joe, 223–5, 227
Clough, Margaret, 223–5
clubs, 209–18; Bedford Boys Club, 211
Coley, Mrs, 165, 169–70
'colour': issues and problems, 12–13, 23–5, 97, 99–100, 102, 106, 107, 111, 115, 128, 139, 150, 153, 155, 169–70, 183, 201, 212, 214, 216–17, 218, 219, 222, 224, 226
Community Relations Commission, 216–17
confinements (Bedford Hospital), 196
Convent of the Holy Ghost, 164

Cranfield Institute of Technology, 85 n
Croatia and Croats, 68–71, 77
Czestochowa, Our Lady of, 33, 40

Dachau, 33, 78
Department of Education and Science, 231–5
Djilas, Milovan, 14, 68, 71 n, 76, 219
drugs, 92, 113, 200; cannabis, 113, 200; opium, 200

East Africa, 116–17
education, 160–74; adult education, 172–3. See also Bedford Corporation: educational policies
Elek, Andrew, 29
Eliot, T. S., 219
employment, 19–31, 145–59, 213, 219; apprenticeships, 157–8. See also brick industry
Estonia, 44
European Voluntary Workers (EVWs), 29–31, 51-2, 72, 78, 148–50, 226

Farrar, Rev. C. F., 19
Fisher, Stanley, 167

Garnett, Alf, 212
Germany and Germans, 33, 37, 42, 44–7, 58–60, 69–72, 77–9
Govind Singh, 118. See also Sikhism
Granada, 102–4
Groovers (West Indian music group), 109
gurdwara, 118–20, 124, 196, 221
gurus, 118–26
Guyana, 12

Harpur Trust schools, 21–2, 164
Harte, Dr John, 188–94, 223
health, 133, 135, 188–97, 221; anaemia, 192, 193; clinics, 190–5; health visitors, 194–5, 221; tuberculosis, 192, 205; venereal diseases, 135–6, 190–1, 202–3. See also Bedford Corporation: Public Health Department
Hendriks, A. L., 115
Herbert, George, 211
Hindi, 123, 130, 194, 195
Hinduism and Hindus, 116–17, 225
Home Office, 65, 231–5
housing, 37–8, 50–1, 62, 83–4, 108, 133, 135, 175-87. See also Bedford Corporation: housing policies

Howard, John, 20, 22
Hungary and Hungarians, 30-1, 199
Hunt Committee Report on 'Immigrants and the Youth Service', 214

illegal entry, 225
India and Indians, 11, 15, 66, 97, 116–31, 140, 148–9, 151–2, 164, 168–9, 172, 186, 190–6, 205, 207, 209, 210, 213, 214, 223, 224, 231–2; Athharmis, 117; Balmikis, 117; Bengali and Bengalis, 116, 133, 141; Indian Workers Association, 130; Jats, 117; Jullundur, 116–17, 129; Kashmir, 135; Punjabi and Punjabis, 116–17, 123, 124, 128, 130, 132, 134, 135, 139, 141, 194, 195, 224, 225; Rangharhia, 117; Untouchables, 117, 128; Young Indian Association, 126–30, 209. See also Sikhism; Hinduism
Irish, 11, 23, 180
Islam, 116, 132–3, 139, 141, 224, 225; law, 141; Mecca, 133; Mohammed, 132; Ramadan, 132. See also Pakistan
Italy and Italians, 13, 14, 71, 72, 77, 82–97, 120, 148, 150, 152, 153, 154, 158, 175, 177, 183, 189, 190, 199, 224, 225, 231–2; Abruzzo, 82; businesses, 88, 150, 183; Busso, 83, 85–6, 89, 97; Calabria, 82; Campania, 82; Campobasso, 83–5; Catholic Mission, 86–7; groups and clubs, 87, 89, 93–5, 209, 215; Naples, 83; St Angelo, 85, 89. See also Scalabrini missionaries

Jackson, J. Hampden, 44
Jamaica, 97–106, 109–11, 150, 183, 225

Kazakhstan, 36, 63
Kempston Hardwick Hostel, 49, 60–2, 83, 176
Kenya Asians, 162, 225, 232; Indians, 117, 124–5, 160–8, 180
Koestler, Arthur, 58

Lampedusa, Guiseppe Di, 14, 82
Latvia and Latvians, 11, 14, 44–55, 66, 175, 177, 189, 226
Lesins, Knuts, 14, 45, 55
Levi, Carlo, 14, 82, 83

Lithuania, 44, 45
Ljubljana, 77, 78
Luton (car firms), 150, 183

Majewski, Father Marian, 33, 39
Mander College, 125, 126, 127, 172
Martinique, 99, 106
Mihailovic, Gen. Draza, 28, 70-5
Monte Cassino (battle), 28, 38, 40, 43
Montserrat, 103
Moravian Church, 54
Mortimer, Dr J. G. M., 196 n
Muslims, see Islam

Naipaul, V. S., 14
Nedic, Gen., 70
Nevis, 103, 105, 111, 115
NKVD, 35

Obrenovic, Milos, 69

Pakistan and Pakistanis, 11, 15, 97,
116, 120, 130, 132-42, 145-6, 147,
148, 150, 151, 155, 160-2, 165, 183-4,
185, 190-2, 202-4, 205, 223,
224, 225, 229-30, 231-5; Cultural
Society, 138, 185; Mirpur and
Mirpuris, 132-4, 136, 225; shops,
183; Sylhet and Sylhetis, 132-
137, 141, 225
Pavelic, Ante, 69
Peter, King of Yugoslavia, 71, 75
Petrovic, George, 69
Plantation Society, 13, 98-101, 109,
115, 223-4
play groups, 216
Poland and Poles, 11, 28, 31, 32-43,
57, 66, 146-7, 149, 150, 160-2, 164,
175-6, 177, 189, 226; clubs, 38, 39,
209; Joint Council, 40; newspapers,
38; Resettlement Corps, 37; Youth
Club and youth organisations, 40,
41-2, 209
police, 61, 198-208, 221
Powell, Enoch, 169, 212
prisoners-of-war, 28, 88, 146
prostitution, 113-14, 135, 201-3
Putnoe School, 162, 166, 232

Queens Park School, 162, 164, 231

Race Relations Act, 153-4
Race Relations Board, 114
Red Cross, 210-11
Redlands Fletton, 148-9, 155

Robertson, W. H. A., 21
Rousseau, Jean-Jacques, 32

St Kitts, 98, 101, 103, 111
St Lucia, 98, 99, 112
Scalabrini missionaries, 86-7
Serbia and Serbs, 34-6, 68-76, 77, 78,
81, 226; Church, 75; School, 75
Shevchenko, Taras, 57
shop stewards, 154-5
Shukhevich, Gen. ('Taras Cuprinka'),
59
Sicily, 82-9
Sikhism and Sikhs, 116-22, 126, 131,
140, 149, 151, 155, 173, 196, 206,
221, 223, 224, 225
slavery, 98-9
Slovenia and Slovenes, 68, 76-81, 198,
226; Cultural Association, 80
Speight, J. ('Till Death Us Do Part'),
212
Stefanowicz, Jan, 40
Stewartby, 11, 27-8, 146, 147, 149
Sutcliffe, Harry, 127 n, 209

Tapsell, Mrs Anna, 216
Texas Instruments Ltd, 152-3
Times, The: supplement on southern
Italy, 83; 'Why Immigrant Statistics
Are Unreliable', 231-5
Tito, Marshall, 71-2, 74, 76, 79
Tobler Meltis Ltd, 89, 159
toilets, 151, 166
trade unions, 28, 153-5, 158
Trinidad, 28, 101, 103
Turner, Alderman Richard, 20 n, 23,
40

Ukraine and Ukrainians, 42-3, 53, 54,
56-67, 175, 177, 189, 226, 227;
Church, 64-5; community organis-
ations, 64-7
UNESCO, 196
United Counties Bus Co., 150
Urdu, 134, 139, 141, 184, 193, 194,
195
USSR and Russia, 32-6, 39, 44-8, 51,
53, 55, 56-60, 63, 65, 70, 71

Vico, Father, 86, 93-5

West Indians, 11, 12, 13, 14, 23-5, 43,
67, 97, 98-115, 120, 130, 139, 147-
152, 154, 155, 156, 162, 164, 166-70,

172, 175, 177–80, 182–3, 185, 188, 190–1, 194, 195–6, 200–3, 207, 209, 211, 214, 217, 222–4, 225, 226, 227, 231–2; groups and clubs, 105, 109, 185, 209–11; churches, 111–13. *See also under individual islands*

Whitehead, A. N., 219

Yalta, Treaty of, 28, 37, 67
Yugoslavia and Yugoslavians, 11, 14, 68–81, 175, 189, 226. *See also* Serbia; Slovenia